Real
Preseli

For Ewan and Seren, Ioan and Osian

Real
Preseli

John Osmond

SERIES EDITOR: PETER FINCH

Seren is the book imprint of
Poetry Wales Press Ltd
Nolton Street, Bridgend, Wales

www.serenbooks.com
facebook.com/SerenBooks
Twitter: @SerenBooks

ISBN 978-1-78172-497-2

A CIP record for this title is available from
the British Library

The publisher works with the financial assistance
of the Welsh Books Council

Cover photography: 'View from Fishguard Fort' by James Samuel.

Printed by Latimer Trend & Company Ltd, Plymouth.

CONTENTS

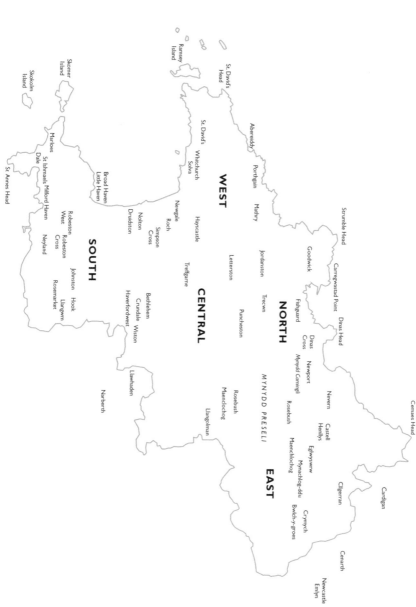

SERIES EDITOR'S INTRODUCTION

In a tent on a football field in Upper Solva I'm listening to John Osmond talk enthusiastically about devolution. We are in the far west where there's not much land left before the oceans start, where drowned worlds lie, where there are dragons roaring, and beyond them across endless water is shining America. This is Preseli and we are at Solva's Edge Festival, a mix of family fun day, music, drink and spoken literature. John is part of the literature component. This place is in the heart of the parliamentary constituency he has stood for many times. He has never won but he's certainly increased his party's market share. In the pursuit of this enterprise he has walked Preseli's every significant street, climbed all its hills and trekked its entire coast. Talking about the land he loves comes as second nature.

This is just as well. Immediately outside the canvas walls is the band stage on which a four piece are giving it wellie. Listening to John discuss devolution and the part played by MP Leo Abse against such a rhythmic thrum resembles listening to *Newsbeat* on Radio One. Undaunted John sails on. The book he's promoting is the first volume of his great triple-decker Welsh documentary novel, *Ten Million Stars Are Burning*. It's a fat doorstop. He's brought six copies and sells the lot.

Preseli, the subject of this present volume, John defines as everything west of a wavy line running from Neyland on the north side of the Cleddau to Poppit Sands at the mouth of the Teifi estuary. It's North Pembrokeshire writ large. He follows the advice I give to all authors of *Real* books. Make your geographical spread as wide as you can. If in doubt include. Your market will be bigger and you'll sell more books.

North Pembrokeshire, of course, is a much wilder place than the county's pasteurised south. There are fewer cafés, fewer pubs, roads seem longer, the cliffs are taller, the coast path rucks along them like a roller coaster. In winter it's here that the great storms make landfall. They hammer at St Ann's, St David's, Strumble and Dinas Heads in a perpetual battle for dominance. If the alluvial coast at Cardiff is forever moving outwards, here it is slowly wearing back.

Preseli for most outsiders is known for its central and defining range of hills. The Preseli Mountains are south west Wales' manageable versions of the great rocky peaks of northern Snowdonia. At 347 metres Mynydd Carningli is a stroll when compared to Eryri's 1,085. Yet these hills have a mystic appeal totally missing from their northern fellows. Walk the Preseli ridge, the Golden Road, extended from the hillfort cairns of Foel Drygarn to the volcano-like top of holy Carningli, to get the full experience. Ingli was where fifth century Saint Brynach communed with angels. That was my destination when I did it. Eight miles extended. Took all day but was full of marvels. King Arthur's Round Table Knights are here, frozen in stone and scattered along the trail. They will wake when the need arrives. Some may say that is sometime soon. There are hillforts and standing stones. Hut circles. Ancient grave markers. Ingli itself appears as a volcano might. Indeed, there's evidence that long ago this is just what this eminence once was.

Brian John, who lives on its slopes, has written about it extensively, basing his spectacularly best-selling *On Angel Mountain* saga on the greater Carningli district. From Ingli's peak you can see the sea. If you try this out, then keep looking at that horizon. The smudge you can discern out there could be distant Grassholm, uninhabited except by seabirds, or maybe the tip of Ireland or even Amerika, shimmering in the fuzzy light. We are, after all, in the place above which flying saucers circle and where, in the depths of solstice nights, the many burial chamber capstones rise up and mysteriously rotate.

Out here are the Neolithic quarries where the famous bluestones that form the inner circle at Stonehenge were cut. At Graig Rhos-y-Felin one lies unfinished amid the spikey grass. Latest research has suggested that some of the builders of the great ancient monument actually came from this place. Stone shifting travellers rolling their giant slabs through the Preseli countryside before somehow floating them over the Bristol Channel to stand upright on the plain of Salisbury. When I visited Carn Rhos-y-Felin I am sure I could sense an ancient connection in the air. But John will have no such truck. He is a realist, he tells me, levitating stones and all that magic are for the hippies. For his money the stones were moved by glacial action at the time of the last ice age. Given their huge size how else?

The towns of Preseli, hardly cities, are ones that somehow stick in the Welsh consciousness. Neyland and Milford Haven are bastions of an oil importing and refining industry that has seen its fair share of difficulty (the *Sea Empress* grounding off St Ann's Head in 1996 perhaps being the best recalled). To them John adds

Newport, Fishguard, St Davids, Crymych and Haverfordwest. After that all we have left in ancient Preseli are villages.

John has a caravan at Talbenny, near Little Haven, into which he has retreated from the wilder world for decades now. It's got wi-fi, central heating, an electric toaster and double glazing so he's snug. We meet in the car park at Whitesands to amble along one of the greatest walks in Wales. The site of St Patrick's Chapel, just over the hedge from the ice cream stall, out to the hillfort on the headland itself, through the spectacular heather, Celtic field markings everywhere, pass the cairn of Coeten Arthur, and then zip up across Carn Llidi to return to where we started. Way less than two hours but the views and copious Preseli spirit come in waves.

Back at Solva we discuss St Elvis and the Preseli hinterland. His chapel was barely a mile from where we stand. St 'Elvis' is a corruption of St Eilfyw, the baptising priest for St David. 'How great thou art' sang his American cousin. Rock and Roll and religion have always been close bedfellows.

John's Preseli, of course, is as much about people as it is about landscape. In *Real Preseli*, which you hold, he talks to Jamie Owen, broadcaster and farmer; Anna Mari Huws from the Cwm Gwaun Christian retreat; Chris Gillham, former Port Admiral at Haverfordwest; Derek Rees, one-time President of the local show; Glen Peters, Rhosygilwen concert hall owner; Myles Pepper, gallery operator and visual arts entrepreneur; Hatty Woakes, tapestry embroiderer; Tao Wimbush, animator of the Lammas off-grid eco-village, and to many others. Follow him to the amazing Teletubby House on the coast path at Druidston, to Skokholm looking for the shy Manx shearwater, to Bethlehem, the religious settlement that Preseli barely knows it has, to Poyston Hall to view the skull of Sir Thomas Picton's horse, to the Spitfire museum, to Rosebush's amazing corrugated Tafarn Sinc, to the saint's bones at St Davids Cathedral, and to Viking Fiskigarde, the Fishguard of today. In the event John's Preseli does not need to be artificially enlarged, this place is huge anyway.

John has a reporter's way of getting to the heart of any story. His guides and guests are inveigled to tell us just what we want to know. In a landscape so replete with its Neolithic past it is good to hear the living actually breathe. You'll find John at his best, however, striding around Atlantic-facing Cemaes Head or taking the long breath-stretching run from Nine Wells to St Non's Well at Porthclais.

Writing about Pembrokeshire or, more particularly, writing in Pembrokeshire puts John in the company of a good many others. John Tripp, Brian John, Tony Curtis, Trevor Fishlock, Sarah Waters, Waldo Williams, D.J. Williams, and Niclas y Glais have all found inspiration in the Preseli Hills. Tripp, who John knew well, did readings here, ate apricot sponge in local tea shops and wrote the whole experience up. Tony Curtis edited *The Poetry of Pembrokeshire*, Seren's anthology which encapsulates the entire county. Amy Wack has edited *Poems from Pembrokeshire*, a gift book of contemporary verse. Waldo took the land's spirit and turned it into some of the best verse Wales possesses.

Creativity does not affect writers alone. Painters flock, drawn by the light as if this were a sort of Welsh south of France. With its balmy climate and picturesque scenery the place has that air. Preseli roads are dotted with viewing galleries, signs pointing up lanes to the showrooms of the painters, sometimes the rooms in which they actually work. In Preseli it can often be hard to tell reality from paint. John Knapp-Fisher, David Tress, Chris Neale, Sarah Jane Brown, Graham Sutherland, John Piper, Stan Rosenthal and Brendan Burns along with hundreds of others have worked the landscape here. It's a magic land.

At the tent the audience have applauded and we're out again standing in the sun ravaged field. There really is something about Preseli that elevates the spirit. If you doubt this conclusion, then read John Osmond's book for yourself.

Peter Finch

INTRODUCTION

The place to start is Foel Cwmcerwyn, the highest point in Mynydd Preselau, the Preseli Hills. It's two-hundred-and-forty feet short of the necessary two thousand feet for the Ordnance Survey to call it a mountain. But it feels like one. It's known as Preseli Top.[1] Looked at from the east its slopes have a sharp, glacier-cut curve, reminiscent of the Brecon Beacons. From its summit on a clear day you can see Ireland, Lundy and Devon, and most of Wales. But more to the point, from here you can see the whole of Preseli.

This is magical country, a land of enchantment. The hills have a mystical quality, due as much to the sky as the bare, rolling landscape. Together the sea, land and heavens produce a luminous light, changing with the weather and seasons. No wonder Preseli is a Mecca for artists.

Looking north from Cwmcerwyn you can see well beyond the River Teifi which marks Preseli's border with Ceredigion. To the east are the hills of Carmarthenshire. To the south is the silvery line of Milford Haven and the chimneys of its oil refineries. And to the west is the coastline, with Carningli above Newport in sharp focus. A little further south is Carn Llidi and St Davids Head.

The day I climbed Foel Cwmcerwyn the coast was obscured by a sea mist. It crawled inland where river valleys open to the sea, and circled round Carningli into Cwm Gwaun. The sun made the mist look like water blending into the sky.

You can see Preseli whole from Foel Cwmcerwyn. But what exactly is it? Some think Preseli is the Welsh language term for Pembrokeshire. But that is Penfro, Sir Benfro being the official Welsh name for the county. Centuries ago Penfro, which means land's end, actually referred to the territory south of the Milford Haven waterway. Preseli is to the north, stretching as far as the Teifi. It is most clearly identified with Mynydd Preseli.

The name Preselau appears in *The White Book of Rhydderch*, the earliest collection available of the Mabinogion tales. However, there is no agreement about the exact meaning or origin of the word. According to one explanation, which I rather like, the original was *Pred-sel-au*. In this formulation *Pred* means 'passageway' and sel means 'gaze' or 'watch' (extending it to *selau* gives you the plural form). It follows that Preseli is a place where you keep a lookout, perhaps for approaching enemies from the sea.

In constitutional terms Preseli first emerged in 1976 when Pembrokeshire was abolished and merged with Ceredigion and Carmarthenshire to create the new county of Dyfed. As part of that reorganisation district authorities were created, among them Preseli, the northern part of the old Pembrokeshire. It was made up of what had been the borough of Haverfordwest, the urban districts of Fishguard, Milford and Neyland, and the rural districts of Haverfordwest and Cemaes to the north. Then, in the 1996 reorganisation, the Preseli District disappeared, to be combined with South Pembrokeshire to reconstitute Pembrokeshire once more. Today, in a political sense Preseli survives as the name of the constituency, especially significant for me since I have stood here as a candidate for Plaid Cymru on three occasions. So the constituency boundary is the one I use to delineate *Real Preseli*.

The geography and settlement patterns are a mirror image of Wales as a whole. The north is mountainous and Welsh-speaking. The south has industry and the largely English-speaking majority. Like the north of Wales itself, northern Preseli has old slate quarry workings, on the slopes of Cwmcerwyn above Rosebush. And in the south there's a coalfield, a worked out anthracite field that stretches from Hook, on a bend of the Western Cleddau River, in a narrow band to Little Haven and Newgale on the coast.

The west is bounded by bays: Cardigan Bay for Wales, St Brides for Preseli. Meanwhile, in both cases, their eastern frontier is defined by rivers. For Wales it's the Severn; for Preseli the Cleddau. For both, too, their southern shores have large estuaries, the Bristol Channel for Wales, and Milford Haven for Preseli.

For both Preseli and Wales as well, their northern and southern territories are quite distinctive. In Preseli they are divided by the Landsker, which literally means a cut in the land. It marks the northernmost advance of the Norman invasion. In the west it begins where Brandy Brook flows into the sea at the northernmost point of Newgale beach in St Brides Bay. It skirts to the south of Mynydd Preseli, and moves eastwards in an irregular line. It is at one and the same time a political and linguistic frontier. Its political path is dotted with castles at Roch, Rudbaxton, Rath, Wiston, and finally Llawhaden on Preseli's eastern boundary. Then it crosses into Carmarthenshire, and ends on the coast at Laugharne.

It is said that the Landsker is the only linguistic frontier of its kind that has not hardened into a national border. To be sure it changed position many times. It moved northwards into the foothills of Mynydd Preselau during the Norman military campaigns of the early Middle Ages, and retreated southwards in more peaceful times.

The castles were set back some distance from the disputed territory. Behind them were the richer farming lands. Although the line varied, it still established a firm linguistic divide. To the north were the Welshry, to the south the Englishry. These were designations given by George Owen, of Henllys, in his *Description of Pembrokeshire* in 1603. This was the first psycho-geography of the place. The distinction Owen drew survives to this day, albeit that the 'Welshry' are now interpolated by English incomers seeking the good life in youth as well as in retirement.

Although it is invisible, the Landsker frontier line is crucial to understanding many of the dynamics that operate in Preseli. The artist Meirion Jones, who has his studio near Cardigan, told me that when he ventures south of the Landsker, 'It feels like I'm going abroad.' Many southerners regard themselves as from 'down below', and when they go north it is to travel 'up in the Welsh'.

It is intriguing how closely the Landsker follows a geological boundary, with the different rock strata reflected in the relative height and corresponding agricultural value of the land they have produced. The rocks to the south of the line are Silurian, relatively young and mostly carboniferous, while the ones to the north are Ordovician, far older, or even Cambrian or pre-Cambrian, older still.

There is certainly a different sensibility between north and south. The landscape and buildings on either side of the Landsker vary a good deal. To the south are nucleated villages, established by the Normans, with small green fields, high wooded hedgerows and sunken, flower-fringed lanes. Every village has its church, often with a high battlemented tower that served as a place of sanctuary against attack by Welsh raiders.

To the north the settlements are more dispersed, with farms scattered across bare hillsides. Small hamlets lie in deep-sided valleys. The churches are often completely separated from the settlements, and located on sites of old monastic cells. This is replicated in parts of the south as well, most notably on the Dale peninsula, where the small churches at Walton West, Talbenny, St Brides, Marloes, Dale and St Ismaels are built on ancient Celtic foundations. They are made more beautiful by their isolation. Most of the religious houses of the north are chapels dating from the seventeenth century revival. They are simpler, more remote, and represent a democratic impulse. The language, of course, is the thing most separated by the Landsker. To this day it defines a border between overwhelmingly English-speaking Preseli in the south, and the still many Welsh-speaking communities in the north.

It may seem extraordinary how persistent have been the differences between the north and south of the Landsker, lasting the eight hundred years since the Normans invaded. One simple reason was the superb harbour at Milford Haven. This made possible easy sea communications between southern Pembrokeshire and Bristol. Given a fair wind and a good tide it was possible for a sailing vessel to make the journey there and back within forty-eight hours. For the whole time the territory was disputed most, of the Englishry's communication with the outside world was by sea.

Yet, despite all these differences Preseli has tended to grow together more than apart in recent times, certainly since I was a boy. In the 1950s the place I knew above all others was Little Haven where I frequently stayed with relatives. In those days it was very much inside the Englishry. The Union Jack invariably flew above the beach. Today, however, the flag is the Welsh *Ddraig Goch*. There's even a suggestion that the place's name could one day become bilingual. A bus timetable I saw recently, directed me to Aber Bach as well as to Little Haven.

A critical moment for the survival of Preseli came in the aftermath of the Second World War when the War Office tried to make permanent the firing range it had established on Mynydd Preseli. There was a powerful, and ultimately successful campaign of opposition, a story I relate later (see pages 20-24). It is noteworthy that those who defended Mynydd Preselau also had the wider community in their minds. For instance, one correspondent to the Welsh language journal *Y Faner* (The Flag) declared:

> Another important aspect to me is that the Preselau have always, rather than split Pembrokeshire into two parts, kept her as one. Of necessity, the people from both sides of the Preselau are one people as there is constant interaction between them. If the Preselau to all practical purposes were to be taken out of Pembrokeshire, she would be split into two areas apart, and the Welsh on the lowlands would lose a good deal of the Welsh spirit that is part of them,

particularly when, moreover, monolingual English-speakers would be in their midst. Gradually the subconsciousness of being Welsh will be lost – it is a subconsciousness rather than conscious awareness, since relatively few Pembrokeshire Welsh people realise they are actually Welsh – it is something quite natural and unforced, but at the same time motivates their whole lives, and preserves their own particular characteristics.[2]

Preseli is a place for visions, as many writers and artists will testify. The poet Waldo Williams was particularly susceptible to gaining spiritual inspiration from the landscape. One instance was when he gazed at the far horizons from the summit of Carn Llidi overlooking St Davids (see pages 157-58). In the mid-1980s I had a vision of my own, which has stayed with me down the years. After spending a night at the Salutation Inn in Felindre Farchog, I woke early and found myself drawn outside to the morning air. I walked into the hills and was entranced by the earth seemingly coming alive around my feet. A low-lying mist was disappearing in the gathering warmth, while a breeze in my face still felt chilled. High above the sky was azure blue but around were colours of green and yellow. The gorse was in full spring bloom, emitting its yeast-like scent, and contributing to a swooning haze. The sound of robins and blackbirds completed a reverie of motion and I seemed to float above the ground.

It was a kind of epiphany, but suggesting what? I had no straightforward answer. Maybe the experience reflected my pondering at the time on the meaning of what was becoming known as the Gaia hypothesis. This is the notion, associated with the work of James Lovelock, that the planet should be regarded as a living organism.[3] It had developed out of the first space programme in the 1960s. For the first time astronauts were able to look back at earth and take their famous photographs of the blue and white planet floating in the endless blackness of space.

Lovelock's theories included studies of the way the biosphere keeps the chemical composition of the air and the temperature on the surface of the earth, influenced by air and oceanic currents, at optimum levels to sustain life. Thus, for example, the atmosphere's oxygen concentration is kept stable at 21 per cent, just the right level to maintain life. A few percentage points less and the larger mammals, birds and flying insects would not have enough energy to survive. A few percentage points more and even wet vegetation would burn well.

The idea that the earth was a living organism seemed a fantastic notion. But the more I thought about it perhaps it was not so far-fetched. Certainly, it provided an under-pinning for the ecological movement that was then gathering pace, especially in Preseli, the need for a balance between our behaviours and their impact on the environment. It also seemed to touch something elemental in my experience of the sheer physicality of the Preseli coast and countryside.

I really began to get to know the place when I stood as a candidate, first in the National Assembly election in 2007, and later for the Westminster Parliament in 2015, and for the Assembly again in 2016. Campaigning took me to every corner of the constituency. In particular, I walked every street of the larger communities – St Dogmaels, Cilgerran, Fishguard, Crymych, St Davids, Haverfordwest, Johnston, Milford and Neyland – something I otherwise would never have done. And I spoke with hundreds of people.

One abiding memory during the first campaign in April 2007 is walking in the open countryside. The weather that month was one long, dry, blue day. Lack of rain kept the grass in the hedgerows back and in its place were an effusion of wild flowers: red campion, white cow parsley, stitchwort like small white daisies, yellow buttercups, primroses, bluebells.

Miles up in the blue sky streaked lazy white trails of passenger jets, making their way to America. Many seemed to converge on the high cliffs of Strumble Head, the northwestern tip of Preseli. I discovered there was a reason. Here is a navigation system, known as a VHF omnidirectional radio range. It allows aircraft to determine their position and stay on course, invaluable when setting off on a transatlantic flight.

When I first considered standing as a candidate I met Paul Sambrook, Plaid Cymru's constituency secretary, in the Llwyngwair Arms in Newport. I explained that although I had many associations with the place, I was not actually from Preseli. 'I wouldn't worry about that,' he replied. 'Hardly anyone is.'

That was an exaggeration. But it is true that over the years Preseli has welcomed incomers from most parts of the world. They come for all sorts of reasons. But most quickly share one thing: an appreciation of Preseli as a unique place. It's where landscape and people mix. Incomers tend to share native attitudes after they've been here for a while. There's a common sense of living in a far-flung territory, sometimes even of being cut off. It's the end of the line, and not just for railways. It often makes people feel abandoned, for instance when it comes to the provision of schools and hospitals. But it also makes them feel different, and a bit special.

Three writers – Waldo Williams whom I've already mentioned, D.J. Williams, and Niclas y Glais – are an abiding presence in these pages. They were contemporaries and friends during the first half of the twentieth century and had close ties with Preseli. They've left their mark on all who have written about the area since. The artist Aneurin Jones produced a famous line drawing of them in the 1960s (see page 119). Niclas y Glais and D.J. are shown together, deep in some affable conversation. Waldo is alongside them, but really he is alone, gazing outwards, as if in a puzzled trance. They were quite different personalities. Nonetheless, they had in common a deep, steady independence of mind. That I think is a quality characteristic of the people of Preseli. It is connected with the remarkable landscape in which they live.

Notes

1. As naturalist Ronald Lockley observed in the opening paragraph of his book *Wales* (Batsford, 1966), 'After a long absence, when I return to my native Pembrokeshire I like to walk, on the first fine free day, to the peak of the highest mountain – a third of a mile high – for there returns to me, standing on the sacred mountain of Prescelly Top, the "feeling" of Wales, land of brooding mountains and the eternal sea.'

2. *Y Faner*, 27 November 1946. Quoted in Hefin Wyn, *Battle of the Preselau*, Clychau Clochog, 2008, page 37.

3. James Lovelock, *Gaia: A New Look at Life on Earth*, Oxford University Press, 1979.

NORTH

BATTLE OF THE PRESELAU

On a meadow strewn with rocks, close to the summit of Carn Menyn, we form a circle. In the middle is Hefin Wyn, writer, journalist and community activist, reading a poem. His voice echoes against the stones that stand at our backs.

It is the ninth occasion since 2009 that a group of walkers have met towards the end of June to hike six miles across the high ridge of Mynydd Preselau. They start at Croes Mihangell on the slopes of Foel Drygarn, and finish at Bwlch-gwynt, below Cerrig Lladron. Usually around twenty people take part, sometimes as many as thirty. It depends on the weather. Today is hot and airless. We're down to a faithful dozen.

Over the years Hefin Wyn has read and read again the same poem in this place. It was written by Waldo Williams (see pages 106-112) to encourage the campaign against a War Office plan to take over Mynydd Preselau as a gunnery range in 1946. The poem ends with a warning and an exhortation:

> *Mae rhu, mae rhaib drwy'r fforest ddiffenestr.*
> *Cadwn y mur rhag y bwystfil, cadwn y ffynon rhag y baw.*

There's a roar, there's a ravening through the windowless forests.
Keep the wall from the brute, keep the stream clear of filth.[1]

The War Office plan was to possess a total of 58,800 acres of northern Preseli, much more than the 16,000 acres usually referred to that are close to Mynydd Preselau themselves. It enclosed an area from the outskirts of Fishguard and Letterston in the west, to Crymych and Hebron in the east. Specifically, the War Office would take permanent possession of 105 of the 204 farms on and around Mynydd Preselau. The other ninety-nine would lose part of their land.

Mynachlog-ddu with its shop and primary school would be within the range. So, too, would be thirty-eight sites of archeological interest, including Craig Rhos-y-felin and Carn Menyn, among the sources of the Bluestones that are at Stonehenge. Twelve places of worship would be disrupted, most severely Bethel Chapel in Mynachlog-ddu. Of its one hundred and ninety congregation, eighty-five would lose their homes, and a further seventy-nine would be badly affected.

There was fierce resistance. The gunnery range was widely regarded as wanton despoliation, an act of state-sponsored vandalism, an attack upon one of the most sacred parts of Wales. Even so there was a good deal of pessimism. There had been protests at a RAF proposal to build a bombing school at Penyberth in the Llŷn in 1936. Plaid Cymru leaders Saunders Lewis, D.J. Williams and Lewis Valentine had been imprisoned for setting fire to it. But it had still gone ahead. More immediate was the experience of the farmers of Mynydd Epynt in Breconshire. In 1940 the War Office took over 40,000 acres of their land, despite a Wales-wide protest. Four hundred people from twenty-four farms were forcibly evicted to make way for a firing range there. The boundary of Welsh-speaking Wales was pushed twelve miles westwards.

Yet the campaign in Preseli was different. In the first place the Second World War was over. Then there was the determination of the inhabitants. They made it clear they were simply not prepared to leave their homes, though their resistance would be non-violent. In other parts of Wales, the main argument against War Office incursion relied on the economic impact. In Preseli the case was overwhelmingly religious and cultural. A resolution passed by a public meeting at Maenclochog in December 1946 put it this way: 'We are not prepared to be the executioners of the Welsh language and we do not intend to be present at its funeral.'[2]

The 2018 commemorative walk began with a meeting in the car park at Bwlch-gwynt, the highest point where the road from Haverfordwest to Cardigan crosses Mynydd Preselau. The plan was to use a few of the cars to take the party to Croes Mihangell where the walk begins. But before we set off we were joined by Rev Ken Thomas who looks after the four Cylch Bro Cerwyn chapels, two each side of the mountain. His congregation elected him as their Minister. He read Psalm forty-six. 'God is our refuge and strength,' he began, and continued:

> He maketh wars to cease unto the end of the earth;
> He breaketh the bow and cutteth the spear in sunder;
> He burneth the chariot in the fire.

Reverend Thomas's choice of reading was as appropriate as his presence. For the campaign against the firing range was led by Ministers. One was Rev R. Parri-Roberts, Minister of Bethel

Chapel in Mynachlog-ddu. He was a pacifist, known as the 'Ghandi of the Preselau'.

Another was Rev Joseph James, Minister at Bethesda, Llawhaden. He is remembered for his stammer which, it is said, added much to the melodrama of his sermons. In a field above Maenclochog there is a standing stone to his memory. It has the words *Cadwodd fur Preselau rhag y bwystfil* (He kept the ramparts of the Preselau from the beast), a reference, of course, to Waldo's poem.

It was Joseph James who advocated direct action. At a meeting of the Preseli Preservation Committee he declared that he, his wife Ethel and Rev Parri-Roberts, would occupy the first farm whose tenants had been driven out by the authorities:

> And if they dared to th-threaten shooting two m-ministers then the whole of W-Wales would be bound to rise,' he said triumphantly before taking his seat. He leapt to his feet again in an instant and said: 'And if it's n-necessary for Ethel and I and P-Parri Bach to go to jail to d-defend you, well s-so be it – and remember they say visitors can c-come in on Thursdays.[3]

Parri Bach was evidently held in much affection. He gained the soubriquet 'Bach' because of his diminutive stature and his crooked back caused by childhood meningitis. His photograph is included on plaques that were placed at each end of the Preseli commemorative walk in 2009. At first the National Park authorities resisted, but finally relented. They were persuaded that without the campaign Mynydd Preselau would never have been made part of the National Park.

During the walk I discovered that five of our company were among the thirteen that undertook the first walk in 2009 and have been on many of them since. They were Eileen Curry, a part-time administrator in Withybush hospital; Eurfyl Lewis, a youth worker with Urdd Gobaith Cymru at their Pentre Ifan farm; David Llewelyn, a retired primary school headmaster; Rhythwyn Nicholas who worked for many years in the stores of an agricultural company in Crymych; and Suzanne Walters, a retired accountant from Mynachlog-ddu.

They share a dedication and adherence to values that cannot fail to impress. During the campaign there was a meeting between the two leading ministers, Rev Parri-Roberts and Rev Joseph James, and representatives of the War Office. It began with Rev James announcing, 'Let us pray', a move calculated to put the men from Whitehall off their stride.

When the discussion began in earnest, the civil servants pronounced their opinion that the mountain land was of little agricultural worth, apart from fattening stock in the summer. At this Rev Parri-Roberts beckoned his fellow minister to interject. 'You tell them that we rear souls along these slopes, tell them Joe.'[4]

MYNYDD CASTLEBYTHE

The outlines of the old field pattern on the thirty-acre sheep farm in the Preseli uplands can be clearly seen. Their small scale is quite different from the larger lowland farms to the south where the fields have been amalgamated into bigger acreages. As a result, many of the hedgerows and the wildlife they supported, have been obliterated.

Even here all that remains of the hedges are two to three-foot mounds overgrown with grass. Previous generations of farmers ploughed as near the edge as they could. In the process they removed the trees and shrubs that provided cover for bees, butterflies, insects, voles, shrews and birds. They destroyed what might be called the ecological superstructure.

Today's owner, broadcaster Jamie Owen, has a box camera photograph of the farm taken towards the end of the nineteenth century. It shows the fields much as they are today, except that the hedgerows are in abundance. Jamie's life's passion is to restore them to their former glory. Over the years since he bought the farm he's been fencing along either side of the turfed mounds that line his fields. In between he's planted native shrubs and saplings, blackthorn, rowan and willow, white may, hawthorn, holly and oak. Jamie is a new kind of farmer. His land produces a crop but no money. He has ninety sheep and and a handful of beehives but they run at a loss. You might say he is in the business of altruistic husbandry, farming the landscape for the peace of mind it brings. The height and thin soil means that no farmer here can make a living just from the land. They or their wives have other occupations that bring in cash. Much of the time Jamie is far away plying his trade as a broadcaster. For nearly a quarter of a century he was a familiar face fronting the news on BBC Wales and an easygoing voice on Radio Five Live. Then at the start of 2018 he went global with the Turkish-based international broadcaster TRT International, working out of Washington, London and Istanbul.

Jamie's voice draws in the listener. He has the rare quality, too, of appearing effortlessly natural under the harsh gaze of the television cameras. Such gifts come with a price. For Jamie Owen it's the need for constant retreat to the lonely silence of the Preseli hills, made more pressing by his new globetrotting role.

He was brought up in Pembroke Dock where his father was a local solicitor and his mother a health visitor. He read English and History at the University of Gloucestershire. After directing student theatre at the Edinburgh Festival he became a trainee announcer in London with Radio 3 and then Radio 4. A stint with BBC Wales followed but after a year he fell out with his boss and was sacked. Aged twenty-six he went back to university in Cardiff to train as a journalist. Then he returned to BBC Wales, but this time to the newsroom. He also spent time abroad with the BBC World Service Trust. He worked with broadcasters in conflict zones including Ramallah on Palestine's West Bank, in Libya, and Egypt.

At the same time two close friends died of cancer. It concentrated the mind. 'Life is short and you need to grab your dream if you're ever going to realise it,' is the way he puts it. In 2007, aged 40, he took the plunge. Mortgaging himself to the hilt he bought Slade farm in the shadow of Mynydd Castlebythe, a few miles from

Puncheston up the headwaters of the Cleddau.

One of the first farming lessons he learnt was the importance of neighbours. Survival is dependent on co-operation. Jamie made common cause with five other holdings that farm the slopes of Mynydd Castlebythe where each have a share in its three hundred acres of common land. However, for more than a generation its usefulness had declined as its fences deteriorated. Over many meetings in the nearby Tufton Arms Jamie persuaded the others that it would be worth the effort and expense to renew the fencing to regain control of the summer grazing.

The land is inside the Pembrokeshire National Park and it, too, saw the virtue of bringing the land back into productive use. That way the bracken could be reduced and the land recolonised by ground nesting birds. Over seven years a partnership between the farmers and the National Park worked wonders. But first the ownership rights had to be made legally watertight. Who owned the land? No-one could be sure. Claims went back centuries to the Marcher Lords of Newport. It was the National Park that provided the legal backup to secure the rights. It also helped with the costs of gates and cattle grids on the roads.

Now, during the summer months the sheep from the six farms that surround Mynydd Castlebythe graze the common land. In mid-October the farmers bring them down to their winter pastures

in the fields below. It is a return to the old Preseli practice of transhumance. And the birds are on the increase as well. There are wheatears, stonechats, skylarks, barn owls and red kites. Jamie says he has heard a cuckoo for the first time in years.

Renovating the farmhouse has been another preoccupation. Its origins go back some three hundred years when the stones of the rough hut for the first shepherds were laid down. As times became more prosperous, during the nineteenth century when wool prices were high, the structure developed into a typical Welsh longhouse, with two storeys and a slate roof at one end. However, in the 1960s council-inspired improvements nearly wrecked the place. Concrete rendering and double-glazed windows caused condensation and damp. Jamie has undone these changes and restored the house to its appearance a century ago. Inside, heating is provided by a wood-fired stove. Wifi reception is irregular and there is no television.

Towards the end of my visit, as evening draws in, Jamie takes me on the road that marks the upper boundary of his farm. The common land rises to the mountain above where it merges with the clouds. Eventually we reach the lip of the hill where the road begins its descent. Far to the south the stacks of the Milford Haven refineries pierce the darkening evening sky. To the west are the outlines of Strumble Head and Carn Llidi on St David's Peninsula. And apart from the wind coursing through the bracken and grass, there is just the sound of a great stillness.

CWM GWAUN

Ffald-y-Brenin is a Christian retreat on a hillside overlooking Cwm Gwaun, a glacier scooped valley that drives into Mynydd Preselau to the east of Fishguard. In the foyer Anna Mari Huws, a Welsh-speaker from Pontypridd, is smiling at me. She is a confident woman, perhaps in her early thirties.

'I'll give you a blessing,' she declares, closing her eyes. 'I bless you in the name of Jesus to know God, his purpose for your life, and his blessings on you and your family and the situations of your life.'

Ffald-y-Brenin is a place of blessings, set amidst attractive gardens and lovely countryside. Its elegantly converted farm and outbuildings are home to around twenty or thirty visitors at any one time. It's been going for about thirty years and is never empty. Anna is one of twenty staff who organise the place, responsible for front of house, meeting and greeting people, settling them in. They come from all over the world, from the United States, Australia, Norway, the Far East. More than two thousand people pass through its doors every year.

'How do they hear about the place?' I ask.

'Word of mouth,' Anna answers. 'And then, of course, there's Roy's book.'

She hands me *The Grace Outpouring* by Roy Godwin, director of Ffald-y-Brenin. It is published in Colorado Springs in the United States. The blurb inside tells me, 'The Celts used to speak of *thin places*, where heaven brushes earth so closely you feel its breath, hear its whisper. Ffald-y-Brenin – *the Sheepfold of the King* – is such a place.'

A little earlier I had run into a couple from Canada. 'What brought you to Ffald-y-Brenin?' Without a pause they answered, 'Oh, we read *The Grace Outpouring*.'

Alongside me is Bonni Davies with whom I've come to Ffald-y-Brenin. She has lived for fifty years in Penlanwynt farm directly across the valley. At a thousand feet on the slopes of Foel Eryr it's so high up it was once the most elevated dairy farm in Wales. However, they stopped milking twelve years ago. Now they keep about eight hundred sheep and eighty cattle.

Bonni Davies attends meetings of Rocesi'r Fro at Ffald-y-Brenin, along with thirty other women from Cwm Gwaun. She tells me it's like the Merched y Wawr. In England it would be the Women's Institute. The word *rocesi*, meaning girls, is a throwback to the old Demetian dialect that was current in Preseli a century ago, and still lingers in Cwm Gwaun. Demetian for boy is Rocyn. So you could say that around here boys and girls are Rocynau and Rocesi.

They do things differently in Cwm Gwaun. Most famously, the place follows the pre-1752 Julian calendar and celebrates *Hen Galan* (the New Year) on 13 January. It's partly because Cwm Gwaun is so isolated, only reachable by narrow, winding roads. Its individuality also derives from its unusual landscape. The valley is about six miles long, half-a-mile wide, and in places more than three hundred feet deep. Much of it is forested. Geologists call it a sub-glacial melt water channel that was created during the Ice Age. The ice did not come down from the mountains, but in from the sea, hence it is known as the Irish Sea Glacier. At the end of the glaciation, about a hundred thousand years ago, vast quantities of melt water were produced. It was this that created Cwm Gwaun. The melt water was under such great pressure far below the ice surface that it actually flowed uphill. This explains why Cwm Gwaun has no head and why its lower slopes are so flat. In the southwest it opens into Fishguard Bay, in the northeast into the amphitheatre of Cilgwyn.

The valley has a scattered population of about three hundred people, and Bonni Davies knows them all. She edits the local Papur Bro *Llien Gwyn* (White Sail). Cousins run many of the farms. Diversification is the way Cwm Gwaun's farmers survive. Next door to Ffald-y-Brenin is Penlan Uchaf, a farm that diversified more than thirty years ago with a garden and tearoom. Dilwyn Vaughan runs it and assures me that the venture is as hard work as farming. Its visitors peaked at around ten thousand-a-year some time ago. Today they're down to five thousand. But still it's a going concern.

'It's mainly older folk who come,' Dilwyn says, as he watches his granddaughter Ella, a student, serving tea and cakes. 'They're the ones interested in gardens.'

A more recent intervention is the Bluestone Brewery at Tyriet farm, a few miles up the valley. It builds on the long tradition of brewing in Cwm Gwaun, especially at haymaking time. Originally from Yorkshire, the Turner family have been farming here for thirty years, most of the time as tenants. In 2011 they managed to buy the farm and in 2013 diversified into brewing. Simon does the brewing while daughter Amy looks after sales and marketing. Kerry, his wife, keeps their organic sheep farm going. A unique selling point is the water from their well on the farm. Otherwise the association with the Bluestones of Mynydd Preselau, has given an edge to the marketing. Whatever the explanation, sales of Bluestone beers have been increasing by thirty per cent a year. It sells throughout Pembrokeshire, Wales and increasingly abroad, especially Denmark.

Bonni Davies' own farm is an example of diversification in a more conventional but no less innovative way. It outsources its farming skills. Bonni's son Hedd has grown a business scanning sheep between November and February on farms throughout southwest Wales. The scans show how many lambs the sheep are carrying, whether they're singles, twins or more. Grandsons Llyr and Gethin have developed a shearing business.

Just down the road at Pentrisillt farm is Siop Siafins[5], a carpentry business run by the farm's eldest son, Tecwyn James. His brother Euros runs the farm with his parents while Tecwyn makes handcrafted dressers, bookcases, chairs, windows and stairs. He made a new pulpit for Caersalem Chapel in Cwm Gwaun when they replaced the pews with chairs in 2007.

An obligatory stop is at the Dyffryn Arms in the small hamlet of Pontfaen. This ancient pub has been in the hands of the same family since 1845. Bessie Davies, now eighty-eight, married into the business sixty-eight years ago and has become a fixture, though it's her granddaughter Nerys who pulls us half-a pint. I say 'pull' advisedly. In fact, the beer is poured directly into a jug from a keg below the bar. Tourists come from miles away to experience this living piece of the early twentieth century.

However, the quintessence of Cwm Gwaun is the post office a mile away, towards Fishguard. It must be the only post office in the whole of Britain to be located in a farmyard. Indeed, it's the apotheosis of agricultural diversification. It was originally next door to Tŷ Gwyn farm. When the proprietor decided to give up, in the mid-1970s, the farm took it on. Gwenda Morgan has been running it ever since.

I ask her how she's kept going when it has only about five or six customers a day. After all, the Post Office has been busy closing post offices in much bigger communities up and down the land. Gwenda's answer typifies Cwm Gwaun. In the last round of cuts it was decreed that sub-post offices more than four miles distant from their nearest major settlement could survive. Cwm Gwaun's farmyard post office is equidistant from Fishguard and Newport by four-and-a-half miles.

'The people of Mynydd Preselau are very loyal,' Gwenda says. 'They come from as far away as Maenclochog and Puncheston.

Lots of people refuse to have their state pensions paid directly into their bank. They prefer cash from me instead.'

FACHONGLE ISAF

I first heard the name John Seymour, in his day a one-man rebellion against modernity, in the bar of the Golden Lion in Newport. I was there to quiz the proprietor Glyn Rees about the way the political winds were blowing ahead of the general election in February 1974. He had been Agent to Pembrokeshire's Labour MP Desmond Donnelly and had followed him when he led the breakaway Democratic Party in the 1960s. Donnelly fought and lost the seat in the name of his new party in the 1970 election. In the process he split the Labour vote and let the Tories in. It was melodramatic politics and Glyn Rees had been at the heart of it.

But what I remember about our conversation is Glyn's comments about a larger than life character who had bought a farm at Fachongle Isaf a few miles away. 'Don't know how he does it,' he remarked. 'Gets all these young people from all over the world to go there and work his land for free.' What Glyn didn't realise was that it was John Seymour who was losing financially and not the young people who were flocking to his farm. They were supposed to pay at least for their bed and board in return for learning from the renowned guru of self-sufficiency. But John was so disorganised and, ultimately, generous that he rarely collected any money from many of them.

John earned large amounts from his writing, but he was always in debt. When he bought Fachongle Isaf in 1963, for £4,500, he had no money at all. 'Buy first and pay later,' he recalled. In this case the vendor, a squire who was selling off his estate, gave him a mortgage at six per cent for half the amount. The rest he borrowed from the bank.

Seymour arrived in Pembrokeshire with his wife Sally, a potter and artist, and three small children. They left behind a farm in Suffolk where they had lived successfully in a self-sufficient way for six years. So why did they move? They wanted to own their own farm for one thing and in those days Pembrokeshire was one of the cheapest places to buy. Good farming land sold at £60 an acre. Moreover, some friends had already moved there. When the

Seymours visited that sealed it. 'This was a smiling sunny country,' was the way John put it. 'It had hills of a humane size, splendid wooded valleys, sweeping fertile uplands and a coastline that makes the Mediterranean look dowdy.'

His early life laid the foundations for his thinking. He was born in north London but spent much of his childhood at Frinton-on-Sea in Essex. There he experienced a sepia farming world that included shire horses and people living directly off the land and sea. After agricultural college he went, aged 20, to South Africa to manage a sheep farm. He became a deckhand and then skipper of a fishing boat operating from Namibia. Then he worked in a copper mine in Northern Rhodesia (now Zambia). Later he joined the South African veterinary service. He also spent time with Bushmen in the Kalahari Desert, and was much influenced by their hunter-gatherer lifestyle.

He served with the King's African Rifles in East Africa and Burma during the Second World War. Afterwards he travelled overland from Europe to India, through cultures still dominated by peasant farming. Back in the UK, he worked on one of the last sailing barges on the east coast. Later he sailed the Baltic with Sally and seven-year-old daughter Jane exploring the islands of Sweden and Denmark

A stream of books flowed from these experiences, all of them pointing to the coming ecological crisis. In west Wales he became the acknowledged leader of the environmental movement. As he explained, 'We were consciously trying to break away from industry-dominated society and form a new kind of culture – a simpler, less materialistic, less polluting, less dangerous kind, in close touch with the soil.'

His books gained a worldwide audience, especially *The Complete Book of Self Sufficiency*. It was published in 1976 and has never been out of print. One person who read it was Vicky Moller. She was living in London with three small children, having fled from a relationship in Anglesey. She wrote to Fachongle Isaf asking if she could visit. The community had decided they could take no more people but found her letter persuasive. She came, and after three days John Seymour, by now separated amicably from Sally, proposed marriage.

'It was brave of him to take me on with three children,' Vicki recalled. 'But he was trusting and impulsive. He needed help and I shared his vision.'

We are talking forty years on from that moment. Their relationship lasted three years, after which John moved away with a much younger woman, Angela, to County Wexford in Ireland. His three daughters and Vicky combined to buy the farm, releasing him finally from his debts.

Years later I asked him why he'd gone. 'West Wales was becoming far too crowded,' he replied, with a twinkle in his eye.

Vicky still lives at Fachongle Isaf, with some of her children close-by, including a son she had with John. And the place still functions as a loosley connected self-sufficient community. It produces milk, butter, cheese, yoghurt, meat, fruit, vegetables, and preserves. It has a shared electric car, a community hall, and a business selling wood-burning stoves. There are around twenty people making a living in various ways, including craftspeople, plumbers, electricians and carpenters. Among those living there are a local produce market manager, a prosthetic limb designer, an eco-shop manager, a shiatsu therapist, a flower grower, and a marine ecologist. And within a few miles there are a number of innovative enterprises including an artisan brewery and an off the electricity grid land-based community.

Also still living next door to Fachongle Isaf, in a smallholding known as Pantry Fields, is John's daughter Anne. She is a potter, following in the footsteps of mother Sally, while husband David

Sears is a cabinetmaker. Together they run the Carningli Press, named after the mountain that overlooks them. It keeps some of Seymour's books in print. A shelf in their kitchen is lined with his forty-four complete works.

Drinking coffee, we chat about the way Fachongle Isaf has changed over the years. Anne recalls that when she went to school in nearby Newport in the 1960s no Welsh was taught. 'When we first arrived we got on well with our neighbours,' she says. 'But later, as the numbers moving in increased, issues around the language seemed to mount and we were a bit like separate peoples living apart. But these days we're coming together again. I think it's partly to do with a new generation growing up who were born here and attended schools that now teach Welsh.'

Wandering around Fachongle Isaf I bump into John Spikes who is busy making a circular tent-like wooden structure that could be used as a garden shed, summerhouse or even a small dwelling. John lives in one himself. 'They can be divided into a kitchen, living and sleeping area,' he says. 'You can fit a stove whose pipe goes through the roof. It's a low impact design.' The materials and building costs come to around £3,000. But crucially it covers 8.3 square metres of floor space, which is below the ten square metres that would require planning permission from the National Park.

John Spikes has been at Fachongle Isaf for fifteen years. He tells me the place is like a university, but without the structures or hierarchy. 'People come and go, but however long they stay they take a bit of the place away with them,' he says. 'It changes you.'

I reckon John Seymour would nod his head in approval. Something of him seems still to hover above Fachongle Isaf. Vicky Moller says she missed him terribly when he left to go to Ireland. 'It wasn't just our personal relationship,' she said. 'He belonged here. His influence was all around. In a way he's still here.'

In an Afterword to one of his books *The Fat of the Land*, daughter Anne recalls Dan, a friend who lived with them for a while when they were young, saying:

> John was one of the most alive people I ever met. He could be an instant party. He would listen to you as if you were one of the most important people on the planet. And his laugh was so infectious it would draw you into his humour and hold you there, until you shared the conviction that the world was a most wondrous place, and that to laugh was a great glory to be shared.

Towards the end of his life, when he was approaching ninety, John returned to live with his daughters at Pantry Fields next door to Fachongle Isaf. Anne and David brought him back from County Wexford where he was still living with Angela, though she had remarried. He was glad to spend time with his children and grandchildren and help out a little with the garden. He organised the planting of some apple trees at a high point of the farm where he said he wanted to be buried.

When it came, the occasion was as self-sufficient as he could have wished. A coffin had been ordered but was dispatched to Newport in Monmouthshire, rather than Newport, Pembrokeshire. So on the day friends prepared an alternative. The shroud was cloth made of wool from his own sheep and they rolled him in a carpet he had brought back from India. They dug his headstone out of the grave. It is overlooked by Carningli, the Mount of Angels.

MARTHA MORGAN COUNTRY

Martha Morgan, whose name has come to personify the area around Carningli, arrived fully formed in the course of one night. She appeared as if she might be a reincarnation, a disembodied voice in the darkness. She insisted that what had happened to her between the years 1778 and 1855 should finally be told. Oddly, the moment she chose to appear was after Brian John had stepped off an aircraft in Gran Canaria in the winter of 1998. 'I suddenly felt terrible[7];' he told me. 'It was as though I had flu. My temperature shot up, I had a headache and began to shake and shiver. I now think I was affected by what they call Aerotox syndrome, from breathing in the contaminated air they pump round the aircraft.' When Brian and his Swedish wife Inger reached their holiday apartment he went straight to bed. But he didn't sleep. Instead he became delirious, and it was at this point that Martha appeared. 'It wasn't a dream,' he said. 'I was wide-awake. My mind was buzzing. It was almost as if I was in a state of drug-induced consciousness. I had a heightened sense of awareness.'

Martha was a compellingly beautiful and passionate young woman with long dark hair and brown eyes. 'As I lay there in the warm darkness gazing at the bedroom ceiling she was talking to me,' Brian recalled. 'At breakneck speed she told me the story of her life, with details of places, people she knew, twists and turns in her life, even snatches of conversation.'

In the morning he felt better, but Martha's message was firmly fixed in his mind. 'Somehow I knew her story had to be told in her own words, not retrospectively, but with immediacy, through the entries of a diary she had kept,' Brian said. 'You see it wasn't a dream. If it had been I wouldn't have remembered.' So he took out his laptop and started writing, and didn't stop for eight years. By that time eight full-length novels had appeared, creating the *Angel Mountain Saga*.

When he embarked on Martha's story Brian John was already a well-established writer, though in very different fields. He had published approaching eighty books on glaciers and the Ice Age, and the Pembrokeshire landscape, folklore, fauna and flora. Bestsllers include his *Pembrokeshire Coast Path* (National Trail Guides), continuously in print since the 1970s, and *Pembrokeshire* (Pan Books, 1978). Brought up in Haverfordwest, he had studied at Oxford in the 1960s, become a field scientist with the British

Antarctic Survey, and then a Geography lecturer at Durham University. But in the mid-1970s he made an unusual career move, leaving the security of academic life to return to Wales with Inger. They joined a growing band moving into the Preseli hills to adopt a more self-sufficient, ecological lifestyle. On their smallholding on the same slopes of Carningli frequented by Martha, Brian established a publishing enterprise, supplemented by Inger's candle-making business.

At first, Brian found writing fiction difficult. He had to discover ways of developing character, plot and pace, and a sense of place. He also had to think himself into the eighteenth and early nineteenth centuries, researching patterns of speech, social customs, beliefs, farming routines, food, clothing and the political events of the time. Most difficult was portraying the character of a pregnant, suicidal mistress of a small country estate, and to speak through a diary format. Yet, as Brian put it, 'I felt to do otherwise would have been to betray what I can only think of as the gift of that story I was given one night in Gran Canaria.'

The undertaking is reminiscent of Winston Graham's Cornish melodrama *Poldark*, set in the same period with its tempestuous female character Demelza. *A Scots Quair* comes to mind too, the 1930s trilogy by the Scottish writer Lewis Grassic Gibbon, describing the life of another feisty woman from northeast Scotland in the early twentieth century.

They all rely on their settings. In the case of the *Angel Mountain Saga* it is the mountain itself with its myth that if you spend a night at its summit you either become a poet or go mad. It has one of the largest Iron Age hill forts in west Wales, with a volcanic profile that can be seen from miles around. The name comes from the legend of Saint Brynach who used to climb the mountain to find serenity and commune with the angels. In Brian John's stories his heroine Martha also has a special relationship with the mountain. At one climactic moment she struggles with and kills a bitter enemy close to its summit.

Brian wondered if she might have been a real person and searched the records. He found several Martha Morgans from the early nineteenth century. However, they were all people of a lower class who lived as far afield as St Davids and St Dogmaels. There was one who lived near Newport but much later than his heroine.

It took him eighteen months to complete the first volume, *On Angel Mountain*. Then came the challenge of publication. He contacted more than fifty agents and about the same number of publishers but to no avail. 'Nobody was interested in reading even a chapter'. So Brian decided to self-publish. The first print-run of two thousand disappeared in two weeks, and the book had to be reprinted three times. Encouraged Brian carried on, producing four more novels at the rate of one a year.

At the end of the fifth novel *Flying with Angels*, Martha Morgan dies. However, popular demand forced her resurrection. Brian wrote three more novels, in part by going back to fill gaps in her story. Whether there are more novels to come is moot, but I suspect there may be.

By now the *Angel Mountain Saga* has attracted a cult following. Sales exceed eighty-two thousand. More than that, Martha has given her name to a large tract of northern Preseli. She has been pressed into service as a cultural tourism initiative, supported by the National Park and the county council. They're hoping the area will become known as Martha Morgan Country in a similar way to Poldark Country, Shakespeare Country, Hardy Country, Wordsworth Country, Jane Austen's Bath, and Charles Dickens' London.

'It's good to have something from Wales that has nothing to do with Dylan Thomas,' Brian remarks.

An elaborate website features Rhiannon James of St Dogmaels, a former Miss Pembrokeshire, who happens to have long dark hair and brown eyes, acting as Miss Martha. She has been photographed, suitably garbed, in multiple locations associated with the *Angel Mountain Saga.*[6]

Will the idea of Martha Morgan Country catch on? I suspect the answer comes down to authenticity. Will the hallucinations of one man in Gran Canaria, subsequently published to local acclaim, have a wider impact? Naturally, Brian John has no doubt. His conviction

is reinforced by a sense that Martha Morgan's story is an allegory for the story of Wales itself. A plot running through the novels is her clinging on to the estate she has inherited against the depredations of rival claimants to the land.

'It seems to me that much of the history of Wales has been about it being a desirable bit of real estate which other people, especially the English, have been trying to get their hands on,' Brian explained. 'In the face of such a persistent assault, over decades for Martha and over centuries for Wales, how do you sustain your integrity, your self-esteem, your identity? That is a central issue for Martha as it is for Wales itself. As time has gone on, I feel that in telling the story of Martha on her rough piece of land in far-flung Preseli, I've been telling the story of Wales as well.'

And he adds, 'I did not realise it at first, but as the writing proceeded, I came to appreciate that Martha is actually Mother

Wales, personifying all that is good and bad about my native land. A key thing about her personality is her sense of *hiraeth*, of longing and belonging. She really feels that her home Plas Ingli, and Carningli are a part of her, as she is a part of them.'

ROUNDHOUSE

The wooden, grass-covered Roundhouse is in a tree-lined wilderness on the northern side of Carningli. You reach it by way of a lane a couple of miles inland from Newport. There's a narrow gap in the hedge and a short track leads to a parking place. Then you walk. First you pass old farm buildings that now constitute the Brithdir Mawr community. Then you negotiate a muddy path overhung with trees for about half-a-mile downhill.

Eventually you reach a large circular clearing. In the late Spring it's waist high with vegetation, some evidently planted by human hand. The trees are alive with birdsong. The Roundhouse is most clearly evident by a few glass panels that form part of its wall. They glint in the sun. Otherwise it looks for all the world a natural part of the rest of the chaotic greenery that envelops this place.

When its owner Tony Wrench steps out of the doorway it's hard to credit that for a while his Roundhouse was the centre of a global media frenzy. In the early 2000s TV channels from Hong Kong to New York were fascinated by what they saw as a bunch of visionary hippies leading a Stone Age lifestyle in the face of government officialdom.

The Roundhouse is an experiment in low impact living. Made of locally sourced wood and an earth roof, it uses a small wind turbine and solar panels for its heating and lighting. It cost just £3,000 and was built without a thought directed at the planners of the county council or the National Park. Predictably, they decreed the Roundhouse failed to meet their regulations.

So Tony and his partner Faith applied for planning permission. They were refused twice. Then they were told to demolish the structure. That was in 2002. Legal appeals delayed execution until Tony finally gave up. On the Easter weekend of 2004 he was poised to demolish the house. That was when a 'hippyish but well-organised group of eco-warriors', as *The Times* called them, intervened.

Protesters from This Land is Ours descended. First they occupied the Iron Age village at Henllys a few miles away. There the National Park authorities had given themselves planning permission to re-create a group of Iron Age circular huts very similar to Tony and Faith's Roundhouse. The protesters flew a huge banner declaring *Roundhouses Aren't History*. An impromptu 'ideal

low-impact home exhibition' appeared in a nearby lay-by. Then the protesters marched to Brithdir Mawr to prevent Tony and Faith from destroying their Roundhouse. It had become a symbol of the struggle for low impact living.

Tony and Faith stayed their hand. This Land is Ours marched on Haverfordwest and squatted in the car park of the local authority, complete with yurt and tents. Their protest made further headlines and a mockery of the council's commitment to sustainable development. It had just given permission for two-hundred-and-sixty-eight luxury wooden cabins at the Bluestone theme resort. This was set in five hundred acres partly within the National Park, complete with restaurants and a large swimming pool, only a few miles down the road.

Tony and Faith were fined a modest £150 by a sympathetic County Court judge. At a later Crown Court hearing, when the National Park brought an injunction against them, the judge refused permission for the case to proceed. At this point the

National Park said they would review their decision. Tony and Faith were allowed to appear in front of them for the first time. But their application was refused again. This was on the technicality that they didn't have sufficient woodland from which to derive a livelihood. Finally, they won on a further appeal in 2008. It was conceded that, after all, they did have enough woodland, by sharing with their neighbours at Brithdir Mawr.

This long struggle contributed to the inclusion of a Low Impact Development policy as part of the National Park's and the county council's Joint Unitary Development Plan in 2006. Twelve years later, Tony and I are sitting outside the Roundhouse, coffee in hand, contemplating the extent to which the world has changed. The principles of sustainable and low impact living have been won for sure, but how much is actually being done in practice?

Nevertheless, I sense that Tony has arrived at a sense of equanimity with the world. He has a lifetime of environmental campaigning behind him. Now he's turned seventy and just wants to get on with living. He and Faith pay council tax, but they have no mortgage, and no rent, water, heating, or electricity bills. These days Tony gets by on a small pension, does some wood turning, teaches a bit, delivers the odd lecture, and plays guitar with his circle dance and Ceilidh band Rasalaila.

Living in the Roundhouse also takes up a good deal of time. They grow most of their own fruit and vegetables. A profusion of vines on the turf roof and in a glasshouse behind provide the materials for a small wine making industry. Tony reckons they spend about a day a week coppicing, gathering and laying down wood for the winter months. Faith concedes they have a few gas rings for cooking.

The wind turbine and solar panels need constant attention. 'Living in the Roundhouse is a bit like sailing a yacht,' Tony says. 'You always need to trim the sails. There are infinite subtleties in the adjustments you need to make to achieve the optimum output.'

I ask how well his initial design has stood the test of the past twenty years. Tony says there are three things he would change. First he wouldn't build it into the side of an embankment, but erect it as a free-standing structure. 'It's extraordinary the number of creatures that try to burrow their way in to join us,' he laughs. 'We're had moles, voles, hedgehogs, even a badger.'

Secondly, he would separate the bathroom and clothes washing area, to distance the main living accommodation from damp and condensation. Finally, he would raise the floor from the ground to allow about a foot of free-flowing air underneath for better insulation.

All these principles are being applied to a new Roundhouse Tony has started to build not far from the existing one. The idea is to provide him with a workshop for his wood-turning. However, I suspect that when finished its desirability as a new home will become irresistible, with the old one becoming the workshop.

Tony is keen to explain that they are not about trying to achieve a self-sufficient way of life of the kind his hero, the late John Seymour used to advocate. 'To do that in this climate I reckon you'd have to become a hunter gatherer, and what is there to hunt?'

Tony gets up and points across the clearing. 'At the very least you'd have to keep pigs and they would completely trash the land we have. It would mean the end of our wetlands which contain a mass of invaluable flora and fauna. As it is I think the National Park quite like us precisely because we don't engage in heavy-duty farming.'

Our conversation turns to what living in a Roundhouse will be like with the onset old age. Tony says he's been considering this question quite a lot, how low impact design can be made to address it. 'I think we need to think more in terms of community self-sufficiency,' he reflects. 'We should plan for clusters of low impact homes designed to encourage support and interactivity between people. Roundhouses would be good for that.'

KINGFISHER HIDE

A wide reed-lined pond lies in front of the Kingfisher Hide. It seems empty of life. But suddenly a large grey heron rears up on a small island a few yards away and begins preening its feathers. Then a mallard duck lands with a whoosh. It comes to a halt, and the water gradually resumes its calm surface. But there are no kingfishers. You need patience to catch their flash of blue and orange. Maybe on this May morning I can cultivate it. Certainly, this is a good place to be on the day of a royal wedding.

I'm in the Welsh Wildlife Centre's Teifi marshes nature reserve, just inside Preseli's northern border. Within its 270 acres you can find 130 species of bird, fifteen of dragonfly and damselfly, twenty-five of butterfly, 250 different moths, and 350 kinds of plants. Oh, and there are deer, badgers, rabbits, some water buffalo, and – according to the leaflet – this is the best site in Wales to see otters, though I don't see any.

There are four trails, Explorer, Gorge, Woodland and Wetlands. I opt for the last because it looks the most interesting. The guide tells you it should take forty-five minutes, but I linger and spend twice as long. At first the path follows the line of the old Cardi Bach railway, now part of the National Cycle Network. Most of the cyclists are small children wearing elaborate, colourful helmets, riding with stabilisers. I don't think they've come here for the wildlife.

The twenty-seven miles long Whitland and Cardigan Railway was known as the Cardi Bach line. Part of it opened in the 1870s to connect the slate quarries at Glogue, east of Crymych, with the main Carmarthen line, and was extended to Cardigan in 1886. It linked the villages in between, carrying everything from newspapers and the post to shop goods and farming essentials. The line closed in 1962, another victim of the motorcar and the Beeching cuts. But most of the track bed is still intact and there surely is a case for enthusiasts to re-open some of it to join the other Great Little Railways of Wales. It would certainly be a boost for tourism in northern Preseli.

Before the railway was built the the tidal river flooded twice a day, producing a saltmarsh habitat. The railway divided the marsh, cut off large areas from the sea and created a freshwater lake. The two separated areas then developed a completely different habitat and range of wildlife that today add to the nature reserve's diversity.

One species common to both sides is the dragonfly. When mating they fly in tandem, one behind the other. The female lays her eggs by dipping her rear end into the water. The larvae then spend two years submerged before climbing on to a stem of grass or a water plant. Here the skin splits to reveal a fully-formed dragonfly.

As I continue the circular walk I come to a spot that is home to the reserve's most famous occupant, the cetti warbler. This is a small, brown, rather nondescript bird, very difficult to see because of its skulking habits. And, of course, I don't see it. Apparently, the best time is at dawn when the male will land on a prominent part of its territory and emit loud bursts of an explosive song. This has a unique structure that prevents it mating with other species. If you are a keen birder and willing to get up early then it's good to know that the Teifi reserve has one of Britain's largest colonies.

In a short while, I reach the Curlew Hide that overlooks the main river. It was put on this spot to give it a close view of a mid-river mud bank. However, shortly afterwards floodwater moved the bank a hundred yards downstream. Perhaps that's why I don't see any curlews. But there are plenty of gulls and a few cormorants.

It's a peaceful spot, only broken by the low roar of traffic coming from the A484 on the other side of the river that connects Cardigan with Newcastle Emlyn. The noise recedes as I turn on to a long boardwalk through the middle of a huge reed bed. Pools and creeks break up the expanse of reed, allowing other wetland plants such as marsh marigold to grow at the edges. The reed spreads through seed dispersal, but there are also strong underground root networks that help bind the mud together. Altogether it makes a splendid habitat for birds like the water rail, coot, moorhen and the occasional bittern.

There are seven hides dotted along the route, each selected to maximise the possibility of observing different species. Eventually I reach the last, the Otter Hide. About a hundred-and-fifty-yards in front of it is a grassy bank lined with a hedge, apparently a favourite place for otters to breed. You'd need binoculars to see them. However, I do see three swamp water buffalo. They've been introduced to control invasive plants and maintain open water for the damselflies and dragonflies.

You have to look closely for the water buffalo. Now you see them, now you don't. Following a watercourse, their large brown shapes and white horns bob up and down in the lush landscape of the green marsh. They're a strange sub-tropical sight in this most temperate of lands.

NORTH COAST

The most northern point of Preseli overlooks Poppit Sands and the navigationally difficult bar of the Teifi estuary. Across the water are Gwbert and Cardigan Island. It's a gusty, blue day and I'm about to walk what is generally regarded as the most challenging section of the Pembrokeshire Coast Path. Officially it starts here, at the Lifeboat Station on Poppit Sands. There's a plaque naming the man who opened it, in 1970. He was Wynford Vaughan Thomas, at the time President of the Council for the Protection of Rural Wales. More famously he was a radio and television journalist, known for his wartime broadcasts and for taking on Marxist historian Gwyn Alf Williams in the 1980s television history series, *The Dragon Has Two Tongues*. Wynford was born in Swansea but towards the end of his life made Preseli his home. He owned Pentower, a splendid house with views overlooking Fishguard's Lower Town and harbour. A bon viveur and raconteur, he regarded life as guided by 'pointless optimism', which may be as good a philosophy as any.

The plaque says that from here it's one hundred-and-eighty-six miles to Amroth, the southernmost point of Pembrokeshire's border with Carmarthenshire. I plan to walk the whole length someday, but now I'm just walking to Newport. It's about sixteen miles of steep hills and precipitous cliffs. One guide to the path describes this section as a 'brute'.[7]

Nonetheless, the start is gentle enough. It's a lane that leads up a hill past Poppit Sands Youth Hostel. At my back are enticing views of the Teifi estuary. There's a curious metal sign high in the hedge, complete with leaping dolphins, announcing that I'm passing *Gate Number One of Pembrokeshire's Coastal Path*. Except there's no gate. Instead the lane diverges, with one path descending towards a farm and what looks to be a campsite. Incorrectly I choose the other one, branching upwards to the left. It takes me towards the heights of Pengarn and Cemaes Head. Here, overlooking the plunging cliffs, is a broken-down structure with large window frames empty of glass. At first it looks as if it might be a relic from World War II. On closer inspection I see it's an abandoned coast guard station. Inside there's a small rear room that looks as if it might have been an office. Old electricity cables hang down, and pinned high along one wall is a wooden structure with fifteen cubby holes – some kind of

filing system? From this vantage point, on a clear day, you can see across Cardigan Bay to Bardsey Island and the Llŷn peninsula. To the south you can see as far as Strumble Head beyond Fishguard. Missing the edge of Cemaes Head, from where it's said you can view dolphins and porpoises, I rediscover the cliff path and climb to Pen yr Afr (Goat's Head). This is another promontory with cliffs that plunge hundreds of feet down to the sea. From here I can see my destination, Carningli above Newport, and the line of Mynydd Preselau, the Golden Road that recedes far inland (see pages 51-57). As I walk I occasionally glance backwards to examine Pen yr Afr's massive cliff face. Its rock strata are dramatically contorted and folded, the result of powerful earth movements millions of years ago. At nearly six hundred feet it's the highest point of the Pembrokeshire coast path. It seems to glare angrily at me as I leave it behind.

By lunchtime I'm roughly halfway and clambering down Pencastell, an early Iron Age promontory fort, to Ceibwr Bay. This is a narrow stony inlet, once the port for Moylgrove (in Welsh Trewyddel, town of the Irish settlement) which is a mile inland. Small ships used to discharge coal here, also culm[8], lime, and sometimes contraband. It's a place to look for seals, porpoises and oystercatchers. The National Trust have put up a jaunty bilingual sign above a drawing of a seal pup urging you to keep at least fifty metres away from it: 'DO NOT chase me into the water, I can't swim very well.'

A little further on the sharp stacks of Carreg Wylan (Gull Rock) stand out followed by a number of dramatic natural arches. The path crosses one of these above Pwll y Wrach (Witches' Cauldron), a collapsed sea cave. It's a classic feature of marine erosion, where the sea has invaded shales and sandstones along a fault. At certain states of the tide the waves boil and thrash between the rocks. Not for swimming.

In many places the path is overgrown. On a wet day the grass and bracken would soak you to your armpits. Elsewhere rangers have been strimming and the grass smells like a freshly mown cricket field. I climb another hill to find a stile to which the National Park has pinned a stern notice. It says Newport is seven miles away:

> This is a remote, rugged and challenging stretch of the Pembrokeshire coast path. Avoid the cliff edges. On this stretch there are:

Numerous very steep hills
Sheer cliffs to seaward
No escape routes or exit points
No drinking water or other facilities

The reason for the warning soon becomes clear. After about a mile the path cuts a 500ft contour into the cliff edge and to your right there is just... open air. Over my right shoulder herring gulls with their distinctive back-tipped wings float lazily by, carried by the air currents. If I reached out I could touch them. The cliffs form an amphitheatre for nearly three miles ahead. Far below the sea crashes directly against the rocks at the base of the cliff.

Towards the end of this stretch is Pwll Coch (Red Pool), a small cove also known as Seal Bay that is only accessible by boat. In the early 1980s it became the hideout for an international drug-smuggling gang. The suspicions of local fishermen were raised when they saw a fifteen-foot inflatable with two powerful outboard motors beached on the pebbles.

Tipped off, the police staked out the place and eventually spotted a man on the clifftop carrying a rucksack. He turned out to be Soeren Berg-Arnback, a thirty-five-year-old Danish millionaire, owner of a luxury yacht with homes in Switzerland and Italy. He was also one of the world's most wanted drug

runners. He dropped his rucksack and fled. Inside the police found a radio transmitter. On the beach they discovered a large man-made cave beneath the shingle. The entrance was by a waterproof hatch covered in pebbles. Tons of rock had been removed. The roof was held up with wooden beams and the space made watertight by a lining of fibre glass and resin. Inside was a large quantity of heroin.

Berg-Arnback was an expert at disguise. Danish journalists called him the man with the rubber face. But he and his fellow conspirators were caught red-handed. They were sentenced at Swansea Crown Court to eight years in jail. Pat Molloy, at the time head of CID with Dyfed Powys Police, has told the whole story in his book *Operation Seal Bay*.

This walk is becoming an operation for me as well. My legs are protesting and my feet beginning to ache. At the southern end of the high cliffs I turn the corner at Morfa Head, and with some relief see Newport spreading out before me with Carningli rising above. But there's still some way to go. The tide is out so I avoid another hill by striking out across a mile of Newport Sands. The path then skirts the Nevern estuary before taking me across a road bridge into town.

This is a place for waterfowl, including oystercatchers, kingfishers, curlew, snipe, dunlin, lapwings, golden plover, mallards and Canadian geese. I spot a notice declaring that shooting is forbidden. 'Armed trespassers will be prosecuted,' it says. This stretch of coast has a feel of the Wild West about it.

In the Golden Lion I've never been so glad to see a chair. I've been on the path for the best part of eight hours. 'Come far?' the woman behind the bar asks as she pulls me a pint of bitter. I tell her.

'Ah,' she says. 'That's a tough one.'

GOLDEN ROAD

The Golden Road traverses the seven-mile ridge of Mynydd Preselau, ideal for walking. It is early May and there's hardly a breath of wind – a day for shirtsleeves. The sky is a hazy blue, reflected in the mist rolling off the sea. Obscuring the coastline, the low-lying fog crawls up the valley of the Nevern from Newport Bay. It gathers round Carningli and then spreads along the coast northwards as far as the eye can see.

But on the hill the sun shines. Warbling skylarks flutter unseen, and from Pantmaenog forest above Rosebush comes the unmistakable cry of a cuckoo. It gives me pause to think. I haven't heard a cuckoo in years. A passing walker warns me to keep a look out for adders. I don't see any but I do catch a fleeting glimpse of what looks to be a lizard. Perhaps it's a newt.

I'm heading east on the bridleway towards Carn Menyn, about five miles distant. It's where some still believe the Bluestones of Stonehenge were excavated and then manhandled to Salisbury Plain. Menyn is Welsh for butter. Maybe there were summer pastures here once, where they made butter and cheese. After a long winter much of the grass that swathes the hill is bleached white. It dazzles against the sun. Despite this I pass a heavily pregnant mare, all alone, devouring the first green shoots of spring.

At my back is Foel Eryr, once the 'Place of the Eagles', though only buzzards and red kites can be seen there now. At its summit is a Bronze Age burial cairn, which gives you a clue why this is known as the 'Golden Road'. It was in the Bronze Age about three thousand years ago that metals were first used. Dotted along this route are many burial mounds or cairns from that time. The Golden Road was used for transporting ore, bronze ornaments and perhaps weapons in those early days of trading. The name might also refer to this being part of a long route, from Salisbury Plain to Ireland where gold was mined in the Wicklow hills.

It has been called other things, too, including the Roman Way, the Pilgrim's Track, and Robbers Road. Doubtless, the last is why Foel Eryr is also known as Cerrig Lladron, Stones of the Robbers. Both names are on the map, making it one of only a handful of mountains in Wales known by two names. Perhaps there were robbers because this was a golden road. Then again, in more modern times the route has been named Flemings' Way. The first instance of this as far as I can tell, was by George Owen of Henllys, in his *Description of Pembrokeshire*, published in 1603. 'Touching on the coming of the Flemings,' he continues:

> ...well they might make this unusual way for their passage, for that passing along the top of the highest hill they might better decry the privy ambushes of the country people which might in straits and woods annoy them.[9]

Throughout the ages the Golden Road has been the subject of mythology. Passing Cwmcerwyn, the highest point of Mynydd Preselau, I come across a line of rocky outcrops known as Cerrig Marchogion. Legend has it that these stones are the petrified remains of knights of the Round Table who died in battle with a ferocious wild boar called Twrch Trwyth. The story is told in the *Mabinogion*, a collection of medieval tales first translated by associates of Lady Charlotte Guest in 1846. In one of them Culhwch, a cousin of King Arthur, attempts to win the hand of Olwen, daughter of the Irish giant Ysbaddaden Pencawr. But, forewarned that his death will accompany the marriage, the giant places all manner of obstacles in the way of the match.

One is a challenge for Culhwch to sieze a comb, razor and scissors that lie between the ears of a magical beast Twrch Trwyth. This is an errant king who the giant has transformed into a voracious boar. The scissors are to be used to trim the giant's hair in readiness for his daughter's marriage.

Culhwch enlists the aid of Arthur who together with some of his knights pursues the boar across the Irish Sea. Twrch Trwyth lands with his cohorts at Porthclais near St Davids and makes for Mynydd Preselau. Here a fierce battle ensues in which the knights are killed. Nevertheless, Arthur continues to pursue the boar to Cornwall where he drives it into the sea, though not before he manages to snatch the comb, razor and scissors from between its ears.

This is not the only reference to Arthur along the Golden Road. There is Carn Arthur and, immediately alongside the Road within sight of Carn Menyn, there's Bedd Arthur, a stone oval claimed to be Arthur's grave. In fact, it is a Bronze Age burial site, made of thirteen upright bluestones with two others that have fallen. They're about two feet high. Lower down the slopes on the moorland to the south, between Cwmcerwyn and Craig Talfynydd, stand Cerrig Meibion Arthur, the stones of Arthur's sons. Legend has it that they mark the graves of two other warriors killed by Twrch Trwyth.

It is extraordinary to look at these monuments and imagine their creators, more than two thousand years ago, gazing at the same landscape. Of course, they could have had nothing to do with Arthur who, if he existed as we imagine him, lived between the late fifth and early sixth centuries.

It is equally extraordinary to think that the Carn Menyn outcrop has been partially responsible for a very modern myth that has grown up. It follows from archaeologists and geologists demonstrating they are closely connected with the inner bluestone 'horseshoe' at Stonehenge.

There is no doubt that this is the case. The myth arises from a dispute as to how the Preseli bluestones reached Salisbury Plain. The argument begins with Herbert Thomas, an experienced geologist who in 1908 worked with the Geological Survey in west

Wales. It was he who first suggested that the 'foreign' stones at Stonehenge might have come from Mynydd Preselau. He matched twenty-nine of the forty-three Stonehenge bluestones with the rock outcrops around Carn Menyn, Carn Carnalw and Foel Drygarn at the eastern end of the Preseli hills.

When his work was published in 1923 it was immediately acknowledged to be scientifically rigorous. There was no doubt there was a link, but Thomas's revelation raised a question. How did the stones travel the long distance from Preseli to Salisbury Plain? Without a shred of scientific evidence, Thomas suggested that the Neolithic tribes of Wessex physically manhandled twenty-nine slabs of stone, each weighing more than two tons, a distance of some 250 miles over land from Wales to Wiltshire.

The theory was later elaborated by the archeologist Richard Atkinson who directed excavations at Stonehenge for the Ministry of Works between 1950 and 1964. In 1956 he produced the standard work on the monument, *Stonehenge: Archaeology and Interpretation*. He suggested that though the stones had been partly carried overland, they had mainly travelled over water. He claimed they were dragged to somewhere between Llawhaden and Canaston Bridge and then taken down the Eastern Cleddau river. In this account they were placed on a raft or dugout canoes and floated through Milford Haven. After that they rounded the Welsh coast, passed through the Bristol Channel and taken up the river Avon, before being carried overland once more to Salisbury Plain.

The absurdity of such primitive craft carrying huge stones over so long a distance led another archeologist Mike Parker Pearson to support Herbert Thomas's original theory. In his 2012 publication *Stonehenge: A New Understanding* Parker argues that the stones must have been carried all the way overland to Salisbury Plain.

All these theories are, I think, complete fantasy. They leave you with the question why so many generations of otherwise sober archaeologists, geologists, and geochemists have swallowed such improbable explanations. And the theories, fuelled by intense media interest, continue. There were further excavations of Stonehenge in 2008 when Open University archaeologists imagined that the Bluestones had mystical healing properties. This they claimed, provided the motivation for the tremendous effort needed to carry them from Preseli to Stonehenge.

There was even an experiment to reconstruct a Bluestone 'transport expedition', in what became known as the Millennium

Stone Fiasco, in the year 2000. Around £100,000 of lottery money was spent trying to transport a block of bluestone from Mynachlog-ddu, the village closest to Carn Menyn, to Stonehenge, using techniques that might have been employed by a Neolithic tribe. It took more than a month for more than thirty volunteers to pull the stone along metalled roads – not, let it be noted, through forests and swamps – to the water's edge. Soon after it had been loaded on to a makeshift raft it sank in Milford Haven.

An apparently exciting new development in the controversy came in August 2018. Analysis of the remains of Neolithic people discovered at Stonehenge allegedly demonstrated they came from Mynydd Preselau. Scientists did, indeed, discover that some of the human remains found at Stonehenge could not have come from Salisbury Plain. Instead, they came from somewhere else in the north or west of Britain. Theoretically, they could have come from Preseli, but equally they could have come from many other places. In a paper 'Strontium isotope analysis of cremated remains from Stonehenge support links with west Wales', published by *Nature*, the scientists highlighted Craig Rhos-y-felin in Mynydd Preselau, supposedly one origin of the Stonehenge Bluestones, on an illustrative map of Britain. But they could as easily have identified Exeter, Birmingham, Manchester or Edinburgh.[10]

The most likely explanation of how the Bluestones got to Wiltshire is much more straightforward. They were 'entrained' or

picked up during the Ice Age by the Irish Sea Glacier that flowed across Pembrokeshire and thence to Salisbury Plain, crossing the coasts of Devon and Somerset. When the ice retreated the Bluestones were left behind as erratics. It was then relatively easy for the Stonehenge builders to collect and carry them to their Neolithic building site. Geographer Brian John has explained all this in great detail in his *The Bluestone Enigma* (2008).

So why has the mythological overland adventure persisted for so long? Because, it seems to me, it has provided Stonehenge with a backstory that has helped build up its profile. Indeed, it has helped turn Stonehenge into a global icon, a World Heritage Site, and a tourist honey trap able to compete with the Pyramids of Egypt or the Great Wall of China. It has been underpinned too, by the notion of Mynydd Preselau as a mystical healing place, 'home of the gods', truly a land of enchantment.

Yet, contrary to the inflated assessments of archeological enthusiasts, it is not landscape, rocks, oceans or rivers that possess mystical, spiritual or healing properties. It is people who give them these characteristics in their imagination. In that sense I agree that Mynydd Preseli has a spiritual dimension. Walking the Golden Road is an uplifting, though footsore, experience.

STONES THAT FLOAT TO THE SKY

Leaving aside St Davids Cathedral, Preseli's most iconic man-made structure is undoubtedly Pentre Ifan. It's a Neolithic cromlech overlooking the sea above Nevern to the north of Newport. One of the first structures to be protected by law under the 1884 Ancient Monuments Act, it is certainly dramatic. Erected as early as 3,500 BC, the massive triangular capstone is seventeen feet long, nine feet across, and weighs more than sixteen tons. It is held majestically aloft, in what appears a precarious fashion, by three pointed stone pillars.

The Welsh Government's historic advisory service Cadw has an explanatory notice board on the site. 'It is the remains of a chambered tomb for the communal burial of the dead which would have been used for some period before being finally sealed,' it says. The chamber would then have been covered by a great earth and stone cairn, extending well to the rear. However, all traces of this have long gone, swept away over aeons by the elements and human plunder.

Cadw provides us with an artist's impression of the cairn as it might have been, complete with a small group of Neolithic inhabitants performing some kind of ritual in front of it. 'Excavations in 1936-7 and 1958-9 showed that the burial chamber lay within a large oval pit dug into the sloping ground,' we are told. 'Its sides had originally been constructed of dry-stone walling with a few larger slabs. The forecourt area at the front appears to have been filled with carefully packed stones, which must have caused difficulties each time there was a fresh burial.'

But what if all this was simply not so?

In recent years some archaeologists have speculated that Pentre Ifan could have had an altogether different purpose. In this interpretation its builders did not intend for it to be covered up. Instead, they were motivated by a creation myth, in which the structure is representative of the earth being raised to the sky, or in some sense joined with the sky. And, after all, what is most magnificent about Pentre Ifan is the way the great capstone can be seen as balancing in the air. Seen from a distance it is a stone that is floating towards the sky.

What these archaeologists are suggesting is that, far from creating burial chambers, the Neolithic builders were seeking prestige from their feats of engineering. Their objective was to display to the world in the most dramatic way they could that these great stones had mythological properties. So, far from covering them up they wanted them completely open to the elements. They represented the very creation of the earth.

Vicki Cummings, of the the University of Central Lancashire, and Colin Richards, of the University of Manchester, proposed this startling reappraisal in their *Building the Great Dolmens* project. They re-examined Pentre Ifan and other monuments across Wales and Ireland and asked what, really, are some rather obvious questions. What is the role of the capstones? Why do their upper surfaces invariably remain rough and weathered, while the undersides are always shaped and dressed? Is there a particular significance to the sites in which they are located?

Then there are the uprights that support them. As Vicki Cummings and Colin Richards argue:

> Bearing in mind that many capstones weigh over fifty tonnes, people seem to have deliberately chosen slender stones to support them. Furthermore, many uprights have pointed tops which mean that only the smallest points of the uprights support the capstone. Moreover, many dolmens are only supported by three uprights, even though there are more stones in the chamber. This suggests that people were trying to balance massive capstones on the smallest number of supporters, and having the smallest areas touching. This creates the most extraordinary effect with these monuments, and has led several authors to suggest that one of the primary roles of dolmens was the display of huge stones where stones seem to be almost floating above the ground. The essence of a dolmen, then, is the display of a large capstone, where the technical ability of the builders is demonstrated by balancing the capstone on the smallest points of the supporting stones as possible.[11]

If this is the case, then what what would be gained if the structure was to be buried in a cairn of soil and stones? There seems no doubt that some dolmens, probably including Pentre Ifan, were eventually used as burial chambers. But were they originally designed for that purpose?

The question is underlined by the notion that dolmens seem always to be located in relation to striking features of their surrounding landscape, in particular to nearby seas, rivers, and mountains. In the

case of Pentre Ifan, the monument overlooks the Irish sea, and is
clearly visible from nearby Carningli, and the more distant summits
of Mynydd Preselau. As Vicki Cummings says, this time with another
archaeologist Alasdair Whittle, of Cardiff University:

> The achievement of construction must surely have been a source of
> world renown, but it may also have played on a powerful mythical
> dimension, in stories of the creation of the earth and of original
> creator figures that arose from the earth and waters. These might
> also have been associated with the outcrops, hills, mountains and
> sea visible from portal dolmens. The monuments stand in sight of
> landscape features redolent of beginnings, and the monuments
> themselves recreate central features of this narrative.[12]

A premonition that their purpose was to present an image of the
creation can be seen in the 1835 painting of Pentre Ifan by Richard
Tonge (1795-1873) of Bath. He advertised himself as 'a painter and
modeller of megaliths', an unusual specialism for his day. In it
Pentre Ifan's capstone is shown virtually floating in the sky, with the
supporting stones much taller and slender than they actually are.

The idea that the capstone should be seen as floating towards the
sky is even suggested in Cadw's official description. It notes that the
capstone is thickest at its southern end and slopes downwards to the
northern, thinner end:

This visually unexpected arrangement of the capstone, which appears to float and contradict the laws of gravity, taken together with the delicate way in which the capstone rests on the pointed ends of the supporting stones, gives the monument an illusion of instability.[13]

I think the same can be said of Carreg Coetan Arthur, another cromlech to be found a few miles away at the edge of Newport overlooking the Nyfer estuary. Today it stands in a small, hedged enclosure which disguises the significance of its location. But when it was erected it would have been clearly in sight of Dinas Head to the west, and Carningli rising three-hundred- and-fifty metres to the south. Legend has it that the stones forming the dolmen were thrown from the summit of the mountain. In reality they were undoubtedly found very close to the spot. In all probability the capstone was dug out from the ground beneath. In the course of an excavation carried out during 1980 it was found that a build-up of plough soil, in places over a metre thick, lay around the uprights supporting the capstone. Carreg Coetan Arthur would originally have appeared much taller than it does today.[14]

Another magnificent cromlech lies some ten miles southwest of Pentre Ifan, half-a-mile from Abercastle harbour village, and perched dramatically close to the cliff edge. The fifteen-foot long and nine-foot wide capstone stands six feet high. It has six supports but only rests on three of them. Although the capstone is not as big as Pentre Ifan, its positioning is still highly strategic. It angles downwards towards the cliff and has clear views of the peaks of Strumble Head in the seaward direction and Mynydd Preselau inland. Even a small change of location would have made these sightlines impossible.

An excavation during August 1968 revealed that the structure was built within a large pit, about eight metres long and six metres wide. This led Frances Lynch, the archeologist in charge, to speculate whether the capstone was a large erratic boulder dropped on to the site by a retreating glacier. The fact that there were two more erratic boulders in the field supports this interpretation. She also pointed out that five more tombs were located within a three-mile radius of Mathry and Abercastle, though none were as well preserved as Carreg Sampson. As she says, 'It seems likely that all these tombs belonged to the same funeral tradition.'

Yet it seems to me an obvious question follows: if they were just meant to be burial grounds, why did the people who erected them need six within such a small distance of one another? And to be fair to Frances Lynch, she did add, 'However, it would be foolish to suggest that we yet know sufficient about the history of tomb-building groups or of their motivation to be able to draw any worthwhile conclusions from this.'[15]

Then there's the fact that very little else was discovered as a result of the excavation. All they found were the remains of a ceramic pot about thirty inches in diameter, and a few small piece of burnt, apparently human cremated bone. Moreover, it was not clear whether these were left at the time the cromlech was constructed or much later. If this was a burial site surely there would be more evidence of it.

Much better, I think, to judge that, like Pentre Ifan, this was another cromlech built, in full view of its dramatic environs, to reach to the sky. As Vicki Cummings told me, 'It's on a wonderful site and the capstone is very distinctive. Why cover it up when it looks so impressive?'

So were these monuments deliberately constructed to appear as enormous stones floating effortlessly towards the sky? Conclusive evidence has yet to be established. But to me it is a much more intriguing, romantic and, ultimately, convincing idea than to believe they were intended merely as elaborate burial chambers.

Notes

1. The poem 'Preseli', is translated by Tony Conran in his selection of Waldo's poems, *The Peacemakers*, Gomer, 1997.
2. Quoted by Janet Davies, 'The Fight for Preseli', in *Planet 58,* August-September issue, 1986.
3. Hefin Wyn, *Battle of the Preselau*, Clychau Clochog, 2008, page 41.
4. *Ibid.*, page 109.
5. Literally, *Siafins* means wood shavings, though the description is a play on words since in colloquial Welsh to describe somethings as a siop siafins means it is a total mess.
6. http://www.marthamorgan.co.uk
7. Christopher Goddard and Katherine Evans, *The Wales Coast Path*, St David's Press, 2014, page 120.
8. Fine-grained waste anthracite mixed with clay and rolled into balls, it can sustain a fire for long periods. Known in Welsh as *cwlwm*.
9. George Owen, *The Description of Pembrokeshire* (1603), ed. by Dillwyn Miles, (Gomer, 1994), page 107.
10. For an analysis of the Nature article, see: https://brian-mountainman.blogspot.com /2018/08/strontium-levels-in-cremated-bone-what.html On 2 August 2018 the Guardian carried a story with the headline: *Bones found at Stonehenge belonged to people from Wales*
11. Vicki Cummings and Colin Richards, 'The essence of the dolmen: the architecture of megalithic construction', *Prehistoires Méditerraneenes*, 2014.
12. Vicki Cummings and Alasdair Whittle, 'Pentre Ifan: east or west? The origins of

monumentality in Wales and western Britain', in G. Marchand and A. Tresset (Eds.), *Unité et diversité des porcessus de néolithisation sur la façade atlantique de l'Europe, Buelletin de la Société Préhistorique Française*, 2005.

13. John B. Hilling, *Cilgerran Castle, St Dogmael's Abbey, Pentre Ifan and Carreg Coetan Arthur*, Cadw, page 53.
14. Sian Rees, *A guide to ancient and historic Wales*, Cadw, 1992.
15. Frances Lynch, 'Excavations at Carreg Sampson Megalithic Tomb, Mathry Pembrokeshire', *Archaelogia Cambrensis*, Vol. CXXIV, 1975, page 15.

CENTRAL

PUFFIN SHUTTLE

The Puffin Bus can be hailed anywhere along its route. I stop it on the road above Little Haven. My bus is a taxi. I'm the only passenger. 'Going far?' the driver asks, before telling me he's just returned from holiday in Bulgaria. He's keen to talk.

'I'm hiking from Dale,' I say.

'Never been on the path,' he answers.

I'd say he's in his mid thirties. He's wearing a vest revealing tattooed arms.

'Where are you from?' I ask.

'Haverfordwest.'

At Marloes you have to change to another bus going south. It stops at Dale before looping through Milford to Haverfordwest. Dale is a heartland for 'Little England beyond Wales' that has been Flemish or English speaking since the twelfth century. Before that it was the turn of the Vikings. The name derives from the old Norse *Dair*, meaning valley. Today the village, with a population a little over two hundred, is mainly known for its yacht anchorage and wind-surfing. Sheltered by St Anne's peninsula the water is always flat and the sandy beach ideal for launching craft.

Low tide in September is a time for shrimping. My Uncle Jim brought me here when I was a boy, fishing with wide nets strung between wooden arms. Later I brought my son, but not to shrimp. He was a fanatical windsurfer. I'd just sit on the beach with a book and hope he was OK.

The Puffin Bus follows a meandering route along St Bride's Bay, hugging the coastline. It mainly carries walkers of the coastal path, though there are also some locals with shopping bags. Setting out from St David's, it calls at Solva, Newgale, Nolton, Druidston, Broad Haven, Little Haven, St Brides, and Marloes. Then it heads down to Martin's Haven, launch point for Skomer island (see pages 224-227), turns round and sets off back to St Davids.

Sometimes I walk from a northerly direction, starting in Solva. Along this stretch there are views of the whole bay. To the north Ramsey Island looks connected to the coast, as does Skomer in the south. Together they feel like edges of an encircling rim. South of Solva the high cliffs offer flat walking and steady progress. Then, depending on the tide, Newgale's storm beach offers you two miles of easy passage across the sands. Around the distinctive knob of Rickets Head you discover Nolton Haven, then Druidston with its magnificently located hotel.

I always linger at Haroldston Chins on the high cliffs just south of Druidston. This is the dead centre of St Brides Bay, and there is a long flat cliff walk with exceptional views of the ocean. Walking the coast path at this point feels like being on the deck of a liner with a limitless horizon, where the sea touches the sky in a seamless continuity. Out in the bay oil tankers are parked in line. Normally there are three or four, but I've counted as many as a dozen, waiting their turn for a berth in Milford Haven.

It is one of those places that, whatever the weather, has a spiritual quality. Indeed, it has taken on the character of a secular churchyard. It is full of benches and fences bearing plaques commemorating the lives of people who frequented this place. One is in memory of Paul Blick who helped establish the Pembrokeshire coast path in the 1960s and who was appointed its first warden. The inscription is taken from Shakespeare's sonnet commending a summer's day:

So long as men can breathe or eyes can see,
So long lives this, and this gives life to thee.

A stretch of the path has been tarmacked to provide wheelchair access. At intervals are square benches hewn from tree trunks, all bearing plaques. One is for Sheila Ann Mathias (1942 to 2002), 'In loving memory of a devoted wife, mother and granny who liked to walk this path. Hope you enjoy the view as much as she did.'

Another is for Edward (1913-2007) and Margaret Hier (1921-2012), who were 'Passionate about Pembrokeshire.'

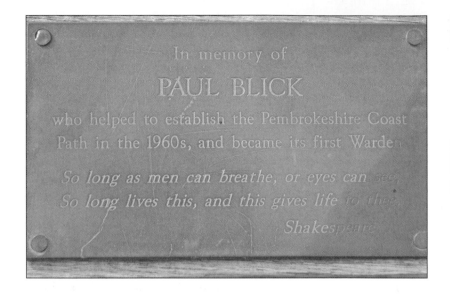

A little further on towards Broad Haven is a standing stone with the inscription, 'In memory of Glyn Charles, Olympic Yachtsman. Lost at sea. 1965-1998. He loved Pembrokeshire.' Charles was drowned, aged 33, after being swept overboard from the yacht *The Sword of Orion*. He was crewing during the 630 mile Sydney to Hobart Race, one of yachting's most challenging contests. Ironically, Glyn didn't much like ocean racing because it made him seasick. He preferred sailing the Star Class, a 22.5ft two-man keelboat, in which he was ranked fourth in the world.

Most of these commemorations are for people who lived for a reasonable time. They had a good innings, you might say. But there is one for a young man who did not reach twenty, Roger Dyer, 1981–2000. His inscription bears a quotation from Nelson Mandela: 'It is not a calamity to die with dreams unfulfilled, but it is a calamity not to dream.'

For me the Puffin Bus is a passport for my favourite occupation of walking these stretches of the coastal path. This is where I come to think. Over the past fifty years I reckon I must have hiked them well over three hundred times. I have walked them so often that they appear regularly in my dreams. If I can't sleep, I imagine I'm striding out on a particular section and count the landmarks before dropping off.

There is something special about where the sea meets the land and sky. The weather contributes to an ever-changing vista. Partly it is the light that, in my experience, is only matched on the west coast of Ireland or along the Llŷn peninsula in north Wales. It's why Pembrokeshire is home to so many artists.

Spring is a joy when the whites, blues, pinks and reds of the wild flowers and the bright yellow of the gorse carpet the land with a veritable rainbow of colour. At the height of summer, the tall grass and hot damp air deliver a heady experience better than any beverage I know. Walking in the gales that hammer the coast during winter is exhilarating as well. Rough seas, dark threatening clouds and driving rain transport you from everyday cares.

Walking the path on a regular basis reveals the permanent inhabitants. The bird life is extraordinarily varied. Apart from the swooping gulls there are finches, tits, and curlews, plus the occasional wren, robin and blackbird. A good place for skylarks is St Brides where if you lie in the grass for long enough you'll see them high in the sky before they plummet to the earth.

Rabbits and voles are common. Once a four-foot long grass snake leapt in a coiled spring across the path in front of me. Occasionally a badger appears. Late one evening, one startled me in Bluebell Wood near Little Haven. I don't know who was most taken aback, the badger or me. For a split second we stared at each other before he dived into the scrub below. During September you might see a newly born seal pup in a closed stony inlet anywhere along the more isolated southern part of the coast. Many years ago I caught a glimpse of a line of dolphins, from the high cliffs north of Broad Haven, skimming through the water with their dorsal fins breaking surface. I've canoed as well as walked up and down this coast. One blue summer day my daughter Elin and I paddled the four or five miles from Little Haven to St Brides. There was no wind and the sea was glassy calm. Approaching St Brides, with the azure sky and emerald sea merging, it felt as though we were sliding downhill. It's not always like this. On another occasion the wind rose and the sea became choppy. Our canoe was built for rivers and not meant for such conditions. We soon shipped water above our stretching legs and the craft stalled. I thought we'd have to clamber out and swim her ashore. Then, miraculously, a lobster fisherman appeared, throttling his healthy outboard motor. He towed us into Nolton Haven.

For me summer always ends precisely on 30 September, the date that marks the end of the Puffin Shuttle's daily forays around the coast. After that it can only be hailed on Thursdays and Saturdays during its winter schedule. So as autumn turns to winter and the days are shortening, I look forward to May when the Puffin Shuttle begins its schedule seven days a week, and summer begins.

HAVERFORDWEST

Haverfordwest Castle stands on an elevated plateau eighty feet above the Western Cleddau. Here is the river's lowest fording point and the highest reach of the tide coming up from Milford Haven. This is what made the place strategically important for the Normans, and why they built the castle here in the early twelfth century. It's a symbol of oppression, of course. Henry I drove the Welsh out of this part of Pembrokeshire. You could say it was the ethnic cleansing of its day. To replace the natives, Henry brought in the Flemings over three years from 1108, while the castle was being built. A further influx came in 1156.

The Flemings had long been associated with the Normans. William the Conqueror used them as mercenaries when he invaded England at the Battle of Hastings in 1066. A large part of their country had flooded and they were encouraged to settle in southern Pembrokeshire and establish their own Flemish-speaking society. The English language came later. The historian John Davies used to say that in the sixteenth century the people of Haverfordwest were still being described as *male Anglice loquentes* (poor speakers of English). Until this time only Normans and Flemings were allowed to live inside the town walls.

Chris Gillham was Mayor of Haverfordwest during 2006. It's a position that goes back to 1213 when the town received its first charter under King John. With the title went the responsibility of Admiral of the Port, reflecting the town's mercantile importance. Accessible to ships of up to two-hundred tonnes, Haverfordwest was one of the largest ports in Wales in Norman times. Wool was a flourishing export and there were weekly passenger services to Bristol, Waterford in Ireland, and a monthly service to London. These only ended with the coming of the railway in 1853. In the past the Port Admiral enjoyed raking in a good deal of revenue from port dues. 'In my year in office I lost money,' Chris, who also chairs the Pembrokeshire Historical Society, tells me ruefully.

However, one tradition, the beating of the bounds, continues. Every year in late summer the Admiral sails down the Cleddau to the White Rock near Boulston that marks the boundary with Milford Haven. This is a transfer point to a boat coming the other way for the return journey. Chris recalls a previous Mayor, a portly woman, being lifted across by six men. Back at the quayside in Haverfordwest the Admiral is presented with a plate of pork brawn. The town Sheriff who accompanys him is presented with a plate of apples. Haverfordwest and Carmarthen are the only towns in Wales to have Sheriffs.

Chris has been Minister at Haverfordwest's Tabernacle Congregationalist chapel for more than thirty years. Built in 1774 it has a unique Romanesque exterior. Inside ornate pillars hold up balconies that overlook dark wooden pews and a carved pulpit. In the nineteenth century the chapel accommodated as many as seven hundred and fifty people. Today the membership has fallen to eighty and a good Sunday sees a congregation of around thirty, many of them elderly. Across the road another chapel, erected in 1865 on a site where John Wesley preached in 1772, is falling into ruin. For a while it was an outlet for antique furniture but that failed.

As he was about to become Mayor Chris attracted some notoriety when he led a delegation from Cytun (Churches Together in Wales) to Syria. At a meeting with President Assad Chris was introduced as the Mayor of Haverfordwest. 'I said that this was not quite accurate since the election was to take place that evening. However, I was fairly certain that I would be elected since I was the only candidate. Assad gave me a little smile and said, "Just like me."' At the time Chris was criticised in the local press for talking with the Syrian dictator, but he is unrepentant. 'I still maintain that Assad is the only hope for the safety of the Christian population of Syria.'

In medieval times Haverfordwest had claim to be the largest town in Wales, with Carmarthen its only competitor. In those days Cardiff had two parishes while Haverfordwest had three: St Mary's, St Martin and St Thomas. A parish was an area with sufficient population and wealth to support a church and a priest. It was the ford, crossed by *haefer* (goats) which gave Haverfordwest its name. The 'west' was added in Tudor times to distinguish it from Hereford in the east. In his play *Richard III* Shakespeare noted the local pronunciation: 'Ha'rford-west in Wales'.

Haverfordwest's heyday was in the eighteenth century when it was more exciting than Bath. It was further away for one thing. Fashionable balls were held in the Assembly Rooms in the winter season. In the summer, sea bathing was just coming in. The blue plaque placed by the Town Council and Civic Society on the wall of the Assembly Rooms says it all: 'Built in the early 18th Century, it was the favoured venue of the local gentry for many social events. Leased to St Mary's in 1925 it was used extensively as a church hall and meeting place until the 1950s. By 1970 the building had become unsafe and remained so until its conversion into flats in 1997.'

Look closely around the back streets and there are many fine Georgian buildings, but a lot of them are in a sad state of decline. A notable example is Grade II listed Foley House, a two-story villa in Goat Street. The Regency architect John Nash, whose family came from Carmarthenshire, designed it in 1790. He went on to be the architect of Buckingham Palace and Regent Street.

The house has some historical importance as Nelson received the Freedom of Haverfordwest in it when he visited in 1802, along with Sir William and Lady Hamilton. Sir Thomas (later Admiral) Foley, a naval commander who had fought with Nelson at the Battle of the Nile in 1798, also received the honour. Foley was Nelson's flag captain at the Battle of Denmark in 1801. It was to him that Nelson, raising his telescope to his blind eye, famously said he did not see the signal of his superior, Admiral Hyde Parker, ordering him to disengage. Foley's brother Richard, a lawyer, owned the house. Nelson gave an address to large crowds from the balcony above the drawing room.

Foley House changed hands during the nineteenth century and was eventually sold to the County Council in 1947. One idea was for it to become the town's museum, but that did not materialise. Instead, it was used as a court and later for administrative offices. During this time it was poorly refurbished without listed building consent. It was re-roofed with concrete tiles, chimneys were removed, the moulded timber base of the pediment lost, and the front door replaced. It was last used by organisers of the National Eisteddfod at St David's in 2002 and has been empty ever since.

At one point the Council had the extraordinary idea of turning its grounds into a car park. Eventually, in 2010 they put the house up for sale but it attracted no offers. Part of the reason might have been that the specification drew attention to a protected bat species in the property. Prospective buyers were advised to engage an ecological consultant to undertake a survey. Mercifully, Foley House has now attracted the attention of the Welsh Georgian Trust. In collaboration with the council it has obtained a grant from the Architectural Heritage Fund to carry out an assessment for its sustainable use.

The whole of Haverfordwest needs this kind of survey. Large out-of-town shopping developments have drained the vitality of the town centre. Like a rotting fish the place is declining from the head down, with many of the shops at the top end of High Street boarded up. A notable exception is Haverfordwest's oldest business, the High Street jewellers Bisley Munt. Founded in 1796, it has remained in the family ever since. The current owner, John Munt began work in the shop with his father Billy Munt, in 1965. 'In those days we took delivery of crystal glass in tea chests at the back,' he told me. 'The glass was put in dry straw and wetted inside to make the whole thing firm. It was darned difficult to get the glass out. The tea chests were in great demand.'

The firm was actually started by one James Bevans. He had three daughters who all worked in the business, mending watches. John's great grandfather Bisley Munt married one of them, Matilda, and eventually inherited the firm. John Munt's other great distinction is that he fires pistols for Wales, using muzzle-loading revolvers. He has represented his country in competitions throughout Europe and as far afield as Australia. Son Paul is carrying on the Munt jewellery business.

At the Castle Museum I meet Simon Hancock, curator for twenty years, who tells me about the last man hanged in Pembrokeshire on Easter Monday 1821. He was William Roblin, of a fiery temper and inclined to drink. In fact, he ran a pub in a small thatched building at his farm at Uzmaston just outside Haverfordwest. Roblin was involved a dispute over outstanding wages with Williams Davies, one of his part-time farmhands. There was a struggle and Davies was shot in the head with a pistol. He died three weeks later.

Claiming his pistol went off accidentally, Roblin hid in Canaston Woods a few miles away but eventually gave himself up. Held for seven months, he was tried, found guilty and executed in Haverfordwest Castle. He was buried in the Castle grounds. The story does not end there. Around 1850, Roblin's remains were dug up and sold as a curiosity. There is a record of them emerging in 1914 when they were sold again, for 1s 4d to a Haverfordwest chemist, Alderman William Williams. The skull eventually came into the hands of Pembroke Castle museum where it was put on display in the 1970s. Simon Hancock remembers how fearful he felt when he saw it there as a child. The skull is no longer on display but kept in a box in a storeroom. It was offered to Haverfordwest Castle Museum but Hancock refused. 'You have to have a special license from the Home Office to display human remains and we haven't got one,' he told me. 'Anyway, I'm against the death penalty.'

Hancock's museum has a list of the one-hundred-and-twenty-two pubs that have existed in Haverfordwest at one time or another. Rev Chris Gillham and I end our tour in the Hotel Mariners, that claims to be the oldest. It used to be the Mariners Hotel. However, it was refurbished in the 1920s and, by mistake, the sign painter got the words juxtaposed. At the same time, plucking a date out of the air, the owner said, 'Put *Established in 1625* underneath.' The earliest recorded presence of the hotel is actually 1729.

The present owner, Andrew Cromwell, tells me about the hotel's role in the Parliamentary election of May 1831 when it was the headquarters of one of the candidates, Robert Fulke Grenville. The other candidate was Sir John Olwen who was based at the Castle Hotel. *The Times* described the contest as the most bitterly fought in the United Kingdom. Grenville lost but immediately petitioned against the result and a re-run was held in October. This time Grenville had to concede defeat. In the meantime, however, he had run up a bill for £1,878 entertaining his electors, including £443 for 'eating for the voters'. In two weeks he got through forty-two barrels of beer, two gallons of whisky, sixty-seven gallons of brandy, fifty-nine gallons of rum, one-thousand-and-sixty-eight bottles of port, and seven-hundred-and-eighty bottles of sherry. He delayed paying and eventually the hotel sued for the amount. But before the case could be heard at Brecon Assizes Grenville fled the country.

My own electoral tale involving the Mariners is not as exotic. It is the location of my selection to be Plaid Cymru's Preseli candidate in the 2007 Assembly election. I made a somewhat dramatic entrance. The week before I had broken my leg, falling out of the door of my caravan, perched on the cliff at Talbenny above Little Haven. So I approached the constituency party meeting on crutches. 'Approach' is a polite way of putting it. The meeting room is on the first floor and I had to climb the stairs on my hands and knees.

I put my case, answered some searching questions, and hobbled back down the stairs to the bar. There I found the constituency secretary and asked him how long I would have to wait.

'We're moving straight to a vote.'

'On the other candidates who went in before me?'

'No, no, its just a choice between you and Ron.'

Ron? I was mystified. A fantastic thought went through my head that maybe the former Secretary of State for Wales Ron Davies,

who had recently joined Plaid, had discovered an interest in Preseli.
However, it turned out that I was the only candidate. Ron simply
meant the option of Re-Opening the Nomination.

LIQUID SUNSHINE

Derek Rees is running a finger down a plaque on the wall of the
County Show office at Withybush aerodrome just outside
Haverfordwest. It lists the Show's Presidents since 1935. He stops
at 1974. 'There, see, that's my father, Trevor Rees.' His finger
carries on until it stops again, this time at 1991. 'And that's me,' he
announces triumphantly, pointing at his name. Derek Rees has a
lifetime's relationship with the Pembrokeshire Show. He tells me it
goes back to 1949 when the event lasted one day and he was a cub
reporter on the *Western Telegraph*. 'I ran back and fore between the
office and the Bridge Meadow site in Haverfordwest carrying copy
for the more senior reporters.'

Today the Show lasts for three days in August and has grown to
cover an enormous two-hundred-acre site on Withybush
aerodrome. Giant sheds house prize cattle, sheep, goats, pigs and
poultry from all parts of Wales whose owners are intent on
winning coveted rosettes. Other sheds contain horticultural, craft
and cookery exhibits all seeking prizes. Outside in the ring men
and women demonstrate their horsemanship. Elsewhere there are
rural activities, from sheep dog trials to demonstrations of
falconry and ferrets. There are stands of all kinds, people selling
everything from sweets to religion, and beyond them the farm
machinery, caravan and four-by-four dealers, plus a fairground.
Above all there are the people, more than a hundred thousand in
a good year. That means not too much rain, what the organisers
call liquid sunshine.

For half-a-century Derek has chronicled the ups and downs of the
Show's survival and growth. He's reported on it for the *Western
Telegraph* and later for Swansea's *South Wales Evening Post*. He was
the paper's west Wales staff man for thirty-eight years. After he
'retired' he continued covering the show, once more for the *Telegraph*.
Before he became president his father, a policeman, was secretary
and his mother assistant secretary. Today Derek is the Press Officer
and has served on the Executive Committee for thirty years.

He's also delved into the Show's history and produced two books. When he began his researches, the founding date on the Pembrokeshire Agricultural Society's badge was 1901. But Derek soon discovered that was merely one milestone along a much longer path. As he looked deeper into old manuscripts he kept passing further milestones – 1884, 1844, 1805, eventually arriving at the Show's starting point in 1784. In each case, for different reasons there was a gap in the Society's existence. So Derek established that Pembrokeshire had one of the longest-lived Agricultural Societies in Wales. The oldest is the Breconshire Society, established in 1755 and, admittedly, in continuous existence ever since.

Derek also discovered that the original Show yard was in the middle of Haverfordwest. It was a one-and-a-half-acre enclosure with a single narrow entrance near the top of the High Street. Bounded by Fountain Row, Barn Street, Albert Street and Dew Street, it has been almost completely obliterated by development, except that sections of the unusually high original boundary walls still exist. Derek discovered that on some stretches of the inside-facing walls heavy iron rings were attached to the masonry. These were used for tethering cattle and horses. The top of the walls was smothered in tar to discourage interlopers evading the entry charge.

The yard was built in 1847. In succeeding decades Pembroke-shire farmers had to get their stock into the enclosure by 9am on the annual Show day. Between nine and eleven o'clock the judges and appointed stock-keepers had the yard to themselves while the exhibitors repaired to the local inns. The exhibition lasted a mere two hours. Stock was allowed to leave the yard from 1pm. At 2pm members of the Agricultural Society retired to the Mariners Inn for a marathon annual dinner that went on until 11pm.

To mark the two-hundredth anniversary of the Society in 1984 Derek arranged for a section of the original wall, complete with a few iron rings, to be moved from Albert Street to a site on the present Show ground at Withybush. The plaque on the replica wall was unveiled by Princess Anne, who attended the Show's bicentenary.

The most significant event in the more recent development of the Show was its move to Withybush aerodrome in 1959. For most of the previous century it had been held at Spring Meadow, the site of today's Haverfordwest Football Club behind Withybush Hospital. But that was frequently boggy and became too small.

During the 1950s the show moved to other sites around Haverfordwest, ending up at the Race Course on the northwestern edge of the town. But the Show there in 1958 was a complete disaster. There was torrential rain and the site turned into a quagmire with mud up to the knees. Tractors had to pull out cars and lorries.

This prompted the move to the aerodrome the following year. It was an ideally level site, initially thirty acres. The runways provided solid roadways with plenty of grass between. Auspiciously there was a heatwave in August 1959 with a record attendance and takings. However, it took the best part of a decade for the Show to establish itself there permanently.

In his account *Fifty Years at Withybush*, Derek Rees describes what happened as a nine-year chess game with the County Council. They had wanted to develop the site as a regional airport. 'Pie in the sky,' says Derek. 'Even Swansea with half-a-million people in its catchment area can't justify such a development at Fairwood Airport in the Gower. Pembrokeshire's population is only just over a hundred thousand.'

The War Office requisitioned Withybush as an airfield in 1939. By the 1960s it was no longer needed for military purposes and was released for sale. The Show executive pre-empted the council in tracking down the previous owners to see if they were willing to sell. 'They button-holed them at marts, farm sales, even barber's shops,' Derek tells me. 'The County Council was handicapped by its ponderous committee structure. Deals were done before they could utter the words Compulsory Purchase.'

As we stroll across the Show ground we discuss the weather. The previous day had been sunny and there were large crowds. But now black clouds were threatening and the wind rising. Spots of rain begin to fall, and soon gather into sheets of driving, soaking Pembrokeshire weather. I shake out an umbrella. 'August is getting worse,' Derek remarks. 'It never used to be as bad as this. Climate change I suppose.'

I suggest the Show could be moved to June when the weather is generally better. However, that would clash with the Royal Welsh. We walk on, until it's pointless to walk any more. 'I love the Show and its complexities,' Derek says as we part. 'It's an annual miracle. Appears quite suddenly, almost magically on these green tarmac-webbed acres.' He pauses, to stare into the misting rain for a while. 'Then, it disappears just as quickly and dramatically, like a mirage.'

SPITFIRE MUSEUM

As you enter the shop strains of Vera Lynn transport you back in time. It's the 1940s. 'We'll meet again…' Newspapers from the wartime era line the walls. Nostalgia is in the air. The large room is erratically lit, spotlights fading into gloom. Racks of clothing look as though they're from two generations ago. There's an exquisite, fading melancholy about the place. This is the National Spitfire Museum of Wales, in downtown Haverfordwest.

A little way into the gloom is Ray Burgess, sitting behind a counter. There's a large colour photograph of a Spitfire pinned to the wall behind his head. In front of him is a cash register. The museum has free entry. But this is also a charity shop. Ray has fifteen volunteers, in this and another shop in Pembroke. All the same, the Welsh Spitfire Museum is essentially a one-man band. Ray has been trying to find a successor for years but with no luck. Who's willing to work seven days a week for even the most deserving of charities?

When you get to look at it, located behind heavy curtains, the Spitfire on show is in pieces. The most striking part is the fuselage, with its cockpit and instrument panel intact. Otherwise parts are scattered around. Fragments of the landing gear and parts of the wings are in a room to the rear (not open to visitors). Impressively on view is a Rolls Royce Merlin MK III engine. This was the aircraft's most important component, the thing that provided its speed and maneuverability. Along with the pilots, it's what clinched the Battle of Britain.

Yet this particular engine does not belong to the rest of the plane. Like many of the other parts it was collected separately. Nonetheless, the Spitfire has an identity, JG 688. It made its first flight in early 1944. More recently, in January 2009, it was registered with the Civil Aviation Authority. The Welsh Spitfire Museum wants to rebuild JG 688 so that it can fly again. But that would take at least five years and cost £1.5 million. It seems an impossible dream. The charitable trust that runs the museum has £7,000 in the bank. The charity shops that support it make just about enough to cover the overheads: rent, heating and lighting. And yet… it is the stuff of dreams that JG 688 has survived at all. There are sixty Spitfires in flying condition around the world. About twenty of them are in the UK. Even Germany has eight. And the global total is gradually going up. Could JG 688 add to its number one day?

The early years were not promising. JG 688 was allocated for use with the Royal Australian Air Force, arriving in Sydney in June 1944. It was moved around to different parts of the country, but apart from that hardly flew. It ended up in the RAAF Oakey

Airbase in Queensland in the late 1940s where its record stops. Until forty years later, when its remains were discovered on a nearby outback farm. Then it began its long road to conservation. It exchanged hands a few times before ending up in Melbourne. Eventually it was sold to an aircraft enthusiast back in the UK, in Oxford. He kept it for three years, during which repairs were made to the fuselage and other components were collected, including the engine.

In 2007 JG 688 was put up for sale once more. That's when Ray Burgess comes into the story. He saw the advert in an aircraft enthusiast's magazine. Together with a group of friends he put in a bid.

Ray was born in Merthyr Tydfil but from eleven was brought up in Oxford. A brief spell in the navy was followed by a series of jobs in the electrical trade. Then, in the early 1970s he was one of the first to take a degree with the Open University, in economics and politics. This led to his becoming a technical author in Robert Maxwell's international publishing empire, writing handbooks for the oil exploration, aviation and space industries. He became a sales executive and in the 1980s moved to a Maxwell outpost in the Netherlands. There he led a management buy-out and went on to win contracts from the European Space Agency, Shell and BP. Along the way he learnt to fly and established connections with Pembrokeshire. A girlfriend led him to Haverfordwest. He made his main home there in the early 2000s after selling his business interests in the Netherlands. By the time the advert for JG 688 appeared, Ray was flying a two-seater Bulldog trainer out of Haverfordwest airport. He had also established a small firm providing certification for aircraft radios. He and four friends put up the £150,000 to buy JG 688. Ray contributed £70,000 from the sale of his Dutch house.

The next hurdle was to find a home for the Spitfire museum. The solution, after prolonged negotiations with the council, was to move a redundant portakabin classroom from St Thomas Picton School in Haverfordwest to the airport outside the town. The museum opened in 2011. But it was far from ideal. The portakabin was on its last legs, cold in winter, and off the beaten track for visitors. Then in 2014 a solution arrived in the form of Jeremy White. He had an ideal location to which the museum could move. For a century his family had owned the Ocky White Department Store in Haverfordwest. Ocky White derived its name from locals who shortened the name of founder Octavius White, Jeremy's grandfather. But now out-of-town shopping stores had forced its closure.

Jeremy suggested that if the museum moved in and also opened a charity shop both sides could benefit. The museum would have a more desirable location and an income stream, while he would be relieved of finding £60,000 a year in rates. It moved in to the new premises in July 2014. The old department store is a vast two-storey building housing a mountain of bric a brac as well as a large library of books about the two world wars and the archives of the Spitfire Society.

Nothing lasts forever, of course. A while ago Jeremy White put the premises up for sale. But when it's sold the Museum will find another empty shop in Haverfordwest. There's plenty of choice.

THE HOSPITAL CAMPAIGN

At about the same time I was selected to be Plaid Cymru's Preseli candidate in the 2007 Assembly election, the local Health Board came up with two options for the future of Withybush hospital in Haverfordwest. One was to concentrate most of its surgical activities at Glangwili hospital in Carmarthen. The alternative was to close both Withybush and Glangwili and replace them with a brand new hospital somewhere in between, probably in Whitland. For most people neither was acceptable. Downgrading Withybush meant, for example, removing maternity consultants to Carmarthen, some thirty miles away. What would happen to a woman in labour who needed an emergency caesarean? She would be bundled into an ambulance and sent thirty miles up the A40. The brand new hospital would cost at least £400 million. No-one believed that sort of money was on the table. Anyway, the proposals as a whole were uncosted.

At an early public meeting organised by the Community Health Council in Fishguard, I proposed a third option. Why not just keep and improve Withybush hospital? This notion was approved overwhelmingly by a show of hands in the hall packed by more than four hundred people. At successive meetings across the county the three proposals were voted on, and my 'third option' was overwhelmingly supported at all of them. The meetings were extraordinary. In an age of political apathy around five thousand people attended them. There were at least two thousand people at the meeting in Haverfordwest. The venue had to be moved, to a giant hanger at Withybush aerodrome. About five hundred attended a meeting in in Milford Haven, three hundred in Neyland and Crymych, about four hundred in St David's. There were more, of course, in the south of the county, outside the Preseli constituency.

Many people had direct personal experience about how vital it was to have emergency services close at hand. Everybody had an experience of travelling on clogged-up country roads to Haverfordwest in a hurry, often in the dark or in bad weather, and dreaded the thought of having to go further, to Carmarthen. All the candidates attended the meetings, including the local Labour AMs whose government was proposing the changes. All supported my third option. Yet the electorate remained deeply cynical. They believed in their hearts that the Health Board's proposals were a done deal.

Throughout the autumn and winter of 2006 into 2007 we leafleted Fishguard, Haverforwest and Milford twice trying to persuade them otherwise. Then into the campaign itself, for six solid weeks across the constituency, I talked about little else but Withybush hospital. *Save Withybush Hospital – Achebwch Ysbyty Llwynhelyg* was on my leaflets and posters. When I announced that it would be beneath my name on the ballot paper the Tories accused me of hijacking the election.

I opened innumerable gates and knocked on uncountable doors to greet whoever opened them with, 'I'm Plaid's candidate and we're very concerned about Withybush hospital'.

'So are we,' they would reply, but then shake their heads and say, 'But what can you do about it?'

The unpopularity of Labour was palpable – especially amongst people who were traditional Labour supporters. It was not just the hospital, though that was emblematic. It was the Tony Blair's prosecution of the Iraq war. In 2003 Rhodri Morgan famously said that Labour had benefited from a 'Baghdad Bounce', a claim that, in the words of President Bush, the mission had been accomplished. By 2007 it was clear that the mission was a catastrophe, and that Blair had dissembled his way through Parliament to bring it about. I lost count of the number of people – especially elderly people – who said to me on the doorstep, in low but determined voices, 'I've voted Labour all my life – but never again, ever.'

Yet it was the hospital that dominated. During the final Saturday of the campaign I found myself manning a stall in Haverfordwest's market square, alongside one of Withybush's doctors. He was Chris Overton, a consultant obstetrician and leading figure in a popular uprising known as SWAT, Save Withybush Action Team. He was handing out a leaflet advising people to vote for whichever candidate they thought best represented the campaign to save the hospital. SWAT was a cross-party organisation. However, Chris and I were duly photographed together. In the course of the morning I suggested that if SWAT could supply us with twenty thousand leaflets we would distribute them before polling day, the following Thursday.

We picked them up the next day. Meanwhile, we arranged for Plaid's Aberystwyth office to print us the same number of last minute leaflets, which included a photograph of myself with Chris Overton. On Monday we leafleted Fishguard. On Tuesday we were in Haverfordwest, and on Wednesday Milford Haven. We finished on our knees in Neyland at gone eleven o'clock on the eve of poll – although just in time to get in a pint.

I reckoned that whoever got nine thousand votes would win. Labour had taken the seat in 2003 with just over eight thousand votes. But I underestimated the impact of Withybush. I underestimated the extent to which our campaign would mobilise the Tory vote. In previous Assembly elections, in 1999 and 2003, it had been artificially suppressed. Tories, hostile to the Assembly anyway, didn't think it was for them and had failed to turn out in their true numbers. But in 2005 they had won the Westminster seat. And our campaign on the hospital gave them a real reason to vote. Tories tend to be getting on a bit and are very keen on hospitals. This was reflected in the turnout, which went up by 10 per cent, from forty-one per cent in 2003 to fifty-one per cent in 2007. And it was Plaid and the Tories that benefited at the expense of Labour. It's just that the Tories benefited more. They got 11,086 votes, Labour 7,881, and Plaid 7,101.

Labour lost Preseli and also the neighbouring seat, Carmarthen West and South Pembrokeshire, mainly because of the hospital issue. Plaid's increased share of the vote in Preseli (up from sixteen to twenty-five per cent) also ensured that we scraped an additional seat on the Regional List in the Mid and West Wales constituency. These changes, combined with others across Wales, ensured that Labour lost its majority in Cardiff Bay. In turn this resulted in lengthy coalition negotiations following the election. Eventually Labour and Plaid reached a deal to form the 'One Wales Government'. A key part of the arrangement was withdrawal of the hospital reorganisation plans.

So Withybush was saved, but not for long. Once Labour got back into government on its own, following the 2011 Assembly election, plans to downgrade the hospital crept back on to the agenda. Today Withybush has lost consultant-led maternity services, its Special Care Baby Unit and some Paediatric services. A threat hovers over sustaining twenty-four-hour Accident and Emergency.

During 2018 the Hywel Dda Health Board came up with what were claimed to be new proposals to downgrade Withybush hospital but build a new one somewhere on the Carmarthenshire Pembrokeshire border, probably at Whitland. They were, of course, a warmed-up version of the same plans we campaigned against in 2007. And as at that time, the Conservatives blamed the Welsh Labour government in Cardiff Bay, while Labour blamed the Conservative Government in London for cutting the Welsh Government's budget.

Driving past Withybush hospital one Saturday afternoon in May 2018 I noticed a bunch of people standing outside with banners declaring that Labour was campaigning to save the hospital. I stopped the car and went across. Among the demonstrators was Philippa Thompson who had come close to unseating Stephen Crabb, Preseli's Conservative MP, in the Westminster election in the

general election the previous year. She had also been Labour's agent during the Assembly election in 2015 when I had stood again for Plaid. We had had many amiable discussions on those occasions when the parties meet during a campaign.

I congratulated her on coming within just 315 votes of beating Crabb, increasing her share of the poll by 14.5 per cent. Then I asked why she was campaigning to save the hospital when it was her Labour government in Cardiff that was behind the downgrading.

'It's the Hywel Dda Health Board's plans,' she said.

'But it's the Labour Government that appoints the Board.'

'You're right, I know. But what can you do?'

COLBY MOOR

Colby Moor lies five miles east of Haverfordwest, between Wiston and Llawhadon. The lane alongside it used to be the main road to Carmarthen. A closely fought battle in the English Civil War was fought here in August 1645. It's called England's war but there's no doubt Wales was very much involved too. In the seventeenth century these fields were open moorland, a traditional gathering place for musters of the County Militia.

Information about the battle is sketchy. But there's no doubt it took place on these fields because quite a few musket and cannon balls have been ploughed up. The authority on the battle is Terry John, author of *The Civil War in Pembrokeshire*. He is a member of Lord Saye and Sele's Blew Regiment of Foote, a Parliamentary regiment of the Sealed Knot. Every year it holds a ceremony at Wiston Church to remember the men who were killed in the battle.

In the preceding year Royalist and Parliamentary forces had clashed across west Wales, with first the Parliamentarians and then the Royalists gaining the upper hand. By the summer of 1645 the Parliamentarians had retreated to their stronghold in Pembroke Castle leaving the Royalists, based at Haverfordwest, in control of much of the county. However, in June the King's forces were defeated at the Battle of Naseby in distant Northamptonshire. As a result, most of the Royalist forces in west Wales were urgently recalled to England. This gave the Parliamentarians their opportunity. The battle at Colby Moor was prompted when the remaining Haverfordwest Royalist garrison burned cornfields around Narberth, to prevent the grain supply falling into Parliamentary hands.

A force of 250 foot and 200 horse and dragoons plus two guns marched out of Pembroke to meet them. They were led by Major

General Rowland Laugharne, a seasoned officer, and reinforced by 200 seamen from a frigate recently arrived in Milford Haven. Even so the Royalists, who had 450 horse and 1,100 foot with four large guns, outnumbered them by more than two to one. What followed is a testimony to the importance of leadership, disposition and morale in a battle. In the early evening, Laugharne placed his men in a line on the high ground above the Royalists, about half-a-mile away on Colby Moor. Then, as he put it in the one account of the battle that has come to light, 'A small party of our horseman, boarded on both sides with a hundred-and-fifty musketeers, charged with their whole body.' The fighting, he reported in a letter to the Speaker of the House of Commons, was 'very fierce and doubtful for near an hour.' But then the Royalist horse wavered, their line broke, and they retreated chaotically. The Parliamentary cavalry pursued them through the narrow lanes, cutting them down. A small band of Royalists took refuge in an ancient earthwork known as the Rath overlooking Crundale. But they too were soon overwhelmed.

In all, the Royalists lost 150 men killed with more than 700 taken prisoner, including a Lieutenant Colonel, two Majors, seven Captains, and twenty-two Lieutenants. Also taken were four field guns, five barrels of powder, 800 rifles and all the carriages and provisions. The Parliamentarians lost only two men dead and sixty wounded. The victory was so complete that for generations afterwards the event was known as the Colby Moor Rout. It's a term that has entered the Pembrokeshire lexicon to describe anything resembling a shambles.

Reading the history, I was intrigued by Rowland Laugharne. Not too much is known about him. He was born around 1610 into a reasonably well-to-do Pembrokeshire family and brought up on an estate at St Brides on the west coast. When he was eight he was entered into the household of Robert Devereux, Earl of Essex, in Carmarthenshire. This was a common enough arrangement, a kind of historical internship designed to improve a young person's education and chances. He accompanied the Earl on various military expeditions to the Netherlands and by the early 1630s had become one of his principal servants. Ten years later he returned to Pembrokeshire and married into a land-owning family in the Dale peninsula.

What I found most interesting about his career was that during the Civil War he switched sides. There were, in fact, three periods of war. The first was from 1642-45 at the end of which Charles I was in the custody of Parliament. Then there was the year 1648-49 during which Charles was beheaded. The final period was between 1651-52 when the future Charles II attempted a restoration. In the first period many Parliamentarians were not opposed to the King as such but rather to his advisers who they believed were influencing him wrongly. They marched under the slogan, 'For King and Parliament.' However, by the late 1640s the King's intransigence eroded this sympathy, though in Parliament there were still many factions. The Presbyterians wished to give the King the benefit of the doubt, while the Independents and Oliver Cromwell's New Model Army made the case for a republic. Laugharne was of the Presbyterian disposition, a view that eventually persuaded him to the King's side.

By 1647 there was also the small matter that Parliament was attempting to disband its Welsh army without settling the soldiers' arrears of pay. The upshot was that in April 1648, when the Second Civil War was imminent, Colonel John Poyer, the Governor of Pembroke Castle, declared for the King. Rowland Laugharne and another prominent Pembrokeshire Parliamentarian, Colonel Rice Powell, joined him.

Aware that they threatened a major rebellion, Parliament sent a substantial force led by Colonel Horton to contain it. The two sides, with Rowland Laugharne now leading the Royalist forces, met at the Battle of St Fagans outside Cardiff in May 1648. This time it was Laugharne's turn to have most men. However, Horton's smaller but more battle-hardened army defeated him. Wounded, Laugharne retreated to join Poyer and Powell at Pembroke Castle. There they were besieged for two months by forces led by Cromwell himself.

Starved into submission, Laugharne, Poyer and Powell were sent to London and court martialled. All three were sentenced to death but General Fairfax decreed that only one should die and they should draw lots. Three pieces of paper were placed in a bag, two of them bearing the words 'Life given by God'. The men refused to draw them so instead a child was deputed to choose their fate. Colonel Poyer was executed by firing squad in April 1649. Laugharne spent most of the 1650s in prison. After the Restoration he was elected MP for Pembroke in the Cavalier Parliament that met between 1661-79. However, he fell into debt and died in London in November 1675.

Rowland Laugharne's life is a central thread in Terry John's account of the Civil War and is testimony to how much of Wales' hidden history is still to be uncovered. His story could be retold as a novel. Certainly there is plenty of action, conflicting loyalties, romance, melodrama and also tragedy – Laugharne lost two sons in the civil war.

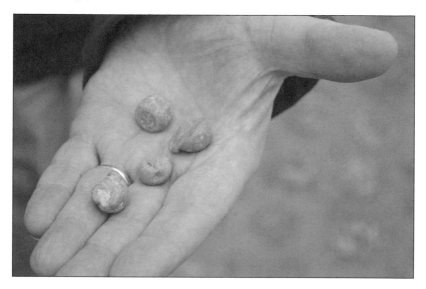

At the end of our tour of the Colby Moor battlefield Terry John opened the boot of his car and took out a small container. Inside were four musket balls. They had been ploughed up in the fields not far away and all were misshapen. 'Result of the impact with their targets,' I suggested. 'Not this one,' Terry replied, holding it aloft. 'We reckon these indentations were made by a man's teeth while he was undergoing some surgery on the battlefield, perhaps having a leg amputated. A case of biting the bullet, you could say. Puts you directly in touch with history.'

BETHLEHEM

Driving through the tiny hamlet of Bethlehem, about three miles out of Haverfordwest on the Cardigan road, I've often wondered how it came about its name. I've wondered, too, how its rather fetching chapel has survived in such an isolated spot. So when I passed by one afternoon and saw a woman standing outside the manse attached to the chapel I drew up alongside. Would it be possible to see inside? 'By all means,' she said. 'Park round the back and I'll get the keys.' Slightly built with a cheerful countenance, Jenny Gough turned out to be the Minister, or rather Pastor, as she calls herself. 'This is a Baptist church,' she explains. 'Church?' I query. 'Oh, yes, the church is the congregation, the chapel the building.'

Inside it has a charming, intimate feel, shaped as a square. Large wooden pillars in each corner hold up a balcony that overlooks the pulpit. I ask if I can take a photograph. I notice a large white projector screen hanging above the pulpit and a drum kit alongside. I question whether this is an evangelical Church, 'Absolutely,' Jenny replies. 'If God created the world in seven days, as the Bible says, then it was seven days. You can't always explain it.'

She has been the Pastor here since 2014. Brought up in London she felt the call of God when she was sixteen. 'I read Luke Chapter 4,' she says, by way of explanation. It tells of Jesus's forty days in the wilderness, when he resisted temptations of the devil, and afterwards when he walked through Galilee performing miracles. Jenny studied for the ministry at the South Wales Baptist College in Cardiff, and afterwards served in a church just outside the capital. Then she moved to Carmarthen to work for a housing association.

Later she joined the Rowan Organisation that supports independent living for the disadvantaged. After a decade she decided it was time to renew her ministry. During her refresher training she was invited to preach at Bethlehem chapel where there was a vacancy. 'It was a call,' she says simply.

I discover that sixty adults and twenty-five children attend, which seems a large congregation for such a small community. Bethlehem has no more than a dozen houses and a population of around thirty. Jenny tells me the church draws people from Haverfordwest, Clarbeston Road, Crundale, and Spittal. She advances two reasons for its popularity. 'Our approach is more modern than traditional, and we're family focused.' She points to an information board in the church hall, an addition built in the 1990s. It advertises toddler and youth clubs, fishing and ladies craft groups, lunch and coffee gatherings as well as prayer meetings.

The Rev David Rees built the chapel in 1820 along with Salem on the other side of Spittal. He was wealthy, inheriting a farm and amalgamating it with two other holdings. A monoglot Welsh speaker from the north of Wales, he undoubtedly would have been traditional from a religious point of view. His large tombstone dominates Bethlehem chapel's graveyard, but I suspect there's little he would recognise in the activities of his church today except, perhaps, the place where baptisms are held. I point, with a querying look, to a hinged wooden structure covering a small piece of ground alongside the chapel. 'Well spotted,' Jenny laughs. 'Would you like to see it?'

She undoes a bolt and lifts the planks to reveal an oblong basin with steps leading to a depth about waist high. Baptisms take place two or three times a year. Jenny's husband part fills the basin with cold water the night before. Then, just before the ceremony, he adds some warm to lessen the chill.

'Why is this place called Bethlehem?' I query. 'I've no idea,' Jenny replies. 'I've never been asked that before.'

In search of an answer I call on artists Maggie and Gwyn Williams at their Old Smithy Studio up the road. I first met them when I stood for the Assembly in 2007. They put up a placard for me, in a great position on one of Preseli's main arteries. As it happens they're also evangelically religious, but eschew any organised church. Instead, they busk to digitised drums on the streets of Haverfordwest, or anywhere that invites them. Gwyn plays rhythm guitar and Maggie bass. One of Gwyn's songs starts with the line, 'You can't go to heaven in a four-wheel drive.'

When I walk into their studio I'm amazed to see suspended from the ceiling an enormous eight-foot by five-foot canvas vividly depicting Christ on the Cross. Gwyn tells me he was compelled to paint it after Clouds, the community cafe and art shop in Haverfordwest which supplies his painting material, gave him the canvas. A woman whose artist husband had died had donated it, with the proviso that it should be passed on to another artist. 'It was a message from God,' Gwyn says. 'A friend, an athletic chap – great body – modelled for me. He stripped and I hung him from the rafters with climbing straps.'

The painting took eight months to complete. That was six years ago. It's still on sale at £8,000.

I put the Bethlehem question to Gwyn. He says that in the 1990s it was decided that the place had grown sufficiently in size to need its own postcode, SA62 5XL. They wanted to differentiate it from Spittal and Poyston Cross, a few miles either side. 'That was when the place needed a name and it was natural to call it after old Reverend Rees' chapel.' All the same, there was a bit of a fuss. Objections came from the other Welsh Bethlehem, near Llangadog in Carmarthenshire. It does well out of people using its post office for their Christmas cards, to have the iconic name printed on the envelopes. An alternative Bethlehem might bring competition. 'The BBC thought there was a story and sent a camera team down here,' Gwyn says. 'They interviewed me, but it never went out. I told them that a place our size didn't have a post office, let alone a shop or a pub, and was never likely to have one.'

THE SKULL AT POYSTON HALL

While being shown around Poyston Hall, a privately-owned mansion on the edge of Withybush aerodrome a few miles north of Haverfordwest, I felt mild disappointment. I'd been drawn there because it was the ancestral home of General Sir Thomas Picton, killed at Waterloo in 1815. But more particularly, I'd come because I'd heard that the skull of the horse that carried him into battle was kept in the mansion's drawing room. And indeed, that had been the case. For many years, going back to the 1970s, the horse's skull was kept under the floor in a rusty biscuit tin, set into a concrete floor.

However, a few years before I visited, the concrete had been replaced with wooden floorboards, and the biscuit tin removed. The grey skull of Sir Thomas Picton's horse now lies on a small sideboard in Poyston Hall's rather grand two-storey library. In fact, that's where it was originally placed some time in the 1820s, on the wooden mantlepiece. An image of it can be seen in a photograph taken at Poyston Hall in 1901, now kept in the National Library.

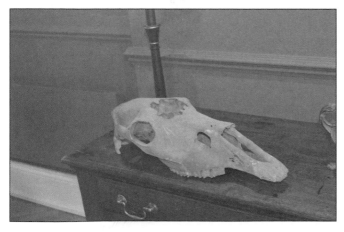

The skull is fascinating to look at. When I picked it up, it was unexpectedly light for its large size. All the same it didn't have the resonance I expected. Somehow it felt more more ordinary than if it were still kept beneath the floor. Whoever placed it there in the 1970s was harking back to a custom that was relatively common between the seventeenth and the late nineteenth centuries. Horse's skulls were placed in the walls, near the threshold, or beneath the floors of houses and other buildings. In the last century there have been about twenty domestic finds across Wales and others in churches and chapels, including at Llandaff Cathedral.[1] They were supposed to ward off evil forces and bring good fortune. It is thought, too, that there are links with Epona, the Celtic horse goddess venerated as a deity associated with domestic prosperity, but also with the passage of life and death.[2]

In Preseli twenty buried horse skulls were found in a house at Jordanston, south of Fishguard, in 1901; four in a house in Glyn Cuch, close to the northern border with Carmarthenshire, in 1979; and one in a cowhouse at Trefwrdan Uchaf farm near Nevern in 1968.

They've also been found in two chapels. At the Ebenezer Independent Chapel in Newport, three skulls were found under the floor in 1958 and regarded as having been buried to improve the acoustics. When the Calvinistic Methodist Chapel at Caerfarchell to the east of St Davids was built in 1827, one Willie Lewis, a sailor and member of the congregation was told to find two skulls 'to kill the echo'.[3]

Why the skull of Sir Thomas Picton's horse was placed beneath the floor of Poyston Hall as late as the 1970s is impossible to know. Perhaps it was for sentimental reasons. Born in 1758 Picton was the eighth of eleven children.[4] He left Haverfordwest grammar school at thirteen and became an ensign in his uncle's regiment, the 12th Regiment of Foot. He was stationed at Gibraltar where he was promoted lieutenant five years later. Shortly afterwards he quelled a mutiny amongst his men, but then retired to Poyston Hall for twelve years.

In 1794, aged thirty-six, he sailed for the West Indies where he eventually became Governor General of Trinidad. Some murky episodes followed. Picton held the island with few men and little money against constant invasion threats by the French and Spanish. His rule was resented by other colonists who accused him of torturing a 14-year-old mulatto girl. Picton returned to London to face trial, leaving behind Rosetta, his Creole mistress, and their four children. He never saw them again, though he made financial provision for the children. There were two, extended trials, but eventually the charges were dismissed. Whatever the truth of the allegations – and it needs to be recorded that friends in Trinidad contributed £600 to his legal expenses – Picton soon redeemed himself by active service during the Napoleonic wars. He was promoted to major general and in 1809 made Governor of Flushing in the Netherlands.

A year later, at the Duke of Wellington's request, he was appointed to command a division in the Peninsular Army in Spain. There his bravery and the exploits of his division at the battles of Badajos, Vittoria, and Cuidad Rodrigo made him a popular hero.[5] However, Wellington disliked his familiarity with his officers and found him 'as rough a foul-mouthed devil as ever lived.' On his return home Picton was the only general not to be made a peer. Nonetheless, in 1813 he was knighted and returned as MP for Pembroke Boroughs in a by-election.

In 1815, after Napoleon escaped from imprisonment on the Island of Elba, Picton was appointed to the high command of the Anglo-Dutch army at Wellington's request. When Napoleon attacked the centre of the allied army at Waterloo, Picton led a bayonet charge on the advancing French column, crying 'Charge! Charge! Hurrah! Hurrah!' They proved his last words. He was shot through the temple by a musket ball, making him the highest ranking casualty on the coalition side. However, his horse survived. Soldiers retrieved the animal from the battlefield and it eventually reached the meadows of Poyston Hall. There it grazed in contented and peaceful retirement. When it died its body was buried between two trees in sight of the mansion's drawing room, and the skull kept in the library.

It's a tangible link with Preseli's imperial and military past. There is also a story in the public record office dating from Victorian times, told by a gamekeeper. He claimed he saw the ghost of General Picton, dressed in a cloak and carrying a sword, in Poyston Hall's front drive on an anniversary of Waterloo.[6] That might be more believable if the gamekeeper had seen the apparition wearing civilian clothes and a top hat. Those were what the General wore into battle at Waterloo. His luggage and uniform had not arrived in time.

TELETUBBY HOUSE

Through a twelve-foot high wall of glass a stream of light is reflected off a gleaming sea. The sun is becoming bigger as it heads towards the horizon. Soon it will slowly disappear, throwing a silvery path across the water. Druidstone Haven faces due west into St Brides Bay and often, as today, has spectacular sunsets.

Watching it, glass in hand, is Bob Marshall-Andrews, the former libertarian-left Labour MP. He defected to the Liberal Democrats in 2017, describing Labour as a 'basket case' because of its failure to oppose Brexit. He is a barrister of whom the Chambers Legal Director remarked, 'Juries love him'. He is also chairman of the George Adamson Wildlife Trust which works in the Kora National Park in northern Kenya. And he's a novelist as well. His fourth and latest book is *Dump* (Whitefox Publishing, 2018). It had its genesis when he was staying at the Greystoke Mahale Lodge, on the shores of Lake Tanganyika, a good place to study chimpanzees. While there, Bob learned the legend of a grossly violent, sexually aberrant, psychopathic alpha male who was so awful he was murdered by the rest of the troupe. The following day he heard of Trump's success in the American election. The allegory was irresistible.

Bob Marshall-Andrews was Labour MP for Medway during the New Labour years from 1997 to 2010. He thought Tony Blair 'dangerously delusional'. That was after witnessing his speech to the 1996 Labour conference in Brighton when he claimed the Labour Party could trace its roots to the Old Testament prophets. I was there, too, and felt the same. In his 2011 memoir *Off Message* Bob recalls how even among the conference delegates, 'by then in a state of semi-tumescence, there was a distinct pause as they digested the hitherto unknown and unsuspected fact that it was Moses, Elijah, Elisha, Jehoshaphat and Co who had founded the Labour party, and not Keir Hardie'. He declared Blair the worst prime minister for a-hundred-and-fifty years. He says the Iraq War more than vindicated this judgement.

But I digress. Bob Marshall-Andrews is the owner of the Malator, an extraordinary turf-covered dwelling that resembles a grounded UFO and overlooks Druidstone beach. It sits above the coastal path along which I have trudged on scores of occasions wondering what this house was like inside.

'You've come on a good day,' Bob tells me. 'But you should be here during a winter gale when ninety-mile-an-hour winds lash spray against us. The glass frontage can buckle in and out by an inch. At first I wondered if it could withstand the stress. Houses along the cliff have had their roofs blown off. But we've been OK.'

Locally the Malator is known as the Teletubby House. Bob had it built in 1997, a year after the popular children's programme was first aired. I glance towards the narrow coastal road that edges round the land at the back. Along it the Puffin Bus swings by. I tell Bob I've been on it many times and it always slows going past, while the driver points out the Teletubby landmark to the passengers. 'I know,' Bob laughs. 'We often get parents with their young children knocking at the door asking if they can peek inside. I imagine they expect to see Dipsy, Tinky Winky or Laa-Laa. Instead they get me, sometimes looking a bit worse for wear after lunch.'

Bob shows me round the open-plan house. I'm surprised to discover it's only on one floor. I'd imagined there would be cellar-like rooms underground. The main feature is the living space and kitchen with a wood burning stove at the centre. Its chimney pokes through the roof like a periscope. Futuristic bright green pods on either side contain a bathroom, cupboards and a utility room. The main bedroom is on one side and there are two guest bedrooms on the other. Overhead the common ceiling slopes upwards from the back, modelled on the underneath of a B52 bomber wing.

Altogether it feels a little like being on board a ship. The futuristic effect is enhanced by an array of woodcarvings from the South Pacific, and paintings from Africa. Bob pauses by a pair of dark coloured etching-like paintings suggesting the struggle against apartheid. He says he bought them at a charity auction for the Nelson Mandela Foundation in London. 'The price kept going up and I sensed I was competing with one other person,' he said. 'Afterwards I discovered it was Donald Woods and I offered to share the paintings. But by then he had bought something else.' Woods was the journalist and anti-apartheid campaigner whose friendship with Steve Biko, leader of the Black Consciousness Movement, was the subject of the 1987 film *Cry Freedom*.

I ask Bob about planning permission. How did he get it when the National Park is so stubbornly resistant to structures that depart from the local vernacular? He answers there was hardly any problem because the Park was so keen to see the back of the building that was already on the site. This was a converted Nissen hut that had been put there during World War II by a London builder to evacuate his family. Eventually it became a holiday let. Bob bought it in 1987 after staying in it several times. 'It had been on the market for ten years, can you believe that?' Intriguingly the Nissen hut's name lives on. I had imagined Malator referred to some figure in Greek mythology. But no, it's merely the combination of the first two letters in the names of the previous owner's three dogs.

The National Park only demanded a few changes to the Teletubby design of architecture firm Future Systems. The main requirement was that its height should be lowered. The design was based on a rough sketch drawn by Bob's son Tom, a graphics engineer. His main suggestion was to shape the large front window to look like an eye.

The nearest I get to a consideration of the cost is when Bob points to the rather expensive-looking semi-circle sofa which is the dominant feature in the main living space. He says that at £8000 it was a bit beyond his budget until a windfall came his way. When the house was first built it attracted a good deal of interest from the London papers. They sniffed around, looking for a planning scandal. Two of them quoted the owner of a caravan site at Newgale, a few miles to the north. 'It's an outrage,' she said. 'You can't get planning to put up a conservatory. But an MP comes down here and gets permission for this monstrosity. It's not a question of what you know but who you know.'

Bob sued the papers for suggesting he was corrupt. As he said, 'I had the permission long before I became an MP.' He achieved an immediate apology and an out of court settlement, half of which he gave to charity while the remainder paid for the settee. 'I think of the case every time I sit on it,' he told me.

Notes

1. Eurwyn Wiliam, 'Concealed Horse Skulls: Testimony and Message', in Trefor M. Owen (Ed.) *From Corrib to Cultra: Folklife Essays in Honour of Alan Gailey*, Institute of Irish Studies Queens University Belfast, 2000, pages 136 to 149.

2. Miranda Aldhouse-Green, who was Professor of Archeology at Cardif University from 2006 to 2013, has surveyed the evidence for the sacrificial deposition of horse remains in the Celtic world. In particular, she has drawn attention to the way horse remains were often associated with situations which could be described as liminal – that is to say, associated with boundaries or thresholds – and that horses have been seen as creatures that straddled two worlds, the civilized and settled on one hand, and the areas outside on the other. One way this is expressed even today is with the *Mari Lwyd* (Grey Mary) ceremony at Christmas and New Year, when a horse's skull covered with a white sheet and decorated with ribbons is taken door to door by a man concealed beneath the sheet and accompanied by a party of wassailers. See Aldhouse-Green's paper 'The symbolic horse in Pagan Celtic Europe: an archeological perspective' in S. Davies and N.A. Jones (Eds.), *The Horse in Celtic culture*, University of Wales Press, 1997.

3. E. Isaac, *Coelion Cymru* (Welsh Customs), London, 1939, page 158.

4. Francis Green, 'The Pictons of Poyston', in *West Wales Historical Records*, Vol X, 1924, pages 53-4.

5. After his death his body was brought back from Waterloo and interred at the family vault at St George's, in Hanover Square, London. In 1859 his body was re-interred in St Paul's Cathedral, lying close to the Duke of Wellington. His marble statue is one of eleven in the Hall of Heroes in Cardiff's City Hall. Along with Henry VII Picton stands in British contrast with the other nine, more Welsh-oriented figures unveiled by Lloyd George in 1916 – Buddug (Boudica), Saint David, Hywel Dda, Gerald of Wales, Llywelyn Ein Llyw Olaf (Llywelyn the Last), Dafydd ap Gwilym, Owain Glyndŵr, Bishop William Morgan, and William Williams Pantycelyn.

6. Francis Jones, *Historic Pembrokeshire Homes and Their Families*, Brawdy Books, 2001, page 228.

EAST

TWO FIELDS

They are two rather ordinary looking fields. In the distance are a few houses of the nearby village of Llandysilio. It was at this spot, at the gate between the two fields, that aged fourteen the Preseli poet Waldo Williams had a vision. It stayed with him and forty years later, in 1956, inspired what many believe to be his greatest poem *Mewn Dau Gae* (In Two Fields).

Waldo often helped John Beynon, the farmer who owned the fields, especially at haymaking time. 'It happened here,' Vernon, John Beynon's son, told me, holding open the gate to let us through. 'Waldo often came with his parents in the summer months. They would sit back-to-back reading, under that oak tree over there, while Waldo wandered the hedgerows. My father told me he often saw Waldo standing just here, where I am now, as if in a trance between these fields.'

When he was growing up Vernon knew the poet well. 'You could always tell when Waldo was coming,' he said. 'He had tacks in the soles and heels of his shoes, to stop them wearing out I suppose. You could hear them clip-clopping on the lanes.'

Waldo made clear that the source of the poem was the intense epiphany he had as a teenager in fields close to his grandfather's house Rhosaeron, near the edge of Llandysilio:

Weun Parc y Blawd (Marshy Flour Field) and *Parc y Blawd* (Flour Field) are two fields on the land of a friend and an old neighbour of mine, John Beynon, The Cross, Clunderwen. In the gap between these two fields about forty years ago I suddenly and vividly realized, in a very personal manner, that men are, first and foremost bound by brotherhood.[1]

Waldo is always referred to by his first name, as though the easy familiarity implies familial possession. This is a common enough trait with loved public figures in Wales, but it is especially the case with Waldo. Those who never knew him, but just read his work and learn about his life, come to love him.

Why is that? In the first place it is because of his otherworldly saintliness. He was probably the nearest Wales has produced to Gandhi, if you exclude Gwynfor Evans. His was the poetry of hope and optimism. Then there was his character, always given to humorous eccentricity, of which there are a host of recollections. But most of all it is the messages contained in his poetry that inspire affection. In essence these are the goodness and sanctity of life, and of brotherhood as the supreme value in human relations. He experienced it in the close-knit, and interdependent Preseli farming community, especially at harvest and sheep-shearing time. He regarded it as an ideal society. He also thought that Wales as a whole could be like that.

Following his death in 1971 a memorial was raised for him at Rhos-fach common on the edge of Mynachlog-ddu. The large stone slab stands in the shadow of the Preseli hills that inspired so much of his imagination. Below the inscription WALDO (1904-1971) is a line taken from his favourite poem, *Preseli*. It was written in praise of the people and the area, in particular the mountains he made famous:

Mur fy meboyd, Foel Drigarn, Carn Gyfrwy, Tal Mynydd,
Wrth fy nghefn ym mhob annybyniaeth barn.

Wall round my boyhood, Moel Drigarn, Carn Gyfrwy, Tal Mynydd,
At my back in all independence of mind.[2]

On a stone nearby is an explanatory plaque, put here by the Waldo Williams Society.[3] They'd heard that foreign visitors thought the name Waldo might refer to a famous horse. The inscription, in Welsh and English, states:

The standing stone commemorates Waldo Goronwy Williams, the poet, patriot, pacifist and Quaker. He spent four years of his childhood in the neighbourhood. This is where he learnt Welsh. Someone said it had taken two thousand years of Welsh civilization to create a person such as Waldo. Someone else said that he was not always of this world. He possessed the attributes of a saint.

Waldo is widely regarded as the pre-eminent and most original Welsh language poet of the twentieth century. But was he a great poet or, merely, a poet who produced a few great poems? The question is prompted by his limited output. Apart from *Cerddi'r Plant* (Children's Poems), published in collaboration with Llwyd Williams in 1936, he produced only one volume of verse, *Dail Pren* (Leaves of a Tree) in 1956.

However, the very frugality of Waldo's work is a reason why he is so admired. For Waldo believed that writing is devoid of meaning without being accompanied by commitment through action. This was reinforced by his experience of living through the Second

World War and the nuclear explosion at Hiroshima. It led him to active protest and eventually more conventional political involvement. He stood as Plaid Cymru's first candidate in Pembrokeshire, in the 1959 election.

A Conscientious Objector in the Second World War, he was released from military service unconditionally after appearing before a Tribunal in Carmarthen in February 1942. But although the tribunal released him, he still paid a price. Pembrokeshire county council education officials objected, with the result that he gave up his headmastership at Puncheston primary school. With his wife Linda he moved to Pwllheli, on the Llŷn Peninsula. There he found work at Botwnnog Grammar School.

In 1950 Waldo was deeply affected by the war in Korea. He resolved that he must refuse to pay his taxes since a proportion of them would contribute towards the cost of the war. So he left his teaching job where he was taxed at source. Instead, he became a lecturer with his salary paid directly by the Extra Mural Department at the University College of Wales, Aberystwyth.

Waldo refused to pay income tax until the last conscript was released in 1963. He was sent to prison in September 1960, and again in February 1961. 'The college for criminals,' he called it. Bailiffs removed his furniture in November 1954, to the value of £41 16s 0d. By this time, he had joined the Quaker Meeting in Milford Haven. Other members went to the auction and bought back his wardrobe, table, chair, linoleum and bicycle – his bed was not taken.

While the Korean War was at its height, Waldo wrote relatively little. He believed that Gandhi's criticism of the great Indian writer Rabindranath Tagore also applied to him: 'You are giving us words instead of action.' Waldo felt his 'action' over the Korean War justified publication of *Dail Pren*. 'I hope it will be of practical assistance to my nation amid the confusion of this age,' he wrote.

More often than not Waldo was to be seen in ragged clothes riding his bike long distances across Preseli and beyond. On one occasion a neighbour in Llandysilio stopped him. 'Why Waldo,' she declared. 'Where on earth are you going, dressed like that?' 'I'm off to Swansea to buy a saucepan,' he answered.

In a letter to D.J. Williams (see pages 180-184), Waldo described how he had to climb onto the roof of Elm Cottage in Llandysilio to cut a tree growing from the chimney. He didn't have a billhook, an axe or saw, only a carving knife. As he stood on the roof he waved his arms and shouted at people passing below, 'Now then, who wants a piece of the breast?' And in 1969 Pembrokeshire's Education Committee invited him to open an extension to the school in Llandysilio where his father had been headmaster and he a pupil. Unwell, he came in slippers, remarking to the crowd waiting for him, 'These are my school opening slippers.'

Waldo Williams has more plaques dedicated to him than any equivalent figure. As well as at Rhos-fach common, you will find them outside the County Archives in Haverfordwest, originally the location of his birthplace in the town, which has been demolished; on Elm Cottage and at his grandparents' home Rhosaeron in Llandysilio; the school at Puncheston where he taught for some years; on his lodgings at 58 Cambrian Street where he stayed while a student at university in Aberystwyth; at Botwnnog Grammar School on the Llŷn peninsula; and even in England, at Kimbolton Secondary School in Huntingdonshire where he also taught.

The Waldo Williams Society will soon run out of places to put plaques. The latest to be unveiled, in September 2018, was on Millin Methodist Chapel south of Slebech, a village straddling the A40 between Haverfordwest and Narberth. Waldo made a habit of cycling there and spending the night sleeping in the chapel. He would wake in the small hours to cycle the short distance to Picton Point, where the Western and Eastern Cleddau rivers join, there to experience the tranquillity of the sun rising amidst the mist and wading birds. The door to Millin Chapel was locked when its members thought a tramp was sheltering there and might entice others to join him. 'If only we had known it was Waldo,' they said when they realised who their visitor had been.

Children loved Waldo. During the 1960s he taught at many schools across Pembrokeshire. A fellow teacher at the Holy Name Catholic School in Fishguard reported:

> Waldo would arrive at the school every morning surrounded by several children – three or four children on each side having managed to grasp his hands or his sleeve; all of them delighted. When Waldo would appear in the classroom, there would be great jubilation, and it was difficult to keep the small children in their places as they were so eager to see what new wonders he had brought them.[4]

Waldo forever found alliterations. A close friend and fellow Preseli poet James Nicholas, recalled a line of 'cynghanedd' – a complex arrangement of sound within a phrase – that Waldo spoke to him after returning from one of his many visits to the Irish Gaeltacht. He had seen some poorly clad children playing barefoot outside their home, which prompted him to say:

Chwi blant troednoeth cyfoethog!

You bare foot wealthy children!

Of course, to Waldo's mind they were wealthy because they spoke Gaelic. Once in a pub Waldo was part of a group who were warned that no singing was allowed. 'Can we sing in our hearts?' Waldo queried. 'Yes, of course,' the barman answered. 'You can do what you like in your hearts.' 'Then it should be no singing aloud allowed,' Waldo declared.

Nearing his end in St Thomas Hospital in Haverfordwest, he was visited by friends who had been regular members of his weekly extramural class at Talgarreg in Ceredigion. They commented on the dim lights in the ward. Quick as a flash Waldo replied:

Gwell golau dim na dim golau!

Better dim lights than no lights!

From all of this it might be concluded that while Waldo was lovable and sincere, ultimately he was a naïve optimist. Nothing could be further from the truth. He was a profoundly realistic, down-to-earth man. He clung to his belief in brotherhood because he sensed it was the only chance of staving off destruction.

Part of this outlook was the result of events in his personal life. When he was eleven his sister Morvydd, only a few years older and to whom he was close, died. In 1941, when he was 37, he married Linda, the friend of a cousin in Llandysilio. But within two years she too died, of tuberculosis. It was an unbearable loss, one from which he never really recovered. He wrote a short elegy for her which he sent to friends. Among the concluding lines are:

Hi wnaeth o'm hawen, ennyd,
Aderyn bach uwch drain byd.

She made of my inspiration
A small bird above the world's thorns.

He referred to his short period of married life as *fy mlynyddoedd mawr* (my great years). Linda's death was the main reason he moved to live in England for seven years. Here he found once more that brotherhood is *Unig falm i fyd* (The only balm for the world). For all that his roots went deep into Preseli, Waldo was and remains a national poet. Certainly, this was the view of Cymdeithas yr Iaith Gymraeg activists in the 1960s and 1970s for whom he represented hope. When they stood trial, they quoted from him as though they were referring to texts in the Bible. As the poet's most lyrical translator Tony Conran put it, 'The poetry of the older nationalists, Saunders Lewis and Gwenallt, had too much tragic clarity to inspire the young. Waldo gave them the joyousness of apocalyptic struggle, in which passive resistance on behalf of the language was linked to anti-imperialism and the campaign for peace.'[5]

Was Waldo a great poet? I think there can be no doubt. His humour gave him an acute sense of life's incongruity, the disparity between the world as it is and the world as it should be. Even read in translation – and Waldo has been fortunate in his translators – his poetry is of the highest quality in terms of intelligence, love, and above all a numinous awareness.

ONE NIGHT IN PRESELI

High in Mynydd Preselau, where the farms edge into the common land, is an historic cottage. At first sight it is little more than a shack imprisoned by encroaching vegetation, a small barn-like structure with a tin roof through which pokes a metal chimney. But this is no ordinary cottage. Some years ago, curators at the Welsh National History Museum wanted to dismantle it stone by stone, and re-erect it amongst the other folk dwellings at St Fagans.

Built on marshy, marginal land, the cottage is surrounded by trees that hide it from view. It is approached by an often boggy, winding track that increases its sense of isolation. Close by is Afon Wern whose waters rush off the Preselau. The hills rise to a skyline that seems so near you could touch it. Along its crest runs the

Golden Road, the ancient pathway that led the people of Neolithic times to Ireland and its gold mines (see pages 51-57). It was at this spot sometime during the 1820s or early 1830s that Thomas Rees raised his *Tŷ Unnos*. That is what they called a house built over one night. It was a tradition whereby a man could gain the freehold to a piece of common land by erecting overnight a structure sufficient to have a fire burning in its hearth and smoke issuing from its chimney. He could then lay claim to the land around by the distance he could throw an axe from the four corners of the house.

Thomas Rees was a powerfully built man and threw his axe far enough to encompass six acres. The structure he threw up over that one night soon became a stone cottage with a thatched roof. It provided Thomas with the nickname he was thereafter known by, *Twm Carnabwth* (Tom Stone Cottage). The cottage was first called *Treial*, Welsh for homestead, but soon became Carnabwth, the name it has kept to this day. It had one room of twenty feet by twelve, with a half ceiling for sleeping space. Here Twm and his wife Rachel scraped a living and raised their three children, Elizabeth, Daniel and John. Twm was not a farmer in his own right, but hired out his labour to the farms around him. The nearest was *Glynsaithmaen* (the valley of the seven stones) across the Afon Wern on the slopes of Cwmcerwyn.

John Penn found Carnarbwth in the 1970s. He was part of a wave of incomers seeking a greener, simpler and cheaper lifestyle

than in the English cities they left behind. John was from London and had spent weeks travelling through Wales looking for a place. Eventually, some friends who had squatted in Carnabwth wrote to him saying they were leaving and he was welcome to try it out. So he came, found a ruin but stayed, establishing a carpenter's business, making Welsh dressers and chairs. The cottage had lost its thatched roof and had acquired an asbestos one. John quickly got rid of that, replacing it with today's tin cladding. At the same time, he repaired the stone walling and woodwork, gradually making the place habitable. 'You could see the original foundations that Twm Carnabwth had put in place,' he said. 'He used the best stones for the corners.'

Thomas Rees, or *Twm Carnabwth*, was a larger than life character. Red haired and heavily built with a deep bass voice, he was well known as a prize fighter across the three counties of west Wales. He spent his winnings in the ale houses afterwards. In his later years he was well known, too, for his devout observance at the Bethel Chapel in the tiny village of Mynachlog-ddu. On Whit Sundays he was the chief reciter of the *Pwnc*, the catechism of the points of the Scriptures. His status in the chapel can be seen today by the well-kept headstone in the graveyard outside. On it is the date of his death, 17 May 1876 aged seventy, and the inscription:

> Nid oes neb ond Duw yn gwybod.
> Beth a ddigwydd mewn diwrnod.
> Wrth gyrchu bresych at fy nginio,
> Daeth angau i fy ngardd i'm taro.

> No one but God knows
> What may happen in one day.
> While fetching a cabbage for my dinner,
> Death came into my garden and struck me.

It is an odd choice of words since, by all accounts, Twm Carnabwth died of an illness in his bed.

When John Penn came to the cottage there was a tricky question of ownership. There were no deeds. After about a decade he decided he could claim squatter's rights and the freehold for himself. He hired a solicitor in Cardigan to draw up the necessary documents. 'All deeds have to start somewhere,' was the way John put it.

I point to a newish-looking, shack-like structure alongside the cottage. 'Neighbours?' I ask. 'Oh, that's the wife,' he replies. 'Or, rather, the former wife.' It seems that when they split up neither wanted to leave Carnabwth. The solution was to build another cottage alongside. 'We were both equally stubborn, I suppose,' John explains.

REBECCA'S SPIRIT

Until the mid-nineteenth century travelling to west Wales was difficult and time consuming. The nearest railheads were at Bristol and Birmingham, each at least a day's journey by stage coach. Travel to Bristol entailed an additional steamer trip across the Severn Estuary. Stage coaches moved at about four miles an hour. The journey from Carmarthen to Haverfordwest took at least six hours. Cardigan was further two or three away. Moreover, stage coaches were far too expensive for most people who had to rely on the much slower team-drawn wagons. In wet conditions they turned the roads, such as they were, into quagmires.

This was the background for the creation of the turnpike trusts, first set up by Act of Parliament in 1707, with powers to collect tolls for the maintenance of the roads. By the 1830s the trusts had reached their peak with more than a thousand across England and Wales administering about thirty thousand miles of roads, and taking tolls at some eight thousand toll gates.

In England the trusts operated with relative efficiency, but in Wales this was often far from the case. They developed in a piecemeal fashion and many of them covered small tracts of road. The result was that toll gates proliferated and seldom achieved their purpose, which was the up-keep of the roads. Owners of the gates became known as 'toll farmers'. Most were English which heightened resentment against them.

These circumstances were designed to create dissension. In 1839 matters came to a head in northern Preseli where the Whitland Turnpike Trust was close to bankruptcy. An English 'toll farmer', one Thomas Bullin, who owned gates as far as London, made an offer to bail out the Whitland Trust with £800 cash. However, in return he insisted that additional gates be placed on roads leading from Carmarthenshire into Pembrokeshire, including one on the

county border at Efail Wen. They were designed to entrap
impoverished farmers as they began carting lime into their fields in
the spring of 1839.

Outrage ensued and there were debates in pubs and fairs across
west Wales. A meeting was called in the barn of the remote farm of
Glynsaithmaen in Mynydd Preselau, a stone's throw from Twm
Carnabwth's cottage. What exactly happened at that meeting and
how many attended is not known. Undoubtedly, however, there
would have been men from the surrounding parishes of
Maenclochog, Llangolman, and Mynachlog-ddu.[6] And certainly, a
leading figure among them was Thomas Rees, Twm Carnabwth, at
that time aged thirty-three and already prominent in the local
community.

They met to consider Thomas Bullin's newly erected toll-gate at
nearby Efail Wen on the road between Narberth and Crymych,
today's A478. In deciding what to do they looked to the Welsh
custom of *Ceffyl Pren*, literally a wooden horse. It was used to
frighten or punish those who had offended in some way against
their sense of *chwarae-teg* (fair play). Typically, offenders were harsh
landlords, adulterers, or men who hid behind a hated provision of
the Poor Law, which made mothers solely responsible for
illegitimate children. In this case the offender was Thomas Bullin
and his toll-gate at Efail Wen.

The use of women's clothing, blackened faces, nocturnal rides
and a generally riotous carnival atmosphere were well-established
features of the *Ceffyl Pren* tradition. So it was, late in the evening of
13 May 1839, a mob charged the Efail Wen toll gate. They were led
by Twm Carnabwth, on horseback and dressed in several layers of
petticoats, his charcoal-smudged face topped with a wig hung with
ringlets. The toll collector and his family fled. Then, to a cacophony
of horns, drums and shotgun blasts, the toll-gate and its house were
torched.

Thomas Bullin quickly had a new gate erected, and this time it
was guarded by seven special constables. But they proved no match
when the mob advanced once more, on the night of 6 June.
Chanting they were 'Rebecca's daughters' they destroyed the
toll-gate once again. A few weeks later they descended on the Maes
Gwynne gate near Llanboidy, five miles from Efail Wen, and
destroyed that as well.

Little of this was new. Riots against injustices were common across Britain. Toll-gates in Herefordshire, Gloucestershire, and Somerset had already been attacked by men mounted on horses using the disguise of blackened faces and women's clothing. However, what was unique about the Preseli disturbances was the adoption of the persona Rebecca. The name soon became known throughout Britain, even by Queen Victoria, and rapidly entered folk-lore.

'Who is Rebecca?' was a question on a thousand lips. It gave the Riots an infamy that set them apart from the other civil disturbances. And the name has echoed down the decades since. An assumption is that the name Rebecca derived from the Bible. And it is certainly probable that Twm Carnabwth and his followers would have been familiar with verse 60 in chapter 24 of Genesis:

> And they blessed Rebekah, and said unto her, Thou are our sister, be thou the mother of thousands of millions, and let thy seed possess the gate of those which hate them.

Yet it is more likely that the name comes from a woman called
Rebecca who gave Twm Carnarbwth the petticoats and other
garments he wore when leading the attack on the Efail Wen
toll-gate.[7] She lived not far from him in Llangolman. Evidence for
this comes from a man called Stephen Rees, who was
twenty-years-old at the time. He published his account seventy-one
years later, in February 1911 in the *Cardigan and Tivyside
Advertiser.*
    As for Twm Carnarbwth, his name was lost to history for more
than a century. The Rebecca Riots were generally frowned upon by
the law-abiding Nonconformist chapels. Then, in the 1970s his
exploits were celebrated in a popular song penned by the folksinger
Tecwyn Ifan. Entitled 'Ysbryd Rebeca' (The Spirit of Rebecca) it
tells how *Daeth gwr o Garnabwth i fynnu ei rhyddid i'r werin i gael
cerdded ei thir* – A man of Carnabwth came to demand freedom for
the people to walk the land:

> *Tra bo haul yn y nen*
> *Tra bo Duw i ni'n ben*
> *Fe fydd Ysbryd Rebeca yn fyw yn yr Efail Wen.*

> Where there's a sun in the sky
> Where there's God as a guide
> Rebecca's Spirit will live in Efail Wen.

NICLAS Y GLAIS

The Preseli hills are littered with stones and cromlechs, many from
the Neolithic period, but some much more recent. The most
famous new one is that erected at Rhos-fach common, on the edge
of Mynachlog-ddu, to commemorate Waldo Williams, the poet,
pacifist and patriot who immortalised the Preseli landscape in his
writings (see pages 106-112). Now a campaign is underway to raise
another stone just a few miles away, for Niclas y Glais. He was a
contemporary of Waldo's, also a poet though not as great, but
nonetheless an inspirational figure. Both were friends of D.J.
Williams, Abergwaun (see pages 180-184). All three were from this
corner of Wales, where Carmarthenshire meets Preseli.
    They are shown together in 'Y Tangnefeddwyr' (The
Peacemakers), a drawing by Aneurin Jones, who taught for most of

his career at Ysgol y Preseli in Crymych. A signed print of it, one of about twenty, hangs above the fireplace in my study. Niclas y Glais and D.J. are shown together, looking as if they are sharing a joke. Niclas is wearing a flat cap and bow tie, with a jacket and waistcoat. Between his thumb and forefinger he holds what appears to be a cigarette holder. D.J. is similarly attired, though he is wearing a trilby. One hand is grasping his jacket, the other open in a gesture, and he smiles benignly.

Aneurin copied the image of Niclas and D.J. directly from a photograph taken by Geoff Charles at a CND rally at Aberystwyth in May 1961. It's now in the National Library's collection, and can be seen online. In Aneurin's painting, Waldo is separate from the other two, staring directly outwards, as though he is among a cloud of witnesses from the past.

Of the three men Niclas y Glais is probably the least known, though in recent years he has come more into prominence. At the Ebbw Vale National Eisteddfod in 2010, a group of Cymdeithas yr Iaith activists launched Cymdeithas Niclas y Glais (the Niclas y Glais Society) to promote his life and values to a new generation. In 2017 the first major biography appeared, Hefin Wyn's *Ar Drywydd Niclas y Glais: Comiwnydd Rhonc a Christion Gloyw* (In Search of Niclas y Glais: Avid Communist and Ardent Christian).

Niclas was born in 1879 as Thomas Evan Nicholas, at

Blaenywaun Felen, Llanfyrnach. Within a year the family of six children – Niclas was the last – moved a few miles to Y Llety, a 57-acre rented smallholding on the slopes of Foel Dyrch above Pentregalar just to the south of Crymych. It is here, where Niclas was brought up, that his stone will be erected. Why is he being commemorated? It's partly because he led such an extraordinary life. Variously he was a preacher, pamphleteer, political journalist, parliamentary candidate (in Aberdare in 1918), trade union organiser, pacifist and anti-war campaigner, anti-monarchist, anti-fascist, anti-imperialist, member of the Independent Labour Party, editor of the weekly *Merthyr Pioneer* and a supporter of Keir Hardie, a founder of the British Communist Party to which he was loyal to the end, a poet, and along the way, a dentist.

But most of all, I think he is remembered because of his beliefs which were rooted inside the heart of Welsh-speaking Preseli. As the historian Kenneth O. Morgan has judged, he embodied a union between 'Nonconformist radicalism and the extreme political left.'[8] His obituary in the Union of Welsh Independents' annual publication *Blwyddiadur* declared:

> He inherited sympathy for the helpless from his mother and learned to love, even when young, the simple honest folk of the Preseli slopes, and detested every power and influence that sought to oppress them and rob them of a full life.[9]

Meanwhile, alongside a large photograph, the *Morning Star's* front-page obituary described Niclas as a champion of the Soviet Union, and bitter opponent of fascism in Germany and Spain.[10]

Niclas y Glais acquired his name during the ten years between 1904 and 1914 when he was a minister with the Seion Chapel at Glais, a village in the Tawe Valley just north of Swansea. During this time, he signed articles in the quarterly magazine *Y Geninen* (The Leek) as Niclas Glais, and thereafter the name stuck.

He had attended school at Hermon, a few miles from his home, until he was thirteen. It was a largely fruitless experience since Niclas was a monoglot Welsh-speaker and the school taught through the medium of English. What education he received, including English, came from home and Sunday school. A premonition of the controversy he was to court throughout his life came when, aged about sixteen, he wrote a disparaging poem about the vicar of the church at the nearby village of Eglwyswen.

Reputedly the vicar had to be carried home in a wheelbarrow due to his inebriated state. This led to Niclas being sacked from his first job as a messenger boy for a shop and the Swan pub just outside Crymych.

He trained for the ministry at an academy in Ammanford and veered towards Christian socialism. He was ordained, aged twenty-two, at the Welsh Independent chapel in Llandeilo and soon after married. Then came a strange episode when, amidst rumours of an affair, he fell out with the chapel elders. He emigrated to become Minister of the Dodgeville Welsh Congregational Church in Wisconsin, about as far from Wales as you could get. But within less than a year he was back. It seems a farmer from Glais met Niclas's father at the Crymych fair and enquired after his son whose preaching had impressed him. Niclas' father persuaded the farmer to get the Glais chapel to invite his son to be its Minister.

During his ten years in Glais, Niclas became famous throughout Wales for his preaching and his exploits as a bard at successive Eisteddfods. He also became politically involved, joining the Independent Labour Party and establishing a friendship with Keir Hardie.

In 1914 he left Glais to become a minister at Llangybi and Llanddewi Brefi in Ceredigion. However, this rural idyll, if indeed that was what he sought, was immediately interrupted by the outbreak of the First World War. Niclas was caught up in an all-consuming campaign across Wales promoting the No-Conscription Fellowship. He was for pacifism, and against capitalism which he saw as the cause of the conflict. At the same time, he was organising the Cardiganshire lead miners and the farm labourers of Preseli and Cardigan into trade unions. All these activities drew the attention of the authorities who made frequent attempts to have him prosecuted. He continued to preach and agitate throughout Wales, contributing a stream of articles to many publications, including a weekly column in *Y Cymro*, though the paper dispensed with his services at the outbreak of war.

By 1918 Niclas' mounting disillusion with the chapels' support for the war – many banned him from their pulpits – caused him to resign his pastorate. Instead, he became an unlicensed dentist. While at Glais he had acted as an agent for a Mumbles ILP dentist candidate for the local council, and picked up a few rudimentary dentistry skills. Later he received a more thorough training from a dentist in Mountain Ash. He first set up a practice in Pontardawe, but soon left to settle in Aberystwyth in 1921, where he remained for the rest of his life, establishing a surgery in a shed in the garden of his house in Elm Tree Avenue. The Russian Revolution was a decisive influence. In 1920 Niclas became a founding member of the Communist Party of Great Britain. All the same he continued preaching, never wavering in his belief that Christianity and Communism were entirely compatible. The former MP for Aberavon, Hywel Francis, recalls that, delivering a sermon one Sunday in Rhigos in 1957, Niclas compared the new Soviet Sputnik with the star over Bethlehem.[11] As well as joining the Communist Party, Niclas continued as a member of the Labour Party. However, in 1926 he was expelled for criticising its leader Ramsay MacDonald for being too right wing.

At the outbreak of the Second World War the authorities finally caught up with him. In July 1940, together with his son Islwyn, he was arrested by the Cardiganshire Chief Constable Captain J.J. Lloyd-Williams. The charges were trumped up under the 1939 Emergency Powers Act that allowed internment without trial. Niclas and his son were accused of impeding recruitment to the forces and being in the possession of a number of swastikas. The latter turned out to have been supplied by the *Daily Express,* along with a map of Europe on which the flags were to be placed to mark the course of the war. Lloyd-Williams is said to have exclaimed on Niclas' arrest, 'I've got you at last. You call yourself a bloody Communist.... You are a fascist.'[12]

Niclas and his son were held for three months between July and October, first at Swansea and then Brixton prison. Their release followed a strong campaign on their behalf amongst chapels and the Labour movement throughout Wales. As it turned out, imprisonment was one of the best things to happen to Niclas. In the relatively short time he was behind bars he composed around a hundred and fifty sonnets that did more than all his other work to establish his reputation as a poet. As writing paper was banned, he first wrote them on a slate in his cell, copied them on to toilet paper, and then passed them to a sympathetic prison officer who smuggled them out. Many of their themes recall his upbringing in the Preseli community of his youth, together with a national identification that approaches the universal. Certainly, they go well beyond the political propaganda that had characterised much of his previous output. As his fellow poet, Gwenallt, judged:

The Marxist sonnets are sincere, but the rural sonnets are deeper. It is these that are his valuable contribution to the recent literature of Wales... Moscow owns the ideas; Crymych owns the senses. Capitalism made Nicholas a revolutionary; Wales made him a pure poet.[13]

CARN AFR'S SWIRLING MISTS

I had intended to explore how the light on Mynydd Preselau influences Elizabeth Haines' work. There is, after all, something mystical, even magical about this place that has inspired generations of painters and poets. What is it about the landscape that drives an artist to her easel? What was it that drew Elizabeth to the terrain in the first place? However, when we met our conversation turned first to questions of identity.

Elizabeth Haines is English, but she has lived in the Preseli hills for more than fifty years. She married a Preseli-born shepherd and together they worked a smallholding at Bryn Morris. It lies at eight hundred feet, near the edge of the common mountain land, with Carn Afr looming above. It was originally a *hafod*, a shepherd's summer dwelling. Today it has been expanded to provide a home, studio and art gallery. Elizabeth's paintings, many of them inspired by the surrounding landscape, line every available wall of her studio. In the adjoining house she has a large collection of other paintings, most of them by contemporary Welsh artists.

She has lived so long in this place, learning the language and by now amongst its oldest inhabitants, that I ask whether she feels she has become Welsh.

'Oh no, I couldn't say that,' she replies.

Originally from Hertfordshire, she took a degree in Graphic Design at Brighton College of Art before moving here in 1966.

So I ask again, 'You still feel English then?'

'Heavens no! I certainly don't feel English.'

She registers my expression and laughs, 'Other than being an artist I don't feel the need to have an identity in that kind of way.'

I protest, 'Surely all art is inevitably an expression of some national identity?'

Elizabeth Haines is used to considering such questions. She researched the relationships between art forms that resulted in a doctorate in Philosophy at the University of Wales, Lampeter, in

2002. Now she says, 'Well, I can see that for the French, say, or the
Welsh or the Jews, it's possible to have an identity mixed with a
strong sense of patriotism. They've all been bullied by other
countries, in one way or another, the French by the Germans, the
Welsh by the English, the Jews by almost everybody. But the English
haven't been bullied in that way, have they? They've never been
invaded, not in recent times anyway.'

I suggest that the English are an odd sort of nationality in other
respects. They don't have a strong idea of territory, for instance.
What child in an English primary school can draw a map of
England? Then again, they speak an international language. And
they don't have a republican sense of the people. In constitutional
terms English people are subjects under the crown. 'Ultimately the
English identity is built around class,' I say.

Elizabeth pauses to think. 'Perhaps that is beginning to change.
Perhaps some of them feel they've been bullied by Europe. Maybe
that's why they voted for Brexit.'

Elizabeth was extremely upset by the vote to leave the European
Union. It led to one of her few politically inspired paintings. It's
called 'Bateau des Imbéciles'. She points to it, leaning against a wall.
It's quite unlike her other work. Large swirling brush strokes have
created a square frame in which a ship appears to be foundering.

'I didn't intend to draw a boat that was slipping backwards and
sinking,' she tells me, picking the picture up and dusting it off. 'It
just somehow came through.'

'From your subconscious?'

'That's exactly right. You can produce your best work when
you're angry. Someone said that for an artist to be angry is to be in
luck.'

Another such moment was when Britain invaded Iraq in 2003.
The event coincided with an extraordinary event she witnessed,
standing in the yard outside her backdoor, contemplating the
appalling thought of fighter planes coming over the Preseli hills. A
line of fantail doves was standing on the crest of the roof of the barn
opposite her. Then suddenly a hawk swooped and seized one,
causing an enormous flurry and cacophony of sound among the
other birds.

The symbolism of this event prompted another, untypical
painting which she shows me. In it the outline of a black hawk is
etched against the sky, reminiscent of a menacing military aircraft.

Our conversation turns to identity once more. Elizabeth says again that she doesn't feel a strong sense of national or cultural attachment. 'I've often thought how blessed are those who are secure and enclosed by a feeling of belonging,' she says.

Yet it seems to me that in her work she has created the rootedness she says she lacks. She is plainly affected by the wild Preseli landscape which is reflected in many of her paintings.

She has also delved into the writers of the area, becoming friends with poets like Eirwyn George of Maenclochog, and the late James Nicholas, of St Davids, one-time head teacher at Ysgol y Preseli in Crymych, and Archdruid of Wales from 1981-84. In 1987 she won a competition to design a piece of work conveying the genius of *Cerdd Dafod*.[14] Nicholas, one of the judges, dubbed her presentation *Llyfrau Maenclochog* (The Books of Maenclochog). This led to a week in residence at the National Eisteddfod in Porthmadog when she produced a series of calligraphic paintings representing the poetic form.

It's difficult to see how anyone could be drawn more deeply into a relationship with Welsh culture and identity. And Elizabeth agrees that her work is influenced by Welsh language poetry in a fundamental way. Her 'partial knowledge' of the language means she can switch off from the meaning and just listen to it as pure music.

She says it's the abstract quality of the sound of the poetry that inspires the link with her painting: 'Looking up at Carn Afr, especially when the mists swirl about, I think of Dafydd ap Gwilym's poem Y Niwl, The Mist: *Cnu tewlwyd, gwynllwyd, gwanllaes, cyfliw y maes* – a pale grey, weakly trailing fleece, like smoke, a hooded cowl upon the plain.'[15]

So, I reckon that after more than fifty years living in the Preseli hills, and despite her denial, Elizabeth Haines has in a profound way become Welsh.

DECOY VALLEYS

A few miles southeast of Fishguard is one of the most isolated valleys in Wales. It can only be reached on foot. Known as Esgyrn Bottom, it is a sub-glacial meltwater channel. That is to say, it was formed a hundred thousand years ago when an enormous glacier, two thousand feet deep, covered southern Wales. At the bottom of the glacier melt waters were under such pressure that sometimes they ran up hill, creating distinctive valleys with high sides. Another one is Cwm Gwaun (see pages 27-32) to the northwest. They have flat bottoms and no obvious head of the valley. They have no obvious mouth either. Such is Esgyrn Bottom.

During the Second World War it was used to mislead the Germans. Small wooden platforms were scattered along the hillsides. Local people described them as oversized beehives. In fact, they held inflammable material. Some say they were filled with explosives such as cordite. More likely they contained rags soaked in oil or tar that would burn steadily. One witness reported what appeared to be electrical connections that suggested an ignition device.[16] The purpose of the 'beehives' was to be lit at night if an enemy air raid was expected.

Why would the Germans wish to bomb this part of Wales? Because during the war it was the site of Britain's biggest ordnance depot, an arsenal of shells, mines, depth charges, cartridges and other explosive devices. They were stored in the Nant-y-bugail valley at Trecŵn, just over the hill. Esgyrn Bottom was a decoy valley. In the event of an air raid it would be lit up to fool the enemy into thinking they were flying over Trecŵn. There were occasions when the beehives were deployed. Another witness, at the time a girl living on a farm within sight of Esyrn Bottom, remembers being lifted by her father up to a window and seeing pin-pricks of light.[17] The Decoy Valley was probably unnecessary. Trecŵn is so narrow, deep-sided and covered with forest that it would be extremely difficult to see from the air. That is one reason it was chosen. Another was its location on the far western side of Britain, as far as possible from the English Channel and yet still close to the rail network.

Survey work in the 1930s confirmed Trecŵn's suitability for storing armaments in underground magazines well out of reach of the enemy. Starting in 1938, cottages were demolished, security fences installed, tunnels bored and railways laid. Finished by 1941, it was a huge armaments depot and yet you could walk on the surrounding hills and be completely unaware of what was in the valley beneath.

The site became readily available because of what had long been known as the Trecŵn Curse. In the early 1500s the owner of the estate, Owen ap Dafydd, threw people off his lands to free them for hunting. As a result, he was cursed by a local witch. Although the lands would remain in his descendants' possession, there would be no male heirs and so the name of the family would constantly change. And this is exactly what happened. Over the years the owners of the Trecŵn estate, although related, were named Johns, Owen, Vaughan, Barham, Robins-Barham, and Barham again. The last Barham, his wife and son and heir all died in a car accident near Oxford in 1933. Later that year the War Office bought the estate.

During the construction of the site coal miners drafted from the Welsh Valleys bored fifty-eight tunnels and chambers into the hillsides, each about two hundred and forty feet long and thirty-five feet wide. The rubble they excavated was used to provide foundations for the factories and warehouses built outside on the valley floor. In some places the ground level was raised twenty feet because of the boggy nature of the land.

Trecŵn was linked with the main Great Western Railway near Letterston, two-and-a-half miles away. Inside the complex a narrow gauge railway connected the concrete-lined tunnels and storage chambers. In all, there were eighteen miles of new rail line. They

were made of expensive phosphor bronze, which doesn't spark. Thirteen miles of roads were laid as well. There were two hundred and fifty thousand square feet of industrial buildings and three hundred and eighty cubic metres of underground storage. Two reservoirs were built on either side of the valley to provide water for fire-fighting. Ten miles of security fence surrounded the site, much of it still there today.

During the war two thousand people worked shifts in Trecŵn. They assembled munitions and repaired weapons. Many of the workers were women, who proved efficient in packing cartridges. There were engineering workshops, canteens, laboratories, offices, and a tailor's shop that fitted out people with flame-proof clothing and spark-proof shoes. Three housing estates were built for workers close by and special trains and buses brought others from Fishguard and the surrounding area.

High standards of safety were insisted upon, though they were often contravened. Possession of cigarettes and matches, and clocking other people in for shifts were the main offences. The *West Wales Guardian* reported Court proceedings under such headings as 'More Trecŵn Workers in Trouble'. One case cited a fine of thirty shillings for possessing a box of three safety matches. Fifty shillings was the usual fine for smoking. Today that would be a mere £2.50, but in the early 1940s the average weekly wage was just over £3.39.

After the war Trecŵn continued as an important armaments depot, though the number of people employed declined sharply to around four hundred. Activity increased whenever Britain went on a war footing, for instance at the time of the Korean War in the early 1950s, and during the Falklands conflict in the early 1980s. However, in the late 1980s as the Cold War was drawing to a close, the Ministry of Defence decommissioned Trecŵn. In 1992 it sold the site to an Irish company, Omega Pacific, for just £329,000. This was an extraordinarily low amount considering that the estate included twenty-six private houses which alone would have been worth at least four times the price paid for the entire depot. Nonetheless, a Public Accounts Committee investigation in the House of Commons led nowhere. Omega Pacific said it would use the surface buildings for aircraft engine maintenance, while the underground tunnels would store nuclear waste. These proposals generated immense local opposition. Eventually, in 2002, Omega Pacific ended up in court when they were ordered to sell the site to the London-based property developers Manhattan Loft Corporation. In keeping with the air of secrecy around Trecŵn, the sale price remains a mystery. However, the 'secure' part of the armaments depot was valued at £500,000 to £700,000, with the houses additionally worth around £80,000 each. So Omega Pacific must have seen a significant return on its investment.

Initially, Manhattan Loft intended to develop the site as a multi-use industrial estate, with the surface buildings leased for light industry, and the caverns for storage and distribution. However, that came to nothing. Meanwhile Network Rail refurbished the railway line to keep alive the potential for Trecŵn to develop as a freight traffic distribution centre.

Some years later Manhattan Loft transferred ownership to a subsidiary company, The Valley (Pembs) Ltd. However, the 2008 financial crash and subsequent recession put whatever plans they had on hold. Then, in 2015, the new company won planning permission to develop the base with an £80 million biomass plant, burning sawmill residues and recycled wood. They claimed this would create two hundred and fifty construction and forty-five full time jobs. It was supposed to be completed within three years. Time passed but nothing happened. Trecŵn remains in limbo.

I've often wondered where the name Trecŵn came from. Of course, *cŵn* is the Welsh plural for dogs. But rather than the *Tre* emanating from *tref,* meaning town, I like to think it comes from

cartref, meaning home. Hence, Trecŵn might refer to the valley being regarded as a dog's lair.[18] It's all speculation, of course. Names change over the centuries. But these days the place has become a decoy valley in its own right.

RHOSYGILWEN

Finding a fully-fledged concert hall in the open countryside is an arresting prospect. To be sure this one is a relatively modest concert hall, with a capacity for just two hundred people. On the other hand, it's in a remarkable location, amidst the rolling hills of the eastern Preseli. It is like a miniature version of Glyndebourne, but without the dress code.

It is made of green oak, hence its name Neuadd y Dderwen (Oak Hall). The double beam crick structure supports the roof without need for pillars that would obstruct the audience's view. Modelled on the sixteenth century Middle Temple of the Inns of Court in London, it cost £1.7 million. It is the only privately sponsored arts venue in Wales. At the performance end of the hall is a grand Steinway piano, imported from Geneva and once played by Rubenstein. During 2018 Angela Hewitt, one of the world's finest pianists, played Bach's *Well Tempered Clavier Part I* on it here in

Preseli. She is just one of a litany of famous musicians who have graced this space since it opened in July 2006.

Neuadd y Dderwen is set in the grounds of Rhosygilwen, a mansion a mile or so south of Cilgerran. The beauty and isolation of the place are undoubtedly part of the attraction, but how does it get its audience? The weekend before I visited, a performance of extracts from *My Fair Lady* attracted 300 people. 'Word of mouth, mainly,' owner Glen Peters tells me. 'People in this area think nothing of driving an hour or more to get here. They come from Cardigan, of course, but as far afield as Tenby as well, even Aberystwyth.'

Glen and his wife Brenda Squires arrived from London in the late 1980s, first to a holiday home in Cardigan. They liked it so much they decided to settle permanently. In 1994 they bought Rhosygilwen. It had been gutted by fire in 1985 and had been on the market ever since, in a ruinous state. It took two years to restore it to something like its previous grandeur and is still a work in progress. One wing is being converted into a music room, with the three storeys previously destroyed in the fire now become one. The walls have been insulated, and a glass roof placed on top. The result is a space that has an extraordinary acoustic quality. At its centre is a Broadway grand piano that came with the house and, miraculously, survived the fire. When Glen and Brenda were considering buying Rhosygilwen, they brought in Mark Morris, a local builder to give them an estimate of what needed doing. He sat at the piano and played Schubert's *Sonata in B Flat Major*. 'That was it,' Brenda said. 'We needed no more persuading. The decision was made. That piece of music has become Rhosygilwen's theme tune.' Glen added, 'Sometimes places and buildings call to you. There was something beckoning about this house.'

The Colby family that already owned extensive land and property in west Wales, built Rhosygilwen in the 1820s. Glen Peters has placed a blue plaque near the front door in honour of Major General Thomas Frederick Colby, 1784-1852. It says he 'was appointed by Lord Nelson to lead the development of the ordnance survey of Britain'. The house was substantially rebuilt in the 1880s when the present Bath Stone door surrounds and window frames were added.

At the height of its pomp, at the beginning of the last century, the house was surrounded by four hundred acres and was looked after by some fifty servants. But like many houses of its type, it fell into gradual decline after the First World War. The coup de grâce was delivered by the fire.

Today Rhosygilwen's grounds have been reduced to sixty acres overseen by three gardeners. In addition, Glen employs five staff to run the estate and arts centre. They deliver a diverse programme of classical, jazz and folk music, literary and art events, plus a thriving summer wedding schedule.

Glen and Brenda enjoy sailing in the Mediterranean where they relax by writing fiction. Brenda's first novel was *Landsker*.[19] It's about what happens when a young woman from a wealthy family in west Wales moves to London during the 1920s. In her relationships she crosses class and political boundaries, experiences alluded to in the title.

Glen's first novel was *Mrs D'Silva's Detective Instincts and the Shaitan of Calcutta*.[20] The idea for it came to him while sailing in the Mediterranean. The starlit skies triggered childhood memories of the night skies over Calcutta. It is set in 1960 in the city's Anglo-Indian community where Joan D'Silva, a teacher, turns detective after her son discovers the unidentified body of a woman. As Glen says, 'There is action, food, politics, sexual intrigue and an insight into a community trying to come to terms with the end of the Raj.' There is a sequel, *Lucknow Ransom*.[21]

Glen was born into this same community, in 1952. As he remarks proudly, he went to a Salesian, Don Bosco school in the slums of Calcutta.[22] But when he was sixteen he emigrated with his family to London. There he won a place at City University, became president of the students' union, graduated in chemistry, and went on to gain a Doctorate in Management Science from Henley College. Later he became an engineer with British Gas, managing major construction projects. When he was thirty-two he published his first book, *Project Management and Construction Control*.[23] The accountancy firm Price Waterhouse Coopers noticed it and headhunted him. Glen became an expert in the North Sea oil business, and eventually a partner with PwC in 1988. That's how he made his money.

Even so Glen couldn't fork out for Rhosygilwen indefinitely. So he looked for a way to put it on a sustainable footing. As well as an arts enthusiast, he is passionate about the environment and renewable energy. Which is why he lighted on the notion of creating a solar energy park at Rhosygilwen, the first in Wales. It was built in 2011, behind a hedge just a short walk away from Neuadd y Dderwen. It has involved importing ten thousand photo-voltaic solar panels from California, digging eight hundred metres of trenches, laying two-and-a-half kilometres of cable, and spending £5 million. Glen Peters operates on a large scale. But it has paid off.

Rhosygilwen gets cheap electricity and at the same time earns money selling it to the National Grid, enough to power six hundred homes. Glen's next project was housing. He noticed that rising prices together with people moving into the area was putting buying a home beyond the reach of many local inhabitants. So he came up with the idea of Tŷ Solar, an affordable eco-friendly house. It's made of locally-sourced timber, insulated using recycled newspaper, and is powered by solar panels.

A prototype was unveiled at Rhosygilwen by former First Minister Carwyn Jones in 2013 and is still there. With a match-funding £141,000 grant from the Welsh Government, Glen's new firm Western Solar established a factory to build six homes in the nearby village of Glanrhyd. They cost £1,250,000 and now a local housing association rents them out for around £350 a month. Western Solar is building ten more houses for councils and housing associations in south west Wales and has another fifty in the pipeline. It wants to build a thousand more across the UK in the coming decade.

Glen Peters tells me he doesn't think he could have achieved all this if he had stayed in England. 'Wales is different,' he says. 'It has to do with the smaller scale. So long as you move with the grain of the way the authorities are thinking you can persuade them to get things done.'

He acknowledges that he lives a privileged life, but says that with it comes responsibility. 'We need to think in the longer term. It's short-termism that is the driving force in this fossil-fueled myopic world.' He pauses for a moment, then says, 'It's only thinking in the long-term that the level of research and investment in renewable energy, for instance, makes sense. It's like planting trees. It's future generations that benefit.'

Glen mulls over these messages while showing me his walled garden. It has two acres of vegetables that are grown for Rhosygilwen's restaurant. He takes me into the restored sixty-foot glasshouse, built against a large wall at one end. Inside are vines, rows of ripening tomatoes, and a line of peach trees. A muslin cloth stretches under them, ready to catch the falling fruit.

Glen reaches in and hands me one. 'A gift from Rhosygilwen,' he says with a smile. It's perfectly ripe, glowing. It occurs to me that it's reminiscent of Glen's philosophy in restoring this place. However much you invest in it, life is transitory and must be lived for the moment. All the same, you're driven by the hope that future generations will carry on making something from it.

LAMMAS

'We were told it couldn't be done,' Tao Wimbush said as I was taking my leave. His piercing blue eyes held mine in a steady gaze. 'But as you've seen, we're still here and we're doing it well.'

Turning, he gestured to the land behind him, seventy-six acres of Preseli hillside close to the Carmarthenshire border. We're a few miles south-east of Crymych, near the village of Glandŵr. Once part of the Pont-y-gafel farm, the land is now the site of Britain's only low impact, off-grid eco-village. It's home to about fifty adults and thirty children. At its core the village has nine families living on separate plots. But there are also visitors and volunteers working a further six plots, people who come and go.

The place is called Lammas because it was conceived in 2005 around a campfire during August, the month of the Celtic harvest festival. Called Lughnasad or Lammas, it is the celebration of the Sungod Lugh, of Celtic mythology, and the first grain harvest. When the village was first established, in 2009, many locals were sceptical that its occupants would be able to grow anything. At a height of six hundred feet Tir-y-Gafel, as the village is called, has a thin layer of topsoil and is exposed to the elements. 'It's some of the poorest land in the area,' one farmer said. 'It's just poor quality sheep grazing.' But its founders thought it ideal. It was south-facing, had water, some woodland, and a derelict hydro-electric scheme ripe for renovation. They took out loans and bought the land for £210,000.

The beginnings were far from easy. There was intense local opposition. Many people felt they were facing an invasion of alien hippies. Stephen Crabb, Preseli's Conservative MP, denounced the project, which was born in a glare of adverse publicity. However, following much consultation, a compromise was reached. It was understood that Lammas would begin with a small number of households, and only expand once these had proved successful.

Today it's a flourishing maze of extraordinarily designed hand-built houses, set amidst hedges and coppicing woodland. These enclose garden plots and polytunnels growing all manner of vegetables, soft fruits, herbs and flowers. Goats, cows, pigs, ducks and chickens occupy enclosures scattered through the settlement. It could be a film set. Certainly, it's a throwback to a time, centuries ago, when rural Wales was densely populated.

'We've demonstrated that it's possible to turn degraded upland pasture into fertile land,' Tao said. 'We're pioneers of what I think will have to be a controlled move back to the land if we're going to tackle the environmental impact of climate change. But, of course, we're just a patch amidst hundreds of thousands of acres of despoiled, depleted land. We're a tiny oasis in a desert of devastation.'

Tao believes Lammas is a signpost to a future in which mainstream and alternative cultures merge. Certainly, it's not just some off-the-cuff initiative and perhaps it has a chance because of that. It's been established legally, with planning permission and with settled, long-term ownership relationships. Initially Pembrokeshire county council refused permission. But following a two-year process involving an appeal to the Welsh Government, the project was allowed to go ahead.

If the application had been made in England it wouldn't have happened. However, in Wales it was approved under Pembrokeshire's 'low-impact development' planning policy, established in 2005. Five years later the Welsh Government scaled it up to cover the whole of Wales with its One Planet planning guidance. Developments outside existing settlements can go ahead so long as they demonstrate natural building techniques, a commitment to sustainable living, and a meeting of basic household needs from land-based livelihoods. Each year Lammas submits a report to the council setting out its progress on these objectives.

Tao gives me a tour of his smallholding. A high privet hedge protects the main growing area with its lines of vegetables from the wind. Above he's created a large pond that collects rainwater. Alongside is a polytunnel containing vines, ripening tomatoes, lettuce, peppers, courgettes, and a small but important pond. It acts as a humidity regulator and a habitat for frogs and toads that eat the slugs and other pests that would otherwise destroy everything growing here.

Tao explains that in each part of his smallholding he is creating a separate permaculture, a self-sustaining ecosystem. 'Basically, what I'm doing is building soil,' he says. 'Composting is a fine art.'

He used to have a milking cow, but is converting to goats which are more cost-effective. 'A cow can make me £2,000 a year from the milk she produces, but it costs me £1,000-a-year to have the raw milk tested and certified,' he explains.

Above the pond is the single storey house he's built, mainly of wood, with the walls filled with sheep's wool for insulation, and a corrugated fibre-boarded roof. There are outbuildings, a barn for animals, a shower cubicle, and a compost toilet that contributes to soil building.

'It's top of the range,' Tao says.

'Meaning?'

'It's airy, has lots of light, is clean, hygienic and graceful in its mechanisms.'

'So what's one like at the bottom of the range?'

'Smelly and full of flies.'

Tao (he's changed his name from Paul – *tao is* Chinese for the 'way', leading to the underlying order of things) is an extraordinary man. In his mid-forties he has spent his adult life pursuing a dream to live on the land as simply and self-reliantly as possible. He had a conventional upbringing, in Berkshire, and studied architecture at Cardiff University. But after that he spent years living in communes, the Tipi Valley in Carmarthshire, Brithdir in Preseli, then in the Sierra Nevada in Andalusia, ending up in a chalet he renovated on Gower. In the process he has honed many essential crafts for open-air living, in particular carpentry.

Along the way he acquired three children and his partner Hoppi with whom he has been living for fifteen years. She is a powerful presence, strikingly open to the world and what it offers. A qualified Integrative Arts Psychotherapist she runs courses in guided meditation. She is a follower of Condace Pert (1946-2013), an American neuro-scientist who investigated relationships between mind and body. 'We've all heard about Psychosomatic Illness, but have you heard about Psychosomatic Wellness?' was her question. 'Since emotions run every system in the body, don't underestimate their power to treat and heal.' To put it another way, she declared that our bodies are linked to our subconscious minds. What we need is emotional integration between the two.

Quite apart from Lammas's role in pointing the way to a more ecologically balanced future, Hoppi's courses attract people interested in holistic mind body relationships. Undoubtedly, the two strands are connected and sustain Tao and Hoppi's relationship.

Under Hoppi's inspiration, Tao has embarked on another initiative. This is to build the Lammas Earth Centre. When I visited it was still a work in progress, a circular, wooden atrium with a wheel-like roof planted directly in front of their house. It's about forty feet high, and when finished will be encased in double-glazed glass. They're crowd-funding on the internet to pay for it.

What's it for? In the first place, to grow exotic fruits. But mainly as a place for the soul, where Hoppi's mindfulness experiments can be given full rein. We're going to need them if we're to face what nature has in store for us. Anticipating the impact of climate change that is to come Tao says, 'We stand at a cusp. We're at the end of one era, and at the beginning of a new age... the first step is daring to dream.'

RHYDWILYM

Rhydwilym (William's ford) is a tiny hamlet in the narrow, glaciated valley of the upper reaches of the Eastern Cleddau river. The valley sides fall steeply and are thickly forested. Along its floor the trees are interspersed with small fields, reminiscent of an Alpine scene. Occasionally, there's a glimpse of Cwmcerwyn, the lowly position making it appear more like a mountain than from any other perspective I know. Its looming presence is a reminder that this is the beginning of the Preseli foothills.

The only way to fully explore this territory is on foot. The circular sixty-mile Landsker Borderland Trail, between Lawrenny and Efail-wen, follows the line of the Eastern Cleddau. The main access road, a single-track from Llandysilio to Llangolman, has very few passing places. It crosses the Eastern Cleddau at Rhydwilym which is just inside Preseli's border with Carmarthenshire.

And right here, on the left bank of the river, located to take advantage of the rushing water, is 'the oldest active Welsh Baptist chapel in existence.' The claim is made in a fund-raising leaflet, and I have no doubt it is true. There are older Baptist chapels in Wales, but none that are active. Alongside the chapel a few steps have been cut into the river's edge behind a small weir. It's here that baptisms still take place.

In July 2018 the chapel celebrated its 350th anniversary. The hundreds of photographs of this occasion that you can see online make it look like a wedding.[24] The chapel is thronged with people who must have come from far and wide. There's even a cake, with an image of an earlier chapel built on this site, with the inscription 1668-2018. The trestle tables in the vestry, which has seating for more than a hundred people, have tablecloths, white plates and teacups, sandwiches, scones, and cakes. The people are almost all of a certain age and there are more women than men. It's mainly women who keep the chapel going.

But it's largely men who started it. I have a particular interest since the men who founded the Baptist community at Rhydwilym were from Abergavenny and the Black Mountains where I grew up. Indeed, William Prichard, who founded the Baptist church at Rhydwilym in 1668, had earlier formed one at Abergavenny in 1652.

The reason for the chapel-founding at this time lies in the Act of Uniformity, passed a century earlier, in 1559. This required the English *Book of Common Prayer* to be followed, and for all persons to attend the Church of England at least once a week, or be fined twelve pence (about £15 today). Those who objected became known as 'Nonconformists'.

Cromwell's Commonwealth Parliament repealed the Act in 1650. However, when the monarchy was restored and Charles II gained the throne in 1660 the repeal was declared null and void. Repression against Nonconformists intensified. This prompted the emergence of sects in isolated parts of the country, such as at Rhydwilym, where members could meet in secret. Nonconformists regarded the Bible rather than the *Book of Common Prayer* as the true source of spiritual guidance. They turned their back on the Established Church and later formed the denominations with which we are familiar today, the Baptists, Methodists, Presbyterians and Independents.

Originally, there was no building at Rhydwilym. The congregation of about thirty met in each other's homes and held baptisms in the Eastern Cleddau. By 1689, the year they began a record book, their number had increased to 133, drawn from as far afield as Llanarth in Ceredigion, Llanllwni in Carmarthenshire, and Slebech and Mathry in Pembrokeshire. People would travel for miles, often over several days, to attend a meeting.

Then, in 1701 John Evans, a local farmer provided funds to build the first chapel. In that year fifteen members led by a Minister, Thomas Griffiths, emigrated to Pennsylvania where they founded the Baptist Church of the Great Valley. Its website acknowledges the church has its roots in Rhydwilym. 'Anyone visiting this attractive rural chapel cannot help breathing in its sense of history, whilst the beauty, peace and solitude capture the imagination of all who survey this ancient site.'[25]

The chapel at Rhydwilym was extended and renovated in 1763 by which time the membership had surpassed 200. No image of what the chapel looked like in those days survives. However, there is a drawing of it when it was rebuilt in 1841. It's smaller and squarer than the present chapel, with outside steps leading to a first floor. Today's structure, Grade II listed, was re-built and enlarged in 1875.

With its first-floor balcony the new chapel was made to hold as many as five hundred people. It was an indication of the strength of the Baptists in Wales during the nineteenth century, by the end of which their membership had reached more than a hundred thousand.

Today, however, Welsh Baptists have declined to ten thousand, and Rhydwilym's congregation is down to just sixty-seven. But it is still, as it declares, the oldest active chapel in existence. What of its future? Some years ago plans were discussed to create a Baptist heritage centre at Rhydwilym. And certainly, there is great potential for such an initiative. Facing the chapel is a stable with an old school house above. Alongside is a small, single story Chapel House and behind that the substantial vestry and a large car park. These buildings could provide the infrastructure for an interpretive museum to tell the story of the Baptists in this part of Wales.

Does it need to be told in our secular age? I think there's no doubt that it should. Quite apart from Rhydwilym's fascinating insight into the religious experiences and disputes of previous centuries, its story throws up all manner of interesting personalities. Not only that, a heritage centre would bring many more people to this most lovely and distinctive part of Preseli.

TAFARN SINC

On either side of me in the bar of Tafarn Sinc in Rosebush, the highest and only community-owned pub in Preseli, are two of its eight trustees. Peter Ward, an IT specialist from Tavernspite on the Carmarthenshire border, has oversight of the finances. Rev Emyr Wyn Thomas, from nearby Hermon, is responsible for six chapels straddling the border. At the initial public meeting he proposed community should buy the pub. Now he regularly brings his caravan so he can stay overnight and drink without having to drive. One is bilingual, Welsh and English, the other a monoglot English-speaker. However, it makes no difference in this easy-going pub. The enthusiastic involvement of the two men in its rescue provides one answer to the question I've been asking. 'How does a pub as isolated as this manage to survive?'

In 2017 the owners, Brian Llewelyn, his daughter Hafwen Davies and her husband Brian, who had run the place for more than a quarter of a century, decided the time had come to retire. It went on sale for £295,000 and the worry was that it would be bought up as another holiday home. So *Clebran*, the *papur bro* (community newspaper) for the Preselau swung into action. It launched a campaign to raise money for the pub to become community-owned, by people willing to buy shares in the enterprise. As Hefin Wyn, the paper's editor and now chairman of Tafarn Sinc's board of directors, said, 'This is the epitome of Welsh Wales. It's the hub of the Preseli area. Here you can hear the dulcet tones of the Welsh language in its natural environment.'

Meetings were held, a web presence was established, and the Tafarn Sinc campaign went global. Plenty of local people bought a share-holding, starting at £200, with nobody allowed to own more than £20,000. But others came in from across the world, from Canada, the United States, Australia… in all there are more than four hundred shareholders.

Celebrities gave their support, including Huw Edwards, the BBC's *News at Ten* anchorman, Trystan Llŷr Griffiths, the opera singer and concert soloist, Wyn Gruffydd the rugby commentator, and Mari Grug the S4C presenter. Actor Rhys Ifans made a supporting video. 'Keep the Sinc in the Pink,' was the way he put it. They raised more than £30,000 in the first week of the appeal, in July 2017, and the whole amount by Christmas. It was testimony to Tafarn Sinc's popularity.

On St David's Day 2018 – delayed for a week because of the snow – they held a celebration. Veteran folk-singer Dafydd Iwan entertained a capacity crowd of around eighty people. The event was memorable, too, for the locally-sourced food. The beef for the cawl was supplied by nearby butcher Beni Thomas, the bread by Llandysilio's long-established Pobty Rhydwen, the cheese by Rosebush's own Caws Pantmawr, and the bara brith was made in-house by the new tenant landlord Jennifer Upshall. Pupils from Ysgol y Preseli in Crymych served with enthusiasm.

Rosebush – or Rhos-y-bwlch, to give it its historical name – is an unexpected place to find a pub like this. A few miles to the north of Maenclochog, it is reached by a lane that continues to the old slate quarry workings. The hamlet, made up of former quarrymen's cottages, developed once the Bellstone and Rosebush quarries began working in 1825. They lasted until 1891 and supplied slates for the Palace of Westminster in London. The old workings on the slopes of Cwmcerwyn can be seen from the Haverfordwest to Cardigan road, as you climb the Bwlchgwynt Pass. They're an alien gash in the hillside only partly alleviated by the encroaching Pantmaenog forest.

An eight-and-a-half-mile railway line was built to transport the slate. Known as the Narberth Road and Maenclochog Railway, it ran from Clunderwen through Maenclochog to Rosebush. The line achieved fame during the Second World War when a tunnel just outside Maenclochog was used as a testing site by Barnes Wallis, creator of the 'bouncing bomb'. It was six months after the famous Dambuster raids and the military wanted tests for a smaller version of the bomb, codenamed Highball, to be used against rail installations ahead of the the D-Day landings. Barnes Wallis himself was a witness as one of his bombs, dropped at 300mph, caused extensive damage to the Maenclochog tunnel. Repairs were made after the war and the line re-opened, only to be closed again in 1949.

However, the old Rosebush rail halt still exists, a Preseli version of Madam Tussaud's, with waxen, life-like figures waiting on the platform, complete with sound effects of a shunting steam train in

the distance. Opposite stands Tafarn Sinc's extraordinary pink structure made of wood and galvanized corrugated iron. It was built in 1876, when the railway first reached Rosebush. Known then as the Prescelly Hotel, it was part of an eccentric scheme by local landowners Colonel John Owen and Joseph Macaulay, to make Rosebush a health resort. Artificial lakes were stocked with fish, rhododendrons planted, and lily ponds created. They're still here, but the tourists never came.

The Prescelly Hotel survived, but eventually went into decline and a bad state of repair until the brewery that owned it decided to sell in 1992. It was bought for £18,000 by locals Brian Llewelyn and his wife Brenda. They did the place up and renamed it Tafarn Sinc, after its unique metallic structure.

Their refurbishment created an atmospheric nineteenth century living museum. Ancient agricultural implements hang from the ceilings. Old photographs and posters line the walls and pewter jugs the shelves. There is an antique iron wood-burning stove and sawdust on the floor. A portrait of one-eyed Christmas Evans (1766-1938), regarded as one of the greatest Welsh preachers, glares from the mantelpiece.

And it may be that Tafarn Sinc will one day double-up as a chapel. The notion was suggested, perhaps tongue in cheek, by Dafydd Iwan, a lay preacher himself, on that opening St David's Day evening.

'There are some communities which have made their village hall a real hub and on a Sunday the Cross will be set up and a religious service held,' he said. 'As I travelled down from Caernarfon I passed several pubs that have been forced to close as rental charges are increased way beyond the capability of tenants to make a living. At the same time, I passed closed chapels. I often feel the denomination headquarters are more interested in acquiring the money from the sale of buildings rather than releasing them into the hands of local congregations who could use their own energy and imagination to breathe into them new life.'

Certainly, Tafarn Sinc has been successful in breathing new life into the community. Perhaps, in due time, it will have a spiritual role as well.

Notes

1. Quoted in Alan Llwyd, *The Story of Waldo Williams – Poet of Peace*, Barddas Publications, 2010, p.75.
2. These are the opening lines from Waldo's 1946 poem 'Preseli'. The inscription on the Waldo stone is in Welsh only. The translation is by Tony Conran, in his *The Peacemakers* (Gomer, 1997), a selection of Waldo Williams' poetry.
3. http://www.waldowilliams.com
4. Ibid., page 217.
5. Tony Conran, 'Introduction' in Waldo Williams, *The Peacemakers: Selected Poems* (translated by Tony Conran), Gomer, 1997, p. 34.
6. Maenclochog means 'ringing stone'. About a mile south-west of the village is St Mary's well, from where holy water used to be drawn for use in the church. There was a great flat stone beside it, which used to ring when struck. Some say it was this that gave the village its name. However, Waldo Williams put forward an alternative explanation. He suggested it derived from the early Irish word *clócoz*, meaning rock-strewn land. A branch of the ancient Irish Deisi tribe inhabited northern Preseli in the fifth and sixth centuries. The tribe is associated with the Ogham script and it is noteworthy that there are two Ogham stones in Maenclochog Church. The place name Llangolman derives from its church dedicated to St Colman of Dromore, a sixth century Irish saint. Mynachlog-ddu means Black Monastery – the parish belonged to St Dogmael's Abbey prior to Henry VIII's dissolution of the monasteries between 1536 and 1541.
7. Moreover, the word 'gate' appears in the English version of the Bible. In the Welsh of the Bishop William Morgan Bible that Twm Carabwth would have been familiar, the word used is *porth*, which translates as 'door'.
8. Kenneth O. Morgan, *Modern Wales: Politics, Places and People*, University of Wales Press, 1977, pages 66-67.
9. Quoted in David Howells, *Nicholas of Glais, the People's Champion*, Clydach Historical Society, 1991.
10. *Morning Star*, 21 April 1971.
11. Hwyl Francis, *Ireland 1916, Russia 1917, Wales? (Aberystwyth graffiti, circa 1978)* Welsh Political Archive Annual Lecture, National Library of Wales, 2010.

12. Diarmait Mac Giolla Chriost, *Welsh Writing, Political Action and Incarceration: Branwen's Starling*, Palgrave Macmillan, 2013, page 59.

13. Gwenallt D. Jones, *Rhagymadrodd* (Introduction') in T.E. Nicholas, *Llygad y drws*. *Sonedau'r Carchar*, Gwasg Gee, 1940, page 18.

14. Literally 'tongue craft', *Cerdd Dafod* is the tradition of creating poetry that observes the strict rules of *cynghanedd*. These entail an intricate system of sound arrangement in respect of stress, alliteration, and internal rhyme within each line. Its history can be traced to the sixth century poets Aneurin and Taliesin.

15. Dafydd ap Gwilym (c1315 to c1350), was one of Wales's leading poets and among the greatest European poets of the Middle Ages, whose main themes are love and nature and his personal response to them.

16. Richard Russill, *Llanychaer in Wartime*, Llais Llanychaer, 2011.

17. *Ibid.*

18. *Ibid.*

19. In Hywel Owen and Richard Morgan, *The Dictionary of Place Names of Wales* (Gomer 2007), Trecŵn is referred to as a 'dog's farm' with historical references being Trefcone, 1524; Trekone,1542; and Trecoone, 1575. They were: 'Presumably places where dogs or hounds were kept, perhaps for breeding. Similar names are Tre-Cŵn (Trecŵn 1739) Llantwyd Pemb and Trecŵn (Trecŵn 1596, Trecoon 1739), St Dogmael's Pembrokeshire.

20. Brenda Squires, *Landsker*, Starborn Books, 2004.

21. Glen Peters, *Mrs D'Silva's Detective Instincts and the Shaitan of Calcutta*, Parthian, 2009.

22. Glen Peters, *Lucknow Ransom*, Parthian, 2013.

23. The Salesian Society is a Roman Catholic religious institute, founded in the late nineteenth century by the Italian priest St John Bosco (1815-1888, canonized 1934) to help children of the urban poor. It operates world-wide and is the third largest missionary organisation.

24. Glen Peters, *Project Management and Construction Control*, Construction Press, 1981.

25. www.helendavies.com

26. http://www.bcgv.org/about/rootsinwales/

WEST

SACRED COAST

I'm walking the cliff path around the St Davids Peninsula in search of holy places. It's a bright blue April day and a strong breeze is blowing from the sea. I need my woolly hat as I stride across Whitesands Bay, the beach for people who visit St Davids. At least they have to pass through the little city to get here. It's one of the best beaches in Preseli, wide and good for surfing if there's a swell. I first came here as a teenager on my bike and was overwhelmed by the grandeur of high craggy Carn Llidi. It has all the appearance of a holy mountain.

In Welsh the beach is called Porth Mawr, the great port. This was the western end of a Bronze-age trading route around 1,500 BC, linking Salisbury Plain to Ireland. Later it was the start of a seaborne pilgrim path to St Davids Cathedral.

Whitesands is where St Patrick is said to have set sail for Ireland in the fifth century. It is also the location for his chapel, now buried beneath the sands. Instructions tell me its remains are close to the car park that runs down to the beach. At first all I can see is a grassy mound and a litter of stones. However, on closer inspection an inscribed stone reads, 'Underneath lies a chapel dedicated to St Patrick built 6th-10th c.'

The chapel originally stood inland and as late as the nineteenth century was described as being in the middle of a field. But today coastal erosion has brought it perilously close to the water's edge. In 2004 the National Park placed large boulders here in an attempt to halt the erosion. But storms washed them away in February 2014, revealing a large burial ground.

When the site was first excavated in 1924, a building with walls of rough stone about thirty-three feet long was uncovered. At the east end was a stone altar and several graves. However, the 2014 storms indicated this was a much more significant burial ground than had been thought. A major archeological investigation began. Excavations were undertaken each Spring for three years. By 2017 the Dyfed Archeological Trust, together with experts from Sheffield University and a host of volunteers, had uncovered the remains of more than eighty people in the wind-blown sand. Many were young children and babies, two of whom lay in well-constructed cist graves with base and lintel slabs. Radiocarbon dating showed that burials at the site began before the seventh century and continued into the eleventh. Most of the graves were orientated east to west with the head at the west end. There were no possessions, in keeping with Christian tradition. Burials of the very young were covered with white quartz pebbles placed over the lintel slabs, perhaps to ensure the top of the grave remained visible.

One of the most significant finds was a well-preserved skeleton of a woman in her early twenties. She was about five feet tall and showed no signs of disease though she'd had problems with her teeth. She was buried in a well-constructed cist grave with her hands crossed. A fragment of copper alloy wire was found nearby. It may have been a pin used to secure the body in a shroud. At the head of the grave was a particularly significant cross marker made from bluish-grey Preseli stone. It's the only example of a cross-carved grave marker in Britain.

I turn and head south for about a mile along the coast path until Ramsey Island comes into view. In Welsh it is *Ynys Dewi*, David's Island, a source of much mythology concerning the life of Justinian. The son of a Breton prince, he settled on the island as a hermit. He was visited by David who, impressed by his holiness, made him his confessor and abbot of the mainland community. However, Justinian soon became disillusioned with the behaviour of the monks and retreated back to his island. There he created a stricter regime, allowing no women. Eventually his fellow monks could stand his rules no more. They cut off his head, but where it fell a spring of pure water welled up. Not only that, Justinian picked up his head and marched across the waters of Ramsey Sound and collapsed on the opposite shore. The spot where he fell was marked by a chapel erected in his name.

Today's structure dates back to the sixteenth century. It is in a field a few yards from the cliff edge. Here, too, is the St Justinian's lifeboat station with its dramatic launch slide, enabling the boat to operate at all states of the tide.

As I approached the chapel it looked for all the world like a well-constructed but roofless barn. A sign on the gate to the field says it is private land, but 'genuinely interested persons' are allowed to enter. The chapel looks more like the remains of a castle. It doesn't feel saintly, holy or in any way religious. It's more like a forlorn relic. What would it have been like in Justinian's time?

I press on. Turning a corner on the path I suddenly encounter an artist, complete with easel, intent on painting the view. Glancing backwards I see it is the St Justinian's lifeboat station framed by the cliffs. The artist is Tony Kitchell who works out of Studio 6 in St Davids. He has been portraying this coastline professionally since 1981. I ask about the virtues of painting in the open air. 'It makes a huge difference,' Tony says. 'You get the reflection of the light off the sea. It changes all the time.'

I take a look at his work in progress. The immediate impression is of vigorous colour. The yellowing bracken has become red, the green of the fields turned to yellow, the blue-back of the cliffs a shimmering white.

'A representation?' I murmur.

'Representational?' he echoes and pauses to think. 'To begin with perhaps, but then what happens is that the canvas takes on a life of its own.'

As I move to leave, I tell him I think this is a sacred coast.

'You don't say?' he answers. 'Well yes, you're right.' He points his paint brush upwards towards the streaming sunlight before adding, 'We're lucky anyway, to be out here, in this.'

Walking on with Ramsey Island a short distance across the Sound, two yachts come into view. They're in full sail, but still have to rely on their engines to negotiate these treacherous waters. It's warmer now and I pause to remove my hat and jacket. Rounding the headland the glittering seascape of St Brides Bay spreads southwards, revealing the full length of Skomer Island. It seems like some kind of revelation.

It is now a short walk to the Porthclais inlet with its Roman-built sea wall. Here St David was baptised and later fostered by St Elvis. He has given his name to this parish. At just 200 acres St Elvis (Llaneilfw in Welsh) is the smallest parish in Wales and perhaps in Britain. Even so its rector was previously superior to the vicar of St Teilo's church in neighbouring Solva. These days, however, it is attached to the parish of Whitchurch and together they make up the community of Solva. St Elvis, who later missioned in southern Ireland and died in about 530, was also known variously as Ailbe, Ailfyw, Elouis, Eiliw, and Elfyw. In relation to the last name there is a proverb that seems to propose tolerance and understanding of homosexuality:

Hast thou heard the saying of Elfyw,
A man wise without a peer?
'Let every sex go to where it belongs'.[1]

Terry Breverton's entry about St Elvis in his *The Book of Welsh Saints* in 2000 led to world-wide publicity that Elvis Presley was of Welsh descent.[2] There was academic scorn, but nonetheless circumstantial evidence. Elvis Aaron Presley had the Christian names of two Welsh saints. The maternal side of his family came from generations of Mansells, a well-known Welsh surname. His mother was christened Gwladys, a Welsh saint's name. And, who knows, could the surname be a corruption of Preseli? In any event, the controversy led to much international attention for the Welsh tourist cause.

Beyond St Elvis is St Non's Bay. She, of course, was David's mother. What remains of her chapel lies in fields above the cliff. They're just a few broken-down walls, but all the same they create an altogether more poignant atmosphere than the one I felt at St Justinian's. Non is reputed to have given birth to David here, during a violent thunderstorm in about 520. Her hands are said to have left their imprint on the rock she grasped.

A few yards away is St Non's Well which, it is said, sprang up at the very moment of David's birth. It was restored in the eighteenth century, and again in 1951 by the Roman Catholic Church. A stone cowl covers the well and nearby is a statue of St Non. Like most holy wells it is reputed to have healing properties, this one specialising in eye complaints.

Not far away, too, is the tiny Chapel of Our Lady and St Non. It is just twenty feet long and twelve feet wide, built in 1934 by a devoutly Catholic local solicitor. It gives you a sense of what a pilgrimage chapel might have looked like in medieval times. Inside, above the altar, is a fine stained glass window depicting St Non. Alongside is a statue of St Mary copied from the original in the

Church of Notre Dame de Victoire in Paris. Built into the altar is a heart-shaped stone taken from above the altar of St Patrick's chapel buried in Whitesands Bay.

As I leave I pass St Non's Well once again and notice a woman kneeling there. She makes the sign of the cross, scoops some water with her hand, and dabs her eyes. It is strange to witness this pilgrim's gesture from time immemorial. It's a sign that the medieval mysteries of faith continue even into the twenty-first century.

CARN LLIDI

Carn Llidi, overlooking St Davids Head, means Carn of Wrath or perhaps Carn of the Gates, which I prefer. From its summit you get a 360-degree view, one of the best in Wales. It's only five-hundred-and-ninety-four feet high, but because the hill rises so steeply and directly from sea level it feels a lot higher.

To the west on a clear day you can see as far as Ireland's Wicklow Mountains. To the north is one of the most spectacular stretches of the coastal path, seven miles of high rocky cliff to Porthgain. Carn Penberry appears in the middle distance like an extinct volcano, which it probably is. These 470-million-year-old igneous rocks are the product of explosive, submarine eruptions and lava flows.

To the east across the flat plain below is St Davids, Preseli's city by the sea. Its Cathedral tower peeps above the rooftops. To the south is Ramsey Island and the open sea. On the horizon across St Brides Bay is the full length of Skomer Island.

Immediately below me, behind Whitesands beach (see page 150), is the large car park where St Davids City Council makes a killing. They charge £5 a time, enough to cover most of their expenditure. This makes the citizens of the fair city among the best-off council taxpayers in the county. It's a tourist tax in all but name and the council admits as much. The parking ticket says it's one of the city's 'main sources of revenue'. It spends the money on 'projects to benefit residents and tourists alike.' Well, that's alright then.

It's is only the third time I've climbed Carn Llidi, and the first by the path from the north. Whichever way you approach it you have to climb the last fifty feet using your hands as well as feet.

I've come to St Davids Head many times, of course, mainly to cast for mackerel off the rocks. When I was a boy we used old spark plugs for weights. If you hit a shoal they'd give themselves up, grabbing the silver bait with a voracious tug. You'd haul them in three or five at a time, some of them slithering off the hooks back into the water. The rest came flapping on the rocks, their blue-grey, white and silvery bodies flashing in the sun.

Before climbing Carn Llidi I'd walked round St Davids Head in search of Coetan Arthur, a Neolithic cromlech dating back to about 3,500 BC. Its large flat capstone is supported at one end by a single vertical pillar, while the other end rests on the ground. It's not as striking as other dolmens in northern Preseli but is still magnificent in its way. I take some photos and from one angle, close to the ground, the capstone does indeed seem to be floating towards the sky, just like Pentre Ifan, Carreg Coetan Arthur, and Carreg Samson to the north (see pages 57-63).

Around Coetan Arthur is an ancient landscape created by the two-thousand-foot Irish Sea glacier that passed this way aeons ago. There are massive glaciated boulders and erratic slabs. There is also evidence of prehistoric people. On the lower slopes of Carn Llidi is Clawdd-y-Milwyr, the Warrior's Dyke, a defensive line of ramparts and ditches, part of an Iron Age fort. Inside are the remains of field systems and perhaps a dozen round huts. Lower down, where the ground flattens towards the small cove of Porthmelgan, just to the north of Whitesands, you can still see the stone walls of the original small enclosed fields. All this suggests that, even in this barren, windswept place there was a mixed farming economy in which stockbreeding played a part.

A little below Carn Llidi's summit is a levelled piece of ground known as Highwinds. Here an early-warning radar station and a Lewis gun emplacement were built during the Second World War. The concrete platform still remains. Did the soldiers who manned the installation ever tire of the view?

It's hard to place this thought alongside the pacifist Preseli poet Waldo Williams (see pages 106-112). But somewhere here in May 1935, perhaps on this very spot, he had another of his mystical visions that led to one of his great poems, 'Tŷ Dewi' (St Davids).

This was the set subject for the *awdl* – a complex metre form of poetry – commissioned by the National Eisteddfod for the Chair in 1936. The Eisteddfod was to be held that year in Fishguard. Waldo resolved to enter the competition. At the time he was teaching in St Davids and one spring evening climbed Carn Llidi. Here he underwent that mystical experience. He felt he had become one with the world around him:

Ar gadernid Carn Llidi
Ar hyd un hwyr oedwn i.
Ac yn syn ar derfyn dydd
Gwelwn o ben bwy gilydd
Drwy eitha Dyfed y rhith dihafal.
Ei thresi swnd yn eurwaith ar sindal
Lle naid y lli anwadal yn sydyn
I fwrw ei ewyn dros far a hual.

I lingered one evening
on the stronghold of Carn Llidi,
and with amazement at day's end
I saw from end to end
throughout Dyfed the matchless vision,
its tresses of sand golden on silk
where the inconstant tide suddenly leaps
to cast its foam over bar and bank.[3]

This extract is from a fifty-stanza poem Waldo completed in just two weekends. But after that he became ill, from a nervous disorder he had probably inherited from his father. As a result, he failed to enter the poem for the Eisteddfod competition. Instead, his friend D.J. Williams (see pages 180-184) submitted it.

Unfortunately, D.J. made a number of errors in his typed copy of the poem. This was the reason it came second in the competition, despite the adjudicators judging it the best poem.[4] However, due to D.J.'s transcription, the poem showed signs of haste, with metrical mistakes and grammatical errors.

Much later Waldo substantially revised the poem before including it in his collection *Dail Pren* (Leaves of a Tree) published in 1956. His biographer James Nicholas reveals that the main revisions were to the section containing the stanza quoted above. He says it was completely re-written:

Waldo quoted it in full to me from memory at the Plaid Cymru Annual Rally, held that year in Bala. There was a gleam in his eyes and he was overcome by emotion as he experienced again shades of the creative ecstasy that he had obviously experienced during the creation of this section anew.[5]

DISPUTED SHRINE

St Davids Cathedral is built on marshy ground which is why it has such a shaky structure. It has two Latin names and both give you the clue. *Vallis Rosina* means 'the valley of the swamp' (in Welsh *Glyn Rhosyn*). Meanwhile, Menevia, the name of the wider diocese, means a thicket or brushwood.

St David originally established a monastery on this site during the sixth century. However, the present Cathedral only started to take shape in the 1180s. By then the wood and stone huts David established were long gone, destroyed in multiple attacks by seaborne raiders.

The Cathedral is the result of centuries of endeavour, an amalgam of Romanesque, Gothic, Renaissance and Victorian architecture. There were periodic disruptions. In 1247 an earthquake caused considerable damage. The Holy Trinity Chapel with its fan vaulted ceiling was built by Bishop Vaughan between 1509-22. A decade later the nave's magnificent Irish oak ceiling was constructed – the marshy ground wouldn't support the weight of a stone ceiling.

The Cathedral survived Henry VIII's reformation, perhaps because it wasn't a monastery. However, in 1648 Cromwell's Roundheads ransacked the place. From then on the wind, rain and frost produced constant decay. There was a major restoration in Victorian times, followed by a more recent £5.5million refurbishment in the early 2000s. The cloisters that had been demolished in 1547 were reconstructed, the West Front rebuilt, the organ renewed, and the thirteenth century octagonal bell tower re-roofed. In addition, St Mary's Hall that used to be a college for clergy alongside the cathedral, was redeveloped as an architecturally striking two-storey refectory and gallery.

This last was aimed at the more than two hundred and fifty thousand visitors the Cathedral receives every year. Their spending in the refectory and bookshop keeps the body if not the soul of the Cathedral together. As you enter the Cathedral's main south-facing entrance there is a large box suggesting you contribute £5. Alongside is information that the Cathedral costs £2,250 a day to maintain. That's £821,250 a year. This pays for a groundsman and his assistant, a verger and assistant who organise the services, an organist plus assistant, an administrator, together with stone masons and other builders who are called in as required, plus all the sundry costs such as heating (a big bill).

When they first built the Cathedral it was touch and go whether they would have many visitors. For it was a shrine without relics. St David's bones had long gone, ferried around a good deal after his death. Possibly they had ended up in St Davids, but that was centuries earlier. In medieval times relics were all important. They provided physical evidence of the spiritual presence of powerful saints capable of intercession in response to prayers. Threat of purgatory was a big thing in those days.

Bishop Bernard consecrated an early Cathedral – not the present one – in 1131. But he had nothing to put in it. Appointed by Henry I in 1115 he spent much of his thirty-three years as Bishop searching in vain for David's bones. The saint was supposed to have been buried on the site but Viking raiders had destroyed all traces. The Bishop negotiated this problem with an astute marketing strategy. He persuaded Pope Calixtus II to give St Davids a privilege. Two journeys to the shrine were to be the spiritual equivalent of one journey to Rome – *Roma semel quantum: bis dat Menevia tantum.* Three journeys were worth a visit to Jerusalem. So began the practice of pilgrimages to St Davids.

In the absence of bodily remains, David's possessions were a substitute, specifically his bell, book, staff and clothing. Some of these were kept at St Davids, but others were held at various shrines around the country, including Llandewi Brefi in Ceredigion, Glascwm in Powys, and Llangyfelach on the Gower peninsula. However, bones were still at a premium. The Cathedral had to wait until the 1270s to get them. It seems that John de Gamage, Prior of Ewenny in Glamorgan, had a dream telling him to go and dig a precise number of paces from the south door of the Cathedral where he would find the bones of St David. This was done and, lo and behold, bones were dug up. Naturally, they were assumed to be those of St David. They were placed in a casket in the Sanctuary behind the High Altar. Henceforth, pilgrims flocked to St Davids in greater numbers.

In the wake of his conquest of Wales in 1282, Edward I made a pilgrimage to St Davids. That was in 1284 and he came away with the skull and some other bones of the saint. A few months later he went on a procession with the relics from the Tower of London to Westminster Abbey. There they were placed on the high altar.

There was a strategic purpose behind this despoilation. According to the historian R.R. Davies, Edward's removal of the relics 'was a calculated attempt to obliterate the symbols of independence and communal memory and thereby appropriate to himself and his dynasty the exclusive claim to be ruler of Britain.'[6] As Davies goes on to say, robbery of this kind undermines the cultural autonomy of your enemies.

Nonetheless, there were enough bones left at St Davids to make them worthy of continued pilgrimage. And all was well for three centuries until Henry VIII's split from Rome in the 1530s. William Barlow, Bishop St Davids from 1536-48, a staunch Protestant, recorded his dismay that the misguided faithful continued their 'abominable idolatry, popish pilgrimages and deceitful pardons.' In 1538 he threw out the relics to counteract 'superstition'. Despite this he could not prevent the people from 'wilfully solemnising' the saint's feast day. The cult of St David ran deep.

Barlow also wanted to move the Cathedral to Carmarthen, a location nearer the centre of a diocese that stretched as far as the Welsh border. Hence, throwing out the relics had an additional motivation. Their removal downgraded the Cathedral's importance. This was somewhat offset two years later. Henry VIII commanded that the tomb of his grandfather Henry Tudor, be moved to the Cathedral from the recently dissolved Greyfriars Priory in Carmarthen. In any event, pilgrimages to the Cathedral dwindled.

Three hundred years went by. Then, during a restoration in 1865 a cache of bones was discovered behind the High Altar in the Holy Trinity Chapel. At the time they were not thought to be important and were reburied in the floor. However, in the 1920s Dean William Williams took it into his head that they were indeed the bones of St David. It is said that for a time he kept them in a box under his bed. Eventually he had them put in a casket, a gift of the patriarchs of the Orthodox Church, and in 1925 replaced them in the niche in the wall where they had been originally found. And there they remain though they're not St David's bones. They've been carbon dated which showed they're from the twelfth, thirteenth and fourteenth centuries.

All was not lost, however. In 2010 an appeal was launched to raise £150,000 to restore the shrine. Artist Sarah Crisp, a specialist in medieval-style paintings, was commissioned to paint five icons. These have been installed within the existing front and rear niches of the shrine. Made on lime wood panels using classic Byzantine styles and materials, they depict St David and other saints associated with the Cathedral. In a commentary Canon Patrick Thomas, Vicar of Carmarthen's Christ Church, says:

> The vision for the Shrine was to make it a clear focus for visitors so they in turn could become the New Pilgrims. Rather than an 'old

bloke with a beard' the vision of the artist Sarah Crisp (whose family have had a long connection with the cathedral) was to create a new and young monk, with the tonsure and garb of the Celtic Monk he was – with the choice of colourful icons reflecting how the cathedral would have looked in the Middle Ages... filled with bright colours.[7]

In the painting St David has a dove fluttering down towards his right shoulder. This recalls the celebrated incident during his life when he went to address a synod of Bishops at Llanddewi Brefi in the Teifi valley. There was such a large crowd that few could hear him. The legend has it that when a boy put a handkerchief on the ground in front of him, David stepped on to it and the ground around him rose into a small hill so everyone could hear him. Moreover, he spoke so eloquently that a dove representing the holy spirit flew down to rest on his shoulder. It is a myth, of course. Much of the story of St Davids Cathedral is compiled of myths. But a defeated people depend on myths to give them something to believe in.

SOLVA

Ifor Thomas is one of those people whose energetic enthusiasm exhilarates and exhausts his friends in equal measure. He's a performance poet who thinks it's the performance that makes a poem. He would read a Severn Bridge poem while lying flat across two chairs. He became famous for cutting up books with a petrol-driven chain saw in all manner of auditoriums and venues, even a school. Those were the days before our obsession with health and safety. He was famous, too, for covering his naked torso with cling film.

Ifor's poetry collection *Body Beautiful* won the Welsh Book of the Year Award in 2006.[8] The poems were written between when he was first diagnosed with prostate cancer, and the surgery to remove the tumour and his recovery. It's a compelling mix of anguish, despair, humour and hope. I reckon the experience explains a good deal of Ifor's full-frontal, boisterous attitude to life. After all, what's the alternative? He's faced it, full in the eye.

Originally from Haverfordwest, Ifor lived for many years in Cardiff working as an architect. Later he ran a consultancy that managed the building of hospitals for the NHS. But for some time he has been back in Preseli where, with wife Gill, he's helping to breathe new life into Solva (the Norse name for samphire which grows in profusion around these shores). It is a community of some eight-hundred people who live in the submerged valley or ria that curves into St Brides Bay. Historian John Davies thought it 'perhaps the most delectable place in coastal Pembrokeshire.'[9] Gill was brought up in Solva and four of her five brothers still live there, one of them a fisherman.

In the summer of 2014 the village was invaded by a film crew remaking *Under Milk Wood*, Dylan Thomas's radio play. It was first filmed in 1972, and starred Richard Burton and Elizabeth Taylor, with Fishguard's Lower Town as the backdrop. The new version stars Rhys Ifans and Charlotte Church, with dozens of Solva villagers hired as extras. For two months the place was transformed. At the end of the shoot, during the wrap party, a group of locals decided the village's new cultural profile had to be continued in some way. The idea for the Edge Festival was born.

Masterminded by Ifor, Gill, and their nephew Josh, who runs one of Solva's three pubs, the festival is held over the first weekend in August. It's called the Edge because Solva lies on the rim of Wales, at the brink, the cusp of the ocean.

The festival's symbol is the first Smalls lighthouse, constructed in 1776 on an outcrop of rock that lies out to sea, about twenty-five miles southwest of the village. It's the last piece of land before America. Although built of wood, on nine oak pillars that allowed the sea to pass beneath, the lighthouse stood for eighty years. It achieved notoriety when one of the two light house keepers died and the other, fearful that he would be accused of murder because they were known to argue, eventually went mad. This initiated the change to always having three lighthouse keepers on light houses, until automation made them redundant.

The question whether the festival will last as long as the first Smalls lighthouse is moot. But thus far it has been an extraordinary success. It hosts rock and folk bands, a six-a-side football tournament, cookery demonstrations and food of all kinds, a regatta and raft race, lectures, films, and poetry readings. A high point is the four-kilometre open water swim from the harbour out to Green Scar Rock in St Brides Bay. This attracts upwards of three hundred entrants from across the UK and is fast becoming a staple event in the Ironman Triathlon community.

For Solva, the festival lasts much more than a weekend. The organisation and fundraising continues for most of the year. The village raises more than £7,000 from a raffle, community events and themed food evenings. There's a turnover of much more than this, with ticket sales and sponsorship. Each year a surplus of about £5,000 is distributed to local charities. The Edge Festival has mobilised the whole community and done wonders for the local economy. As the village's monthly newsletter put it in May 2018:

> The festival last year was our biggest to date and sixty stout Solva supporters chipped in to perform various tasks like ticket collecting, bar work, litter picking, car park attending and support for our specialist events like the bat walk, river walk and beach safari. You don't get paid and there are no perks, but if you put in a good shift you will get a free weekend pass – what is there not to like?

On an early May morning, Ifor Thomas takes me in his small boat into the open sea to check his lobster pots. He is a hobby fisherman, with a handful of pots. Nonetheless, they provide him with enough catch to last family and friends for the season. They're all pretty close inshore and I haul up the first one. Amazingly it contains three lobsters and as many crabs. We throw most of them back, except for one lobster which is just large enough. Ifor explains they have to be a hundred millimetres from eye to tail to allow you to keep them. The bait was a frozen pollock which looks intact to me. Bacon is what they really like, which is why that's disappeared.

We head further out to sea to round Green Scar Rock which this
time of year is dense with nesting gulls (Scar is derived from the
Norse word Sker for rock). Ifor tells me that when he was a boy he
used to land on it at the beginning of May to collect gulls' eggs.
They're light green with black speckles, larger than a hen's egg,
richer and gamier with yolks of vivid orange. 'You have to have a
license to collect them now,' he says. 'But there's always a
temptation. They go for about £7 each at Covent Garden.'

As we pass round Green Scar I wonder at the possibility of
landing at all. The cliffs plunge steeply down into the water and
there's a large swell with a rush of white water around the rocks.

Most early mornings between six and seven o'clock you'll find
Ifor running the coast path towards St Davids, making for an
isolated bay called Porth y Rhaw. In English that's Shovel Bay, so
called because of its shape. There he'll take a skinny dip before
running back. On one occasion Ifor emerged naked from the sea to
catch sight of a man standing on the cliff above him. His black
outline was silhouetted by the morning sun. It was a dramatic
moment that sparked the idea for a thriller that is still a work in
progress.

DAISYBUS GARDENS

On the wall of the tearoom in Preseli's latest garden open to the
public, is a photograph of the American actress Audrey Hepburn.
Underneath is her quotation: 'To plant a garden is to believe in
tomorrow.'

The woman behind this garden is quintessentially English. Sarah
Wint is slightly left field, determined, an individualist in search of
collective meaning. She is pursuing a project she believes has great
significance for our peace of mind. In the autumn of 2016, helped
by husband William, an ecologist who maps human and animal
diseases for the United Nations, she began the garden on St Davids
peninsula.

It isn't any old garden. To begin with, they started it from
virtually nothing. Previously it was a large lawn, alongside the house
and eight-and-a-half acres they bought at Llanddinog, edging the
Brawdy airfield a few miles inland from Solva. Moreover, it was to
be a wellbeing garden. It would be a living demonstration of how

gardening can conquer all manner of ailments, especially those of the mind.

Sarah had found solace in her garden in Worcestershire after the loss of a child. Then she began noticing that many other people benefited in similar ways. She had a brainwave of conducting a survey of healing gardens across Britain. Through the Gardens Scheme, which opens private gardens to the public for charity, Sarah contacted their four thousand members. Four hundred agreed to be included in her survey. She chose fifty and used her VW campervan – the *Daisybus* – to visit them, covering ten thousand miles across England and Wales during 2015.

The outcome was her book *Sunshine on Clover: Gardens of Wellbeing*.[10] In it she recounts how gardens are 'the lifeblood of other people's lives in the same way as mine.' She also ate a lot of cake. 'There is nothing so English as sitting in a garden on a summer's day with tea in china cups and a slice of homemade cake.'

All the same, Sarah decided to pursue the dream of creating her own wellbeing garden in Wales. England was becoming too crowded. 'A large suburb of London,' was the way she put it. And she was desperate to live near the sea. 'There's something very deep and visceral about living where the land meets the sea,' she told me. 'The world is made right in front of you. And I love the wildness and beauty of the Pembrokeshire Coast Path. They say it beats the Inca Trail.'

Less than a year after she and William started work, The Daisybus Gardens of Wellbeing were opened to the public. That was in the summer of 2017. Little had developed by then but in many ways that was the point. One of Sarah's objectives is to persuade people that gardening is not as difficult as they might think. Like her they can start from scratch. 'We don't need a horticultural degree to make a garden,' she said. 'We've been working the land for thousands of years. It's what we're meant to do. If we give ourselves a chance, we can find our way into the flow of natural life.'

One of the most popular parts of the emerging garden is a small patch where there is a demonstration on how to get started. You place cardboard on the ground to rid it of weeds, create a few paths, till, and plant. The most common question Sarah gets is how to deal with slugs. She agrees they're a constant challenge, even to the most competent gardener. But she advises against getting too worked-up. 'After all, gardening is about relieving stress.'

Entrance to the one-and-a-half acres is through a polytunnel full of seedlings. Beyond are small, circular themed gardens. 'Circularity is everywhere in life,' Sarah says. 'Anyway, I was bored with gardens consisting of straight-edged rooms.' The first circle is devoted to a grandparents' garden. 'For many of us this is our first memory of gardening, visiting our grandparents,' Sarah explains. 'It's where we were given most freedom in our early lives, where we were most indulged.'

Next is a circle devoted to Gaia, a grassy mound shaped into a pregnant woman representing Mother Earth. Then there is an Artists Garden, followed by others devoted to healing, memory, hiraeth or longing, tea, family, and sunshine. This last has been planted with flowers which will produce a mix of yellows and oranges.

But I'm most intrigued by the circle dedicated to the Blue Zones.[11] These are the five regions of the world where people live much longer than average. They are mountain villages in Sardinia where a substantial proportion of men live to be a hundred; the Okinawa islands in Japan; the Nicoya peninsula in Costa Rica; the island of Icaria in Greece where one in three make it to their nineties; and Loma Linda, a city (population 24,000) in the San Bernando Valley in southern California, home to one of the world's largest concentrations of Seventh Day Adventists.

Common attributes of the people living in these places are a vegetarian or at least Mediterranean-style diet, constant but moderate physical activity, engagement in family and social life, little smoking, and unhappily for me a low alcohol intake, especially wine. Sarah's first thought was to represent these characteristics by growing appropriate plants from each of the five zones. But she realised they wouldn't survive in the Welsh climate, an indication perhaps of the gardening challenge we face. Instead, she chose what she regards as the top herbs for promoting wellbeing – thyme, lavender, sage, rosemary, and hyssop.

It's early days for the Daisybus Gardens. Sarah's worry is that she thinks that it's lacking in soul.

'What do you mean?' I ask.

'I suppose a sense of place,' she answers. 'Our last garden was so full of itself. We merely suggested plants and arrangements, and the garden dictated how it was all going to look, how it was going to feel.'

But she goes on to say, 'It's only a few months since this patch of ground was just grass, a lawn mown into submission. Sometimes we have to help the land find itself again. After all the earth provides for us. So it a nice feeling to be giving something back.'

MATHRY

My first encounter in Mathry, a mile off the main road between St Davids and Fishguard, was somewhat disconcerting. It was about ten o'clock on a fine spring morning during my election campaign in Preseli in 2007. Bearing my yellow, orange and green rosette on my lapel and clutching a handful of leaflets, I advanced cheerfully into the village's General Stores and post office ... and was met by a torrent of abuse. 'Get out of here! You lot are all the same. Load of rubbish!'

I halted, astonished. And looked round in the hope that someone else might be the cause of the red-faced ire of the rather large woman advancing towards me. 'Interfering busybodies, why can't you leave us alone? What's the point of you anyway!'

She continued in this vein for a while. Then abruptly, she stopped, and retreated into the dark recesses of the shop. I turned and made my way to the door thinking, *Well, you can't win 'em all.* But before I had time to add *Why do we have to lose so many?* the woman reappeared. This time she was in a more emollient frame of mind.

'I'm sorry,' she said. 'It's not really your fault, is it?'

It turned out she was referring to the smoking ban that had only recently come into force and meant she was being prevented from lighting up in her own shop.

'Gets me down,' she explained. 'I'm in an out of the back all the time. I'll have to get a bell put on the door.'

When I visited Mathry a decade later the General Stores had closed and was being converted into a rather desirable cottage. But the old frontage was still there, its blue paint faded somewhat, a throw-back to another era. *The General Stores* was still emblazoned in large capital letters above the shop windows, though a 'Sorry we are closed' sign was stuck to the door.

Through the murky windows I could see on the shelves a handful of items that had once been for sale, kitchenware mainly. The red phone kiosk in front was now a community library. It contained some well-thumbed paperbacks, together with an emergency defibrillator donated by the Milford Haven Port Authority. On the wall a 'Petrol pump switch off here' sign revealed that in its heyday, probably the 1940s, the shop had also served as a petrol station. By the time you're reading this, these traces will most likely be gone. I suppose you can't make a General Stores a listed building. But it seems to me it should have as much a place in our memories as those contained in Mathry's church across the road. Both sit at the pinnacle of one of the earliest hilltop settlements in Preseli, originally an iron-age hill fort.

Today's Church of the Holy Martyrs, built in 1869, is the fifth to occupy the site. As the early nineteenth century chronicler of Pemrokeshire Richard Fenton remarked, the previous church 'was formerly dignified by a steeple, serving as a landmark for mariners from its position on this conspicuous eminence, an exposure that proved the means of its destruction, it being blown down in a storm.'[12]

The church is dedicated to the holy martyrs because it is believed that seven sainted men of the village are buried here. The tale is in the twelfth century Book of Llandaff, now in the possession of the National Library. It describes how St Teilo, a cousin and disciple of St David, and founder of Llandaff Cathedral, was one day walking beside the River Taf at Llanddowror near St Clears in Carmarthenshire. There he came across seven baby boys about to be drowned in the river by their father because he was too poor to provide for them. But instead the Saint intervened, baptised the seven boys, and saw to it that every day they had fish to eat from the river. Thus they became known as *Y Dyfrwyr*, the water men. Eventually they were sent to Mathry where they spent the rest of their lives, becoming known as the seven saints. In the seventeenth and eighteenth centuries a number of cist burials were found near the churchyard, though it's not clear there were seven. Nonetheless, they were instantly called 'the coffins of the martyrs'.

Standing on the road between the Church and the General Stores I reflected on what possible connection there could be between these secular and religious icons. Then it came to me. Both were intensely Irish, the Church because of its Catholic mythology, and the shop because looking at it took me back to the west of Ireland when I first visited in the 1970s. 'Yes,' I told myself. 'This is a small patch of Ireland in Preseli.'

FISHGUARD

Fishguard's Viking name is *Fiskigarde*, straight from the Old Norse, a place for keeping fish. Except there's no fishing here now. Lower Fishguard used to be a herring and pilchard port. At its height in the late eighteenth century, fifty vessels brought in catches, selling them on to Bristol and Ireland.

Then, when fishing declined, Fishguard's role as a ferry port took over. Building the docks began at the turn of the twentieth century when the Great Western Railway reached Fishguard. Rock was mined from the cliff face at Goodwick and the mile-long breakwater constructed. For a while Fishguard became the main port for shipping between Britain and southern Ireland.

Today, however, Fishguard competes with Pembroke Dock and Swansea, and in any event the port's economic impact on the town is small. The lorries and cars just stream straight through. For much of the twentieth century many of Fishguard's people relied on the arms depot at Trecŵn for work, but that closed in the 1980s and nothing has replaced it (see pages 126-130). Fishguard's outlook would be bleak, save for one beacon of hope.

In a word, it's culture. Fishguard needs to become a thriving centre for the arts, activities that are not totally dependent on tourism, that take you right through the year. If that does prove to be Fishguard's future, then Myles Pepper, together with his wife Vicky, a stone carver and letter cutter, will have played a major part in creating it. Over the past three decades they've created Peppers, the arts centre in Fishguard's West Street. It's a combination of art gallery, bar, coffee shop and restaurant, with a space for lectures, debates and the performing arts. It is unusual in ventures of this sort since it has survived and prospered without public subsidy of any kind.

In the 1970s and 1980s the Welsh Arts Council determined that no community in Wales should be more than thirty miles from a performing arts venue. Fishguard fell into an artistic hole between Theatre Mwldan in Cardigan to the north, and the Torch Theatre in Milford Haven to the south. Founded in 1987, Peppers has filled it.

Myles Pepper was also instrumental in founding Y Ffwrwm, a larger but still intimate performance space around the corner, in the former St Mary's church hall. It's a venue for Welsh folk and rock bands. Myles has also had a hand in promoting the Fishguard International Music Festival. Each year in July and August it fills venues across the town with classical music of all kinds.

At Fishguard secondary school where Myles was captain of the rugby team, the coach also taught him metalwork. It was this that prompted his interest in the arts. He trained as a silversmith at Birmingham College of Art and in the early 1970s, at the end of the course, resolved to make his way back home. He got a workbench, put some tools together and started out. At first it was hard going. He lived in a tent in the woods above Fishguard Lower Town before earning enough to afford a bedsit. But work slowly came in, culminating in the run-up to the 1986 National Eisteddfod in Fishguard. The London Pembrokeshire Society commissioned Myles to make the Crown, won by T. James Jones (Jim Parc Nest) who became Archdruid of Wales in 2009.

Myles began teaching one day a week at Carmarthen College of Art and it was there he first became aware of the wider art world. He used to take coachloads of students to London to tour the art galleries. At the College he met Vicky who was studying stone masonry and they decided to set up in business together. Mantrafod, a small holding near Fishguard, became their masonry and metal workshop. Not long after they rented a shop in Fishguard as a centre for craft and applied art. The undertaking met an ambition Myles had always had, to find a way for making art accessible to people. However, the place was never really suitable, too small for one thing.

At this point serendipity stepped in, in the shape of William James. In his late sixties he hailed from Scleddau, just outside Fishguard where he kept a home. However, he spent most of his time in the United States. He was an international tax lawyer, a collector of rare books, and well connected – known to Presidents Kennedy and Johnson. During the Second World War he was a liaison officer between Churchill and De Gaulle. Myles suspects his intelligence activities continued after the war, with MI6.

He dropped into Myles' place from time to time and they became friends. He said it was too small to be an art gallery and told Myles to look out for somewhere bigger and let him know. Eventually, what was to become Peppers, a few doors away, came up for sale. It was a large, three-story building, ideal for conversion into a gallery. But at that stage there was no way Myles and Vicky could have persuaded a building society to give them a mortgage.

Instead William James lent them the £90,000 they needed. They paid interest at the rate he would have received from a bank. By the time James died aged seventy-one three years later, the Arts Centre was well underway. Now Myles and Vicky had an income and a track record sufficient to persuade a building society to lend them the money to buy the place. William James left Myles £3,000 in his will. He spent most of it on a trip to New York to attend his friend's memorial service.

Over the years Peppers has developed a reputation as a restaurant as much as an art gallery. It's very much a family business, with all of Myles and Vicky's six children involved at one time or another. You sense, however, that Myles has found most satisfaction in helping artists who have based themselves in Preseli.

A good example is David Tress. Born in London he studied fine art at Trent Polytechnic. Soon afterwards, in 1975, he hitchhiked to Pembrokeshire, got a job in a pub, and spent a decade developing his distinctive approach to painting. Today he has a studio in Haverfordwest. His work is inspired by nature and the landscape. Swirling mixed-media colours create what looks to me to be a form of abstract impressionism, with wide skies reflecting Pembrokeshire's constantly changing weather. Myles has been influential in the development of Tress's career, promoting exhibitions and persuading London critics to give him attention. In an article introducing Tress's work, *The Times'* art critic John Russell Taylor explained how the interaction between an artist and gallery can have a creative impact:

One might say that the arrival of Myles Pepper in Fishguard and the opening there of his West Wales Arts Centre in 1987 did not necessarily have any radical effect on Tress's attitudes; he would probably have developed in much the same way even if Pepper had never come upon the scene. All the same, Pepper was far from being a conventional art dealer. He arrived with a sense of mission and a desire to test for himself the possibilities of modern art in the area. And thus it was that Pepper and Tress ended up developing very much together.

During the 1980s Tress had had a number of small one-man exhibitions in local galleries, but the scope of the West Wales Arts Centre was much wider, its ambitions more far-ranging. Pepper did not want it to be speaking just to locals, but to provide a national display case for local art, exposing it to a larger and more varied public, as well as bringing in art from further afield to fertilize and enliven the local scene. In all this the presence of Tress was a key factor. He had his first solo show at the Centre in 1991, then again in 1994. He began to exhibit also in Cardiff, and from 1995 in London, at the Boundary Gallery. In 1997 he had a more extensive show which started in Fishguard and travelled to two other venues in Wales. He was beginning willy-nilly to return to the main stream of art, but doing so on his own terms.[13]

Myles Pepper is an inveterate networker. Typically, you'll see him working the phone at his desk behind the large window that fronts on to West Street. He has been a councillor representing Fishguard North East since 2008 and has plenty of calls. On the county council he sits amongst those known in Pembrokeshire as independent Independents.

His lines of communication extend far beyond the county. He has been a member of the Arts Council of Wales and the Crafts Council UK. He has been involved in European funded projects linking Ireland and Wales, and represented Pembrokeshire on the governing committee of the Welsh Centre for International Affairs. Some years ago he was rung up by the Welsh composer John Metcalf, Artistic Director of the Vale of Glamorgan Festival. He had the Latvian Radio Choir coming over but they needed to arrange more performances to make the visit worthwhile. Within a matter of hours Myles had arranged venues in Caernarfon, Lampeter and, of course, Fishguard.

It all comes down to culture and communication. In both respects Fishguard is in good hands.

INVASION TAPESTRY

On the first floor of Fishguard's Town Hall, in a dimly-lit corridor-like exhibition space, is a medieval-looking tapestry. More than thirty metres long and fifty-three centimetres deep, it depicts the events surrounding the last invasion of Britain. That was in February 1797, when one thousand two-hundred French troops swarmed up cliffs in the middle of the night a few miles south of Fishguard.

The first impression is one of a series of cartoon-like images. Using intricate detail and vivid colours, they show ships approaching the coastline, soldiers climbing the cliffs and occupying nearby farmsteads, locals attacking them, Pembrokeshire militia gathering, and the final surrender on Goodwick Sands.

The idea for a tapestry to commemorate the 200th anniversary of the invasion, was conceived in 1992. It took four years to complete and involved the voluntary labour of seventy-seven women from Fishguard and its surrounding area. Hatty Woakes was one. She saw an advert in the local paper asking for volunteers, went to a meeting and was amazed to see more than eighty had turned up in the Community Education Centre. Aged between thirty and eighty-two, the women were Welsh and English speakers, natives and people who had moved into the area, including Hatty. She grew up in California where she attended Berkeley University in the 1950s. There she met and married Mike, from Woking, who was studying to be a mining engineer. Mike's work took them to Canada and then Africa where they lived for several decades in what was then Northern Rhodesia, and in Nigeria.

On a camper van expedition to Britain they discovered Pembrokeshire. Inside the van was a map with coloured climate zones. Pembrokeshire and Cornwall were coloured in yellow indicating they had the balmiest climate. That was in 1990. Hatty soon became a mover and shaker in Fishguard. She set up the North Pembrokeshire Transport Forum which has successfully campaigned for improved train services to the town.

The town proved an ideal location to make a tapestry. Living in the town in the early 1990s were three friends, Audrey Walker, Eirian Short and Rozanne Hawksley. Before they retired they had all been lecturers in the Embroidery Department at London's Goldsmiths College. They became the co-ordinators of the project. Also living in Fishguard was the artist Elizabeth Cramp who had trained at the Royal Academy Schools in London, and specialised in watercolour portraits. The Fishguard Arts Society commissioned her to produce the paintings for the tapestry in what turned out to be the most significant output of her life's work. Her first task was to research the subject, about which she had only the haziest notion. Fortunately, to hand was Bill Fowler, a history teacher at Fishguard High School who lent her a book about the affair.[14]

The French believed that if they landed small forces in Ireland and Britain they would easily provoke an uprising against the Crown. In February 1797 two frigates loaded with well-armed troops set out from Brittany, heading for Bristol with the aim of setting fire to the city. However, strong headwinds pushed them out of the Bristol Channel and round the Welsh coast where a few days later they made landfall in Preseli.

They were first sighted off St David's Head, and then in Fishguard harbour where cannon fire from its small fortress forced them to retreat a few miles to the south. There, at Carreg Wasted Point they anchored in calm weather at 2am and spent the rest of the night ferrying their men and equipment to the shore and up the cliffs.

A mile inland they found the hamlet of Llanwnda with its small Celtic church and scattering of farmhouses. The soldiers promptly looted them, discovering barrels of wine from a recent wreck. Some of them became drunk and deserted. The rest soon found the locals to be far from as friendly as they had imagined. Foraging parties were attacked, one by Jemima Nicholas, a formidable Fishguard cobbler. Legend has it that, wielding a pitchfork, she captured three of the French single-handed and imprisoned them in the town's St Mary's Church.

It is also said that the French were deceived by the appearance of large numbers of women wearing the traditional dress of red shawls and black hats, resembling infantry uniforms. As a result, the French believed the six-hundred or so Pembrokeshire militia who arrived on the scene were far more numerous.

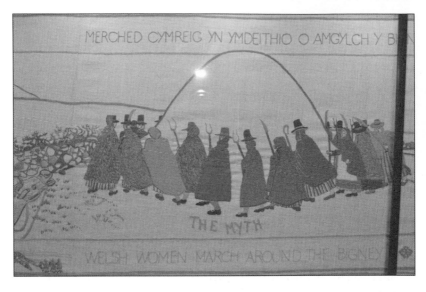

In any event, after a few skirmishes they were persuaded to surrender. Negotiations were held in a house that is now the Royal Oak inn, across the square from the Town Hall in the centre of Fishguard. The French troops, deployed on the heights above Goodwick, marched down and laid their arms on the beach.

Elizabeth Cramp took these events and the myths and stories that surrounded them and produced a series of sketches. To make them manageable the scenes were painted on thirty-seven separate panels that would eventually be joined together. An inspiration was the twelfth century Bayeux tapestry which gives an account of the 1066 Norman invasion of Britain. The design of the Fishguard tapestry follows a similar format and is the same depth. The stitches are mostly the same as those used by medieval embroiderers, with some parts worked in outline while others are solid areas.

It was often the simplest details that were the most puzzling. Would the cows have been Welsh Blacks in 1797? A ninety-year-old man remembered his grandfather speaking of Rowans being the popular breed in his lifetime. Elizabeth declared that memory was sufficiently far enough back for her.

A local builders' merchant donated wood, and husbands of two of the embroiderers constructed frames. Forty metres of an unbleached cotton fabric were sourced in Greece at a fraction of the price it would have cost to buy linen material.

Elizabeth painstakingly traced her drawings which were then transferred to the fabric. This was a crucial process if the quality of the original was to be retained. A number of volunteers helped in what were five processes in all. First came the the original drawing, then painting, tracing, carbon-transfer, and inked outline. The next challenge was to match the crewel wool that would be used for the embroidery to the detail of the painting. Colour charts and instructions were written for every panel. Altogether 178 shades of crewel wool were used. The wool had to be separated into manageable skeins, numbered and compiled to make them readily accessible. Making the colour charts and linking numbers on the drawings with the various wool colours took 150 days. Booklets were produced with recommendations for the stitches that should be used for straight lines, and more intricate and filled-in areas. All this work took months.

When it came to the actual embroidering the women divided into small groups of three or four. They took a few panels each and worked in each other's homes. There were constant references back to Elizabeth and the embroidery co-ordinators to check that details were accurate. Regular meetings between the groups enabled them to compare notes, share ideas, and ensure there was a consistency of approach.

The trickiest bits were the faces of the people, the eyes and moustaches, the rigging of the ships, and the heads, reins and saddles of the horses. Given that so many people were involved, the miracle is the level of consistency of the tapestry as a whole, the vibrancy of the colours and the sense of action and movement. The result is undoubtedly Fishguard's star attraction. Until 2002 it exhibited in St Mary's Church and was seen by 132,000 people. They came from more than sixty countries, many of them from cruise ships visiting Fishguard. Then the tapestry went into storage, until 2007 when it found a permanent home as part of the refurbishment of the Town Hall. Quite apart from the numbers of visitors it attracts, the tapestry is important because of the way it has brought so many people together. They came from the town and the surrounding countryside. The whole thing was only possible because it combined the forces of people native to the area and from outside.

D.J. ABERGWAUN

Number 49 High Street in Fishguard doesn't look particularly important. It's a terraced double-fronted house on the road leading into the town from the south. It has a certain Regency style and was once a pub, The Bristol Trader. Yet, for more than forty years it was the home of D.J. Williams and for that reason alone deserves a plaque.

Williams was so closely associated with the town that he became known as D.J. Abergwaun, its Welsh name. Leaning against a wall in West Street is a stone monument bearing an image of his moon-like bespectacled countenance and the words *Llenor Cenedlgarwr* (Patriotic Literary Man). He came to Fishguard in 1919, aged thirty-four, to teach English and PE in the secondary school.

D.J. was literally a legend in his own lifetime. At five foot six he was a rather diminutive figure and poor eyesight meant he escaped call-up in the First World War. Nonetheless, he radiated warmth and humour and was a fount of stories and anecdotes. His biographer Dafydd Jenkins says he possessed a radiance which won the affection of all who knew him. 'To try and explain that affection is to run the risk of a charge of sentimentality or even blasphemy,' he

wrote. 'But the risk must be taken, and those who felt that D.J. was their friend will not think it improper to say that we loved him because he first loved us.'[15]

In 1925 he became one of the founders of Plaid Cymru. He travelled from Fishguard to the Pwllheli Eisteddfod by train for the inaugural meeting. The train was late so he didn't make it. Nevertheless, he was elected one of the six original members of the executive committee, and became the party's most persistent and industrious campaigner. At that time Plaid Cymru published an annual list of subscribers. In it were pages of contributions sent in by the inhabitants of Fishguard, a shilling here, half-a-crown there, a pound elsewhere. All were the product of D.J.'s ceaseless efforts.

Everyone who knew D.J. has a story to tell. Jane Griffiths, a retired teacher, remembers him from when she was a child living in Goodwick, a mile or so from Fishguard. 'On one occasion D.J. came to our house with a copy of *Y Ddraig Goch*, Plaid's newspaper,' she recalled. 'My father asked how many more he had to deliver that night. D.J. said only one but for a house in Stop and Call, high up

on the steep road above us. My father said he'd take him in the car
and I went along for the ride. We parked in a lane alongside the
house, but instead of going round and down the drive, D.J. just
climbed straight over the wall.'

In 1936 D.J. joined with the leading Plaid figures Saunders Lewis
and Rev Lewis Valentine in setting fire to an RAF Bombing School
in the Llŷn peninsula, following a long campaign of protest. Even
so D.J. had misgivings about taking direct action, doubts that were
overcome by his sense of loyalty. He is said to have declared, 'I
cannot let little Saunders do it all by himself.' The three men served
nine months in Wormwood Scrubs. D.J. claimed he was rather sad
when he was released. Prison life, he declared, had brought him into
contact with a huge variety of fascinating people, all with
enthralling tales to tell.

Throughout his life D.J. prided himself on his physical strength.
When attempts were made to attack Saunders Lewis during
anti-bombing school meetings at Pwllheli, he knocked out one of
the attackers. A bystander protested, 'I thought you were a pacifist.'
To which D.J. replied, 'Yes I am, with the accent on the fist.'[16]

He produced a series of essays and short stories based on
characters he had known as a child. His masterpiece was a memoir
Hen Dŷ Ffarm (The Old Farmhouse)[17], translated by his friend
Waldo Williams (see pages 106-112). An intimate account of the
people of the parishes around Rhydcymerau in northern
Carmarthenshire, it captures the ending of a long period of
community life that had lasted perhaps four-hundred years.

D.J. was not a front-rank politician and neither was he a major
literary figure. So why has he remained in the memory of so many
in Wales? He was quintessentially a man of his own square mile, *dyn
ei filltir sgwâr* as it is put. Yet at the same time he had an
unselfconscious confidence in his Welshness. As he once said, 'It is
impossible to define another national way of life as to define the
smell of flowers. You see the flowers, and you know the difference
between the smell of one and another. Nations are the same. There
is a flavour in a particular society that you don't get in others.'[18]

Then again, D.J.'s social inheritance was more important to him
than his material inheritance. In the mid-1960s he gave the
proceeds of the sale of his family farm at Pen-rhiw to Plaid Cymru.
The £2,000 it realised enabled the party to fight an effective
campaign in the 1966 general election.

Speaking of material possessions D.J. remarked, 'Territorially, my family's inheritance has got smaller over the centuries, until it has almost vanished entirely in my own time. But this has never worried me in the least, since I feel that I have been allowed to keep something that is dearer in my sight than land or possessions – namely the consciousness of the ancient values of our fathers, together with a feeling of responsibility for their continuance.'[19]

Although he was more attuned than most to the sharp contrasts between the different parts of Wales, he saw the differences as enriching a wider unity. This was how he put it:

> As a man from the south who was for some two years a member of a rural and really cultured society in north Wales, and who moreover has for over thirty years the privilege through Plaid Cymru – the only Welsh political party since the days of Owain Glyndŵr – of associating closely with a pretty good number of the people of the north as well as the south, it would be easy for me to succumb to the temptations to pontificate about the differences between south and north, differences in dialect, in temperament and character, as well as in the kind of humour and personal response which springs from those. But at bottom there is in Wales one nation, though it is of mixed blood like every other nation, with all the elements in its destiny and history, since the time before history, woven together into one colourful indissoluble pattern.[20]

Perhaps the most extraordinary thing about D.J.'s life was the manner of his leaving it. It was a Sunday evening in late January 1970 and he had come to his old chapel at Rhydcymerau, to chair a concert arranged for the benefit of the forthcoming National Eisteddfod at Ammanford. The chapel was packed and at the end of the first half he stepped forward to address the audience.

For the first five minutes he had them engulfed in laughter, but then turned to serious matters. He spoke about Rhydcymerau's great characters when he was a boy, about their culture and the things they held dear. He referred to each by name, pointing his finger at the pews where they used to sit. Veteran Plaid leader Gwynfor Evans, was in the audience and later recalled what then happened:

> The long dead were with us again in spirit that evening, he said, a cloud of invisible witnesses who were all about us, and indeed we felt their presence as much as the speaker. He then returned to his seat having put us in a sober frame of mind and at the same time exciting us. He sat down in his corner with his arm resting on the

pine ledge between him and the next pew. He was then seized by a
great shudder and his arm began twitching. And then he died,
sprawled the length of the pew, with his head on my raincoat. D.J.
had himself joined the cloud of witnesses. The circle of his life had
run from Rhydcymerau via the coalmines of Y Betws and Ferndale,
through the Universities of Wales and Oxford, through the schools
of Fishguard and Wormwood Scrubs, and back again to
Rhydcymerau.[21]

Notes

1. Quoted by Terry Breverton in *Wales: A Historical Companion*, Amberley Publishing, 2009, p.164.
2. Terry Breverton, *The Book of Welsh Saints*, Glyndŵr Publishing, 2000.
3. The translation of this excerpt from the poem is by Dafydd Johnston and is contained in Tony Conran, *The Peacemakers* (translated poems by Waldo Willliams), Gomer, 1997.
4. One of them J. Lloyd Jones was convinced that Waldo was 'the competition's greatest poet.' Quoted in Alan Llwyd, *The Story of Waldo Williams, Poet of Peace*, Barddas, 2010, page 103.
5. James Nicholas, *Waldo Williams*, University of Wales Press, 1975, page 37.
6. R.R. Davies (Ed.), *The British Isles 1100-1150: Comparisons, Contrasts and Connections*, John Donald, Edinburgh, 1988.
7. Canon Patrick Thomas, *St Davids Cathedral Shrine and Armenian Memorial*, St Davids and Dewisland Historical Society, July 2016, www.stdavidshistoricalsociety.org.uk
8. Ifor Thomas, *Body Beautiful*, Parthian, 2005.
9. In his entry in the *Encyclopaedia of Wales*, University of Wales Press, 2008, page 825.
10. Sarah Wint, *Sunshine Over Clover: Gardens of Wellbeing*, Orphans Press, 2016.
11. Dan Buettner, *The Blue Zones: Lessons for Living Longer from the People Who've Lived the Longest*, National Geographic Society, 2009.
12. Richard Fenton, *A Historical Tour Through Pembrokeshire*, 1811.
13. John Russell Taylor, Introduction to the monograph *David Tress*, Gomer Press in association with the West Wales Arts Centre, 2002.
14. Commander E.H. Stuart-Jones R.N., *The Last Invasion of Britain*, University of Wales Press, 1950.
15. Dafydd Jenkins, *Writers of Wales – D.J. Williams*, University of Wales Press, 1973.
16. John Davies, 'The inheritance of Waldo and D.J.' in John Osmond (Ed.) *The Preseli Papers*, Plaid Cymru, 2007.
17. D.J. Williams, *Hen Dŷ Ffarm*, Gomer Press, 1953 (a bilingual edition, with Waldo Williams' translation, was published by Gomer in 2001).
18. Quoted in Ned Thomas, *The Welsh Extremist*, Victor Gollanz, 1971
19. *Ibid.*
20. Dafydd Jenkins *op. cit.*
21. Gwynfor Evans, *For the Sake of Wales*, Welsh Academic Press, 1996, page 118.

SOUTH

SAFE HAVEN

Five miles out to sea the four-thousand-ton tanker appeared from the mist like some apparition. I'd been watching the *Joan* on the radar display. Her shape advanced towards us at twelve knots. We were the pilot boat out of Milford Haven, cruising towards the *Joan* at fourteen knots.

They told me it was calm, but I found it impossible to stand as the boat rose and fell. For the crew it was a normal day. Pilot Wayne Lloyd Roberts, a bluff jovial man, stood and donned his coat, a large yellow waterproof that doubles as a life-jacket. It's a piece of kit that costs more than £1,000. Suddenly, he's through the door and moving swiftly round the outside of the cabin. Two deckhands accompany him. The *Joan* looms larger. Both boats slow in the heaving water. This is the crucial moment. Wayne is about to step across the gap between the the two vessels.

'It certainly is dangerous,' he told me. 'But so is crossing the road.'

'I suppose it's relatively calm today.'

'That's when it can be the most hazardous. You think everything is OK. You can lose concentration. If it's rough, you focus more.'

By rough he means stepping between the boats in a winter gale, when a southerly wind can cause a huge swell. Then the distance between the rise and fall of the boats can be as much as twenty feet. I can't imagine what that would be like.

Earlier I'm shown the drill. The deckhands are connected to the boat by wires that follow them as they move around. There's no way they can go overboard. They're either side of the pilot, holding on to him. With one hand he's holding on to a rope attached to the side of the pilot boat. With the other he's reaching out to a rope ladder hanging from the side of the tanker. Seamen are there as well, waiting for him. But he still has to make that step.

It comes down to timing, and the skill of coxswain Rob Evans. He has to judge the swell, choose the moment when to steer close enough.

'Have you ever fallen in?' I ask Wayne.

'Oh, no,' he laughs. 'It does happen though.'

'Do you ever decide not to do it?'

'Most certainly. If it doesn't feel right, I won't go.'

'But don't you feel the pressure? Everything is set up, a big ship

waiting to get in, the expense of putting it all off?'
'It's my life, isn't it? That's what counts. I've got a wife and kids
at home.'
   On this occasion Wayne steps across in an instant. I hardly see
him do it. We pull away and set course for Milford. Looking back, I
see the *Joan* is a liquefied petroleum gas tanker. LPG is emblazoned
across her hull. She left Kaarsto in southern Norway three days ago.
I'm particularly interested in liquefied gas tankers. Especially the
huge ones carrying liquefied natural gas to Milford Haven from the
Quatar gas fields in the Middle East. When I first stood as a
candidate in Preseli in 2007, the project was nearing completion.
Five vast containers, capable of meeting about a quarter of Britain's
gas needs, were being built on the northern shore of the Haven at
South Hook. They're like giant thermos flasks, each having the
cubic capacity of the Albert Hall. Once ashore, the liquefied gas
(temperature −160°C) is warmed up and then pumped through a
long pipeline across southern Wales to the English market.
   Of course, there was no stopping this strategic undertaking. It
had been forced through the planning system at a rapid rate
because of fears that Britain could run out of North Sea gas. What
I was concerned about was that, because of the speed, safety was
not being given the priority it deserved.
   Movement of liquefied natural gas in large tankers around the
world has been going on for decades. And the safety record is
impressive, as Milford Haven Port officials tirelessly point out. The
first LNG tanker arrived in the Haven in March 2009. So far there
has been no major incident.
   However, I discovered there is an industry manual that provides
detailed instructions on the procedures to follow when creating the
facilities for unloading liquefied natural gas. The main fear is if any
of the stuff escapes from a tanker into the sea. There follows what
is called in the industry a 'rapid phase transition'. That is to say, an
explosion. A spill would draw heat from the surrounding water at
an enormous rate. The release of energy would cause an extremely
violent, non-inflammable shock.
   Inevitably, that would take place close to the tanker. There would
be severe damage and the release of a large amount of liquefied gas.
A cloud of gradually warming gas would result, inflammable at the
edges. It would drift in whatever direction the wind took it. South
Hook is located between Herbrandston, Hubberston and Milford,
one of the most densely populated parts of the Preseli constituency.

As soon as the gas cloud met a naked flame it would explode. How do we ensure such an event never happens? The first thing is to prevent a LNG tanker docked at a quayside being struck by another passing vessel, causing a liquefied natural gas spill into the water. The industry guidelines are quite clear:

- Installations should be located as far away as possible from built up areas.
- Jetties where the tankers berth should be located as far away as possible from other passing vessels.
- Jetties should never be located on a bend where passing vessels have to approach towards berthed ships and then turn.

As the guidelines put it: 'The most effective form of protective location is one where there is no possibility of other ships approaching and threatening the security of moored LNG tankers.'

The trouble is that all these injunctions were flouted in Milford Haven. South Hook's jetty is next door to the town of Milford. It juts far out into the Haven in order to reach the main shipping lane's deep water. Here other ships pass within 250 feet, when the guidelines say the minimum distance should be 900 feet. Finally, and most worrying, the jetty is located close to a sharp bend near the mouth of the Haven.

Eight retired Milford Haven Port Authority pilots signed a memorandum drawing attention to all of this, in June 2005. They recommended that the jetty be moved 750 feed northwards, closer to the shore, to bring the risk of collision within an acceptable limit. Of course, this would have required a good deal of dredging. It would also have lengthened the planning application process. There are a protected species of shell fish on the sea bed here. The whole project would have been held up.

Now, a decade later, I'm keen to hear from the professionals about the safety procedures in place to prevent an accident. After all, LNG carriers are really big. At 345 metres, they're more than three times as long as the *Joan*. And at 164,000 tons, they're more than forty times as heavy. They carry 266,000 metres of liquefied gas. All the same, I receive a good deal of reassurance.

When they come into the Haven the LNG tankers are connected to five powerful tugs. One goes ahead, to make sure there's no shipping in the way. These tankers take a mile to stop. Two tugs bring up the rear. If the tanker's steerage were to break down they can take over. They practice this procedure regularly. The fourth and fifth tugs are to the port and starboard. All the tugs are on hand to manoeuvre the tanker into its mooring at South Hook, gently pushing it against its berth.

Moreover, there are always two pilots aboard the tankers when they enter and leave the port. One is in charge of the ship, the other the tugs. So, as I say, I'm reassured. And the track record speaks for itself. You're just left with the question: what is an acceptable risk? As Wayne Lloyd Roberts put it, 'You take a risk crossing the road.' But then, he says, 'If it doesn't feel right I won't go.'

MILFORD

It was a warm April evening in 2006 when I embarked on my first canvassing expedition as an Assembly candidate in Preseli. With me were my seven-year-old daughter Morwenna and my agent Rhys Sinnett. We ambled down Priory Road where he lives in Milford Haven. Everyone knew him, greeted him warmly. We barely got past thirty doors that evening. Every stop entailed an extended conversation, about family, friends, children, how so-and so was doing.

My daughter was impressed. 'I think you're going to get in here Dad,' she said.

I was not so sure. What registered with me was the number of people who were puzzled when Rhys introduced me as Plaid Cymru's candidate in the forthcoming election. 'Didn't know you was Plaid, Rhys,' they said, causing him to laugh. He had been the member for this ward on Milford Town Council since 1999, and on Pembrokeshire County Council since 2004. He had been Milford's Mayor in 2005. But for these people the only label they knew him by was Rhys.

Fast forward twelve years and he and are once more walking through Milford, on another warm April day. This time he was pointing out some of the interesting historical sites. Again we were interrupted, every few yards it seemed. There was a cousin he hadn't seen in a while. A man across the road called, 'Off for a libation Rhys?' A passing car beeped its horn.

'The whole town knows you,' I say.

'I've been here all my life.'

We're leaning on railings overlooking the harbour. For much of the twentieth century Milford was a major fishing port, and as late as the 1980s trawlers packed the harbour. Both of Rhys's grandfathers worked in the port.

'You could walk across trawlers from one side of the basin to the other,' he said. 'Every day was a pay day.'

Today, the harbour is a marina, full of yachts and motor boats and surrounded by new shops and flats, surely a sign of where things are heading. 'Tourism and all its works are the future,' I suggest.

'There's not much else,' Rhys agrees.

Milford's economy has had a chequered history. It started out in the early nineteenth century as a newly-minted whaling town. Then it morphed into a military base with a naval yard and later a munitions factory. With the completion of the docks from the late nineteenth century it became a prosperous port with ships sailing as far as India and America.

For most of this period Milford's main income was from fishing. At its peak, up to and beyond the Second World War, there were more than four thousand people employed in the industry. There were ice factories, a large fish market with auctions six days a week. Catches bound for Billingsgate in London were loaded on to trains at the back of the market. In 1946 the port handled a record catch of 60,000 tons. In 1950 there were still ninety-seven first-class trawlers, and the value of the catch landed was £1,642,080. Hake was the chief fishery and its grounds stretched down the Atlantic shelf as far as the west coast of Africa. However, hake proved too easy to catch, and over-fishing destroyed the grounds. By the end of 1950s it was clear that the Milford's days as a fishing port were coming to an end.

In the 1960s, Milford took off as an oil port, an era that continues with giant tankers carrying liquefied natural gas from Quatar. They anchor at wharfs that stretch into the Haven either side of the town. South Hook is off Herbrandston to the west, and Dragon LNG off Waterston to the east. The chimneys of the oil refineries and the power station line the horizon from virtually every vantage point. But there is a strong sense that the town's oil industry, like fishing, will inevitably come to an end. Depletion is the reason. For fishing it was over-fishing and quotas, and eventually even Quatar's gas reserves will be exhausted.

Meanwhile, Milford with its population of fifteen thousand feels strangely on a limb, even for peripheral Preseli. There is a lot of poverty here, a lot of poor housing, and even poorer prospects for many young people unable to find apprenticeships or even move away. Youth unemployment hovers around twenty per cent. It wasn't meant to be like this.

Until the eighteenth century Milford didn't exist. It came into being as a result of an Act of Parliament in 1790, promoted by the landowner, Sir William Hamilton, Britain's emissary in Naples. As the Act stated, it allowed him 'to make and provide Quays, Docks, Piers and other erections and to establish a Market, with proper Roads and Avenues there to respectively within the Manor or Lordship of Hubberston and Pill in the County of Pembroke.'

That was the grand vision when Lord Hamilton's nephew the Hon Charles Greville began to create present-day Milford, with its grid pattern of streets and its harbour. Greville also passed on to Hamilton his mistress, the famous beauty Emma Hart, muse of the portrait artist George Romney. 'A sweeter bedfellow does not exist,' Greville told his uncle. She became Lady Hamilton when she was twenty-five and he sixty. Later she also became Lord Nelson's consort in a famous menàge-à-trois. This has left its own particular legacy in Milford, to wit the Lord Nelson Hotel that enjoys an imperious position overlooking the waterway.

Milford needs a fresh vision. Perhaps this can be found in the Port Authority's 2017 document *Milford Waterway*. It aims 'to attract world-class events that deliver significant visitor numbers and global online reach to positively impact on Wales' international tourism reputation.'

But that's just gloss. What Milford needs is leadership. Rhys Sinnett says the town had its greatest sense of purpose and cohesion in the 1960s when the Urban District Council was in charge. But this vanished as part of the 1974 reorganisation which created Dyfed County Council, in place of Pembrokeshire, Carmarthen and Ceredigion. In its wake came Milford's powerless Town Council.

This destructive upheaval was partially righted in 1996 when Dyfed was abandoned and Pembrokeshire County Council restored. However, power stopped at Haverfordwest. Milford was still left out on a limb. Now there is a talk of re-creating Dyfed as part of another Wales-wide reorganisation of local government. Rhys says if that happens there must be a rearguard action to ensure some crumbs are cast Milford Town Council's way. I ask him about his own ambitions. 'I might have one more crack at being Mayor,' he says. 'Of course, there's no real power attached to it but all the same it gives you a platform.'

If he gets it I'm sure the people of Milford will be cheering him on.

QUAKER WHALERS

Starbuck Road and Greville Road are not far from the Quaker Meeting House near the centre of Milford. Both are resonant of the town's whaling origins that provide a curious twist to history. Indeed, the story entails a complete reversal of the pattern of migration from Europe to America. For a brief moment at the end of the eighteenth century, a small group of Quaker whalers relocated in the opposite direction.

Charles Francis Greville, the second son of the Earl of Warwick, was responsible for founding Milford in the 1790s. Acting for the landowner, his uncle Sir William Hamilton, he began building a quay and a completely new settlement. Before that there was virtually nothing along the northern shores of the Haven, apart from a few farm houses.

Greville was a chancer and wheeler-dealer. He persuaded a group of whalers from Nantucket Island, off the Massachusetts coast, to use Milford as their base. Samuel Starbuck and his wife Abigail were the first to arrive in August 1792. It is no coincidence that the chief mate in Herman Melville's classic whale-hunting story *Moby Dick*, published in 1851, was of a line of Quakers named Starbuck that hailed from Nantucket.

The Starbucks were closely followed by Timothy Folger and his wife Abial. Then Starbuck's son Daniel came with his wife Alice, and their children. In all about fifteen families arrived in that first year, along with five whaling boats. Over the following decade fifteen more boats and some five hundred seamen joined them. About three times as many settled ashore, working in ancillary trades in the whale-oil business. They were boat builders, sail makers, coopers, carpenters, smiths, whale-oil refiners and candle makers.

They came because they were Quakers. They had refused to take sides in the American War of Independence against Britain between 1775 and 1783 and suffered accordingly. They were harassed and looted by both the American and British navies. Their industry was decimated. A group decamped to Dartmouth in Nova Scotia, and others travelled to London to explore the prospects for establishing a base in Britain. That was when they met Charles Greville.

He must have been persuasive since at the time very little had been done to build the port at Milford. Some advice was sent to the Nantucket whalers by one Thomas Owen, writing from Waterford in Ireland. He described the general circumstances they would find, noting there was a small Meeting of Friends (Quakers) in Haverfordwest:

> People of Pembrokeshire rather comfortable in themselves, civil to strangers and hospitable in their houses having little or no propensity to trade farther than the verge of their respective farms; coal mines, slate or limestone quarry. Great number of hardy watermen employed at herring fishing, carrying lime, coal and culm round the coast, dragging for oisters etc. Wages small.
>
> Manufacturing stockings coarse and fine; all yarn made of wool made in the Country. Great quantity of coarse woollen Cloth made in a neighbouring county of Merioneth sent to the London market undyed, for clothing the Army, use of Slobb Shops etc. etc.

Centrical situation of Milford Haven, about 18 hours sail to Bristol, same to Cork and Dublin, 10 to Waterford, and about 18 to Liverpool. The first mentioned but more especially the last, carry on a very extensive trade to the interior parts of the kingdom by the long rivers and canells; great advantage by getting to her mooring immediately from the sea... It's also well worth observing the contiguity of Milford with Ireland where the Newfoundland Fishermen come from all parts of England to victual or man.[1]

Doubtless this sounded promising. However, when they got to Milford the Nantucket whalers found they had to begin from scratch, building their houses and many of the port facilities themselves.

The small community was given a boost in 1794 when they were joined by a wealthy Quaker family from Dunkirk. It came as a result of the increasing political turmoil in revolutionary France. Benjamin Rotch and his large family, who had already lived in London for a while, established themselves at Castle Hall in Steynton, on the northern edge of Milford. The large house came with extensive gardens, a hot house, conservatories, woods, and an outstanding view of the Haven. There, and also aboard his yacht, Benjamin lavishly entertained his fellow Quakers and leading members of Pembrokeshire society. Seventy years later his daughter Eliza recorded a fascinating insight into the development of Milford and its whaling industry:

A large hotel was built and Mr Greville's influence caused a custom house and post office to be established there. He granted long leases of land, at very low rents, and houses sprang up like magic. My father had all the land he wanted for warehouses, for a mere nominal ground-rent, and Mr Greville obtained for him all the privileges and bounties that he had enjoyed in France... Coopers, sailmakers, ship carpenters, and all the other tradesmen necessary to my father's business, came and settled in Milford, on the prospect of the whaling fishery being carried on from that port, and great was the excitement and satisfaction when the first vessel arrived from America loaded with sperm-oil. The cargo was sent round to London in coasting vessels, and the ship was immediately re-fitted for a voyage to the Pacific Ocean.[2]

Eliza also bore witness to how strange it was for her family, and by implication those of their fellow Quaker whalers to find themselves living in Milford at that time:

Wales being a conquered country, and the peasantry and yeomanry still speaking a different language from their conquerors, their civilization did not keep pace with that of England. It was allowed to be a hundred years behind, and the manners and customs of all classes were of course very different from those of the English.... It was a great trial to my parents to leave a large circle of congenial friends, and the high state of civilization which London afforded, and plant themselves in a strange land and among such a different kind of people.[3]

During these years the Quakers played a major role in Milford's affairs. Timothy Folger was appointed American Consul and a surveyor of ships. He also supervised the large Quaker store-house used for importing grain from America. This contributed to the averting of famine in Pembrokeshire during a period of much social and political upheaval.

Samuel Starbuck founded a bakery and a mill for grinding flour. His son, also named Samuel, was in charge of wrecks and their cargoes. Another son, Daniel, was a merchant and farmer and established a brewery. Benjamin Rotch's son Francis, along with Samuel Starbuck Jnr and others, established the Milford and Haverfordwest Bank.

Quaker meetings were established in Milford from 1794, with Daniel Starbuck as clerk. Both his sons were also involved. Daniel Jnr refused to pay Anglican church tithes, while Samuel had to pay a volunteer to serve in the local militia because he refused to be enlisted.

In 1811 the present-day Meeting House was completed, at a cost of £563, with Benjamin Rotch donating £100. However, this was destined to be the highpoint of the Quaker whaling influence in Milford. In 1812 Rotch suffered a financial disaster when three of his ships were sunk at the outset of another war between Britain and America. The following year, unwilling to comply with the Quaker rule against paying tithes, he resigned his membership.

Then the price of sperm whale oil, which was mainly used for oil lighting, plummeted. The end of the Napoleonic wars in 1815 had led to a flood of imported American oil. At the same time, the Scottish engineer and inventor William Murdoch perfected the use of town gas for street lighting. The bottom dropped out of the sperm whale oil trade as a result. In 1819 Rotch sold up his possessions and with his family left Milford for London. His departure was the beginning of the end of the town's whaling era.

His leaving also marked a point when the distinctive Quaker community began dissolving into the general life of the town. What legacy has been left by Milford's Quaker whalers? They were largely responsible for establishing the core of the new town, the American lay-out of parallel streets, and many substantial buildings. The most important was the Meeting House, a Grade II listed building. It is late Georgian with plain but elegant elevations and high-quality woodwork. Attendance through much of the nineteenth century was sporadic and for long periods the Meeting House was closed. However, a small revival occurred at the beginning of the twentieth century and gradually intensified as the years went by. In the 1950s the poet Waldo Williams became a member. Today the Society of Friends are once again firmly established in Preseli, focused on Milford but with offshoots in Haverfordwest, St Davids, and Fishguard.

Quakerism was founded by George Fox in Westmoreland in the seventeenth century and it remains the Society's heartland. The large Meeting House in Kendal is home to a tapestry created over a period of fifteen years during the 1970s and 1980s. It has seventy-five separate panels, each describing some aspect of Quaker history and service. One is devoted to Milford. At its centre is an image depicting the arrival of the Nantucket whalers in 1792. Alongside is an image of the Meeting House. 'Live adventurously'

is the panel's bold injunction, a reference from *Advices and Queries*, a 1656 text which prompts Quakers on how to conduct their lives.[4] Also on the panel is an image of Waldo Williams (see pages 106-112), sitting amidst the Preseli hills, together with the last two lines of his poem 'Y Tangnefeddwyr' (The Peacemakers):

Gwyn ei byd yr oes a'u clyw,
Dangnefeddwyr, plant i Dduw.

Blest is the generation that hears them,
Peacemakers, children of God.

NEYLAND

' "When the legend becomes the truth, believe the legend." – do you know where that comes from?' Clive James asks, a sparkle in his eye. I shake my head. 'It's a quote from *The Man Who Shot Liberty Valence*, the 1962 John Ford Hollywood Western.'

Clive explains that in the film the Man who apparently shot the outlaw, didn't. Instead it was his competitor for the girl they're both chasing, played by John Wayne. In the end, however, the legend turns out to be more powerful than the reality.

Clive is a volunteer guide with the National Park and today he is showing me around Neyland's waterfront. There's a lot more going on here than meets the eye. And, despite Clive's cautionary warning, I believe everything he says.

He points to a yellow buoy that's bobbing in the Haven no more than twenty yards away. 'Do you know what lies beneath that?' Once again I shake my head. 'A Second World War Sunderland Flying Boat is under the water there, an icon in its day. But it would take more than £7 million to lift it out and restore it, so I don't see it happening.'

I gesture to an interesting looking survey ship moored in mid-stream. In the space of a heartbeat Clive says, 'My wife's sister's daughter's husband used to be the captain.' One half of Neyland he knows, the other he's related to.

Clive then says he's going to show me the man who made the town. We walk along the marina front and gaze at a magnificent near life-size statue of Isambard Kingdom Brunel. Among his many engineering feats he brought the Great Western Railway to these

shores in 1856. In the process he created the town we see today. The
statue was placed here in 1999, following a fund-raising campaign
that took eight years to reach the required £30,000. It was stolen in
2010, for the bronze metal. Luckily it was insured. In 2013 a replica
arrived, now protected by bollards and CCTV cameras.

We walk a short distance further and arrive at a spot on the
quayside where Brunel's station once stood. This was the terminus
of the Great Western Railway, 286 miles from London. Brunel's
vision was that passengers would be able to buy just one ticket at
Paddington and travel from London to New York, changing at
Neyland to a Great Western steamship.

That didn't quite happen. However, Brunel did design the *Great
Eastern* sailing paddle steamship that had a capacity of four thousand
passengers. Launched in London in 1858 she was the biggest ship
built in Britain for forty years. She sailed out of Milford Haven for
New York on a number of occasions in the early 1860s. Great Eastern
Terrace in Neyland is named after her. Thousands of people made
the trip to the town on the train from London just to view her.

When a telegraph cable was first laid across the Atlantic in 1858 only one vessel was up for the job, the *Great Eastern*. She laid 2,500 miles of cable from Valentia in Ireland to Heart's Content in Newfoundland. A smaller vessel completed the link, between Wexford and Abermaw on the north Preseli coast.

Brunel's statue clutches a model of the *Great Eastern* in one hand. The other is holding his earlier *Great Western* paddle steamer, launched in 1838. However, she never came to Milford Haven.

Brunel's famous broad gauge rails are still embedded in the concrete on the quayside. Another line of them make a protective fence along the edge of the dock. But apart from that there's no trace of the station. The shunting yard and the cranes that lifted goods from the trains on to the ships have disappeared.

Clive James takes in the scene and shakes his head sadly. Then, with a dramatic gesture, he takes a red safety vest from his rucksack and puts it on. 'This is the vest my father wore when he drove the last passenger train out of Neyland on 15 June 1964,' he announces, evident pride in his voice. His father was one of a family of six children that grew up in the town and all four of the boys worked for the railway.

In those days Neyland was a railway town, but no longer. For a while it was a trawling town. Clive points across the mouth of Westfield Pill that borders the northern side of the town. We look at Barnlake Point. On the landward side facing us there's a strange cutting that drives deeply into the bank. 'There used to be an ice factory there,' Clive explains. 'Trawlers came from all over to load up. Some came from England's east coast on their way out to the Atlantic fishing grounds.' There's nothing left to show for that industry now. Instead, there's a gently sloping green bank, dotted with executive-style houses enjoying splendid views across the Haven.

These days it's difficult to get a sense of what sort of town Neyland is, though the dockside and Westfield Pill provide one answer. Like Milford five miles downstream, their waters are afloat with yachts and motorboats, leisure craft rather than working vessels.

For most of his life Clive worked for the Midland Bank, in south and west Wales, and later for the ill-fated Welsh Health Promotion Authority. Then he became head of external relations with Torfaen Council. One thing that has stood him in good stead is that he learnt Welsh in Pembroke (Bush) Grammar School. He says he was inspired by the Preseli poet Waldo Williams (see pages 106-112). It was before the Cledddau Bridge was built, so he took the ferry across from Neyland every day.

"I brushed up on the Welsh in my twenties and eventually was seconded by the bank to be financial secretary to the National Eisteddfod,' he tells me, again a touch of pride is in his voice. 'I also wrote Torfaen's Welsh language policy.' I imagine I hear him saying, 'Not bad for a boy from Neyland.' But instead he just remarks, 'I can't complain.'

As we pass further along the marina with its flotillas of yachts – 'Gin alley,' Clive mutters dismissively – I remark that on this very spot I once interviewed Baron Gordon Parry of Neyland, on television. It was the early 1980s and we were talking about the town's forthcoming marina development. Parry was chairman of the Wales Tourist Board at the time.

But Clive tops my story. 'I knew him as a boy,' he says. 'Once he knocked me off my bike.' He pauses, before adding, 'All the same we Neylanders stick together. When he heard I was working in the Midland Bank in Cardiff he came in and transferred the Tourist Board's account to us.'

BLACK DIAMONDS

Hook is four miles down the Western Cleddau river from Haverfordwest, centre of a forgotten industry. It's a village of about six hundred people and today there's no sign of any industry at all. Yet at the beginning of the nineteenth century there were at least fifteen coal mines sunk around here. They had names like Stumpy Audit Pit, American Pit, Sprinkle Pit and Winding Pit. Coal mining carried on until 1948. But today virtually all trace of it is gone.

I say *virtually* no sign except that, as you arrive the Hook village road sign is unambiguous. *Pentref y Diemwnt Du*, it proclaims, the Black Diamond Village. This refers to the coal being anthracite, with its high carbon content and low proportion of volatile matter, making it almost smokeless. It's said Queen Victoria would have no other coal than Hook's 'black diamonds' to fuel her royal yacht. It was particularly suited to drying salt and heating brewery malt houses. Some of it went to the Guinness brewery in Dublin.

Hook has its name because it is located on a sharp, curving bend of the Western Cleddau, just before it meets the Eastern Cleddau

where both flow into the Daugleddau. A few generations ago this was one of the most isolated spots in Preseli, if not the whole of Wales. Its only connection with the outside world was by water. Until 1922 there was no road out of Hook. There were rough tracks through woods to Haverfordwest, but for most of the year they were impassable. Unless you went by boat, you first had to go along the shore to the south via Llangwm, a fourteen-mile journey. Pembrokeshire's chief constable Fred Summers said he felt ashamed that the women of Hook arrived in Haverfordwest covered in mud having been forced to walk over deep rutted riverbanks and cart tracks. Doctors refused to travel to the village after dark.

The village was so isolated it developed its own dialect and vocabulary. It had more than a hundred distinctive expressions. *Beatland* was a bonfire of brushwood; *croglins* were small potatoes; *creath* a scar; *evil* was a three-pronged fork; *enmack* an ant; *squale* a crowd, and so on.

It took sixty years of campaigning to secure a road the few miles northwards to Freystrop, and thence to Haverfordwest. Pembrokeshire County Council only agreed to build it after the Hook Road Committee had raised £1,200 towards the cost. Colonel Lort-Phillips of Lawrenny contributed £200, and the Hook Colliery Company donated £100. But most of the money came from workmen and farmers when colliers at Hook were earning little more than £1 a week.

It was around this time that Hook's production of coal reached its height, rising to 42,000 tons in 1934 and falling back to around 20,000 during the Second World War. At its peak Hook's collieries employed more than 250 men. The early workings were shallow shafts, just four to six metres deep, with the coal hauled up using a windlass. But by the late nineteenth centuries deep mines such as Old Aurora and Amen had opened.

A boost came in 1929 with the building of the Hook Colliery Railway that connected the village with the Great Western Railway at Johnston midway between Haverfordwest and Milford. Before that an aerial ropeway and later a tramroad connected the coal workings to the quay alongside the Western Cleddau. The coal had to be loaded on to small boats, and then trans-shipped to larger vessels lower down the river at Llangwm and Lawrenny. Some coal was loaded into barges and hauled by rowing boat to Haverforwest.

The Pembrokeshire coalfield is a western extension of the main South Wales measures. They fall under the sea west of the Gower and emerge out of Carmarthen Bay at Saundersfoot and Amroth. They carry on westwards in a four-mile wide strip until they reach the coast at Little Haven where they turn north to Newgale. Mining first began here on coastal outcrops in the fourteenth and fifteenth centuries. A hundred years later there were more pits inland of Saundersfoot Bay. But by the nineteenth century mining was mainly concentrated around Hook.

As I drive slowly through the linear village there's no sign of mining. I stop and approach an elderly couple as they're getting out of their car. Neville James turns out to be the son of a miner. His father Jack worked in Hook's mines for eighteen years. Neville tells me his father finished during the war when he joined the army. 'The collieries carried on until 1948 but by then the men were working ankle deep in water,' he says. So close to the coast the ingress of seawater was a continual problem.

Neville points me to a path leading steeply down to a valley below the line of bungalows. He says I might see some remnants of the old workings there. I clamber down but find nothing but woodland, thick scrub and brambles. Pushing through the undergrowth I come across a stern notice: 'Private: Keep Out'.

Later, in the village shop, an austere windowless building, I ask if they have any publications about Hook. The man behind the counter shakes his head but says I should knock on Richard Howells' door a short distance away. 'He's our local historian.'

I find Richard painting his fence. And, indeed, he knows a lot about the village's history. He tells me the old works have become too dangerous to visit, but gives me a locally-produced booklet and DVD.[5] He also points me to a Memorial Garden near the centre of the village. This is sited on the spot where the miners' built their Institute in 1921. Here they had a library, could read the daily papers, hold meetings, and play snooker. The Tute, as it was called, was also a venue for weddings, wakes, dances and amateur dramatics.

By the early 2000s it had fallen into disrepair and there was no option but to pull it down. In its place are a social club and the memorial gardens. Half the village turned out for the unveiling of a plaque, with its image of a winding wheel, in July 2011.

'Anthracite was mined in Hook for over six-hundred years,' it says. 'In far off days, women and children as young as six laboured in appalling conditions to earn enough to survive. The Black Diamonds they dug were exported all over the world. The playing field, the social club and the garden are all part of the valuable legacy of those brave workers who toiled deep underground at Hook colliery. Their sacrifice will not be forgotten.'

DALE PENINSULA

I'm walking the seven miles of cliff path around the Dale Peninsula thinking about the First World War. I was born mid-way through the twentieth century, the most violent in human history. Yet I've never fired a shot in anger and certainly haven't had one fired at me. But that was not the case for earlier generations in Dale.

I pause at the village cemetery, which I think the most poignant in Wales. In fields close to West Dale beach, some distance from St James Church, it's reminiscent of those you find in the Western Isles of Scotland. Lonely patches of green with grey headstones amidst the heather, they flow down to the white sands at the water's edge.

Dale's small cemetery has a similar atmosphere. In the middle is a plinth bearing the white statue of a soldier. His right hand is placed on a rifle that's resting upright. Below is the inscription: 'Far from the land of their fathers these five sleep among the brave.' These five! Dale's population during the First War couldn't have

been more than fifty. So that's at least ten per cent of the hamlet's people, and probably most of the young men. In fact, three of them were brothers. The list reads:

> Private John Codd, Welsh Regiment, fell at Messina Ridge, 7 June 1917, aged 27; Signaller Walter Edwards, Welsh Guards, fell at Passchendale, 1 December 1917, aged 26; Signaller Thomas Edwards, Royal Garrison Artillery, fell at Poperinche, 23 December 1917, aged 29; Bomber Arthur Edwards, Royal Horse Artillery, fell at Ypres, 25 March 1918, aged 27; and Private Clive Reynolds, died of wounds at Trier, 30 July 1918, aged 19.

The cemetery lies in an old river valley on the line of what is known as the Ritec Fault. Responsible for the formation of the Milford Haven waterway, it carries on to Tenby. Then it passes under Carmarthen Bay to the Gower peninsula, which it nearly separates from the mainland. Long ago it separated the Dale peninsula and for a while it was an island.

Walking the cliff path along the peninsula's western edge and gazing across to Skomer and Skokholm islands it feels as though it still could be. Iron age hill forts line the route at prominatories that separate Welshman's from Frenchman's bays. One is at the expressively named Vomit Point. Before long you reach St Ann's

Head and the mouth of Milford Haven, nearly two miles across. It looks a wide enough entry for shipping but the shelving rocks beneath make this deceptive. The channel allowing passage for the huge oil tankers is barely half-a-mile wide. The tankers begin their angle of approach ten miles out to sea. They line up to large navigation towers mounted more than fifty metres high on St Ann's Head. First they follow a north-easterly route, followed by a dog leg change of direction to the east. I sat and watched a large tanker leaving the Haven. It came towards me from its berth further up the Haven, and then took a sharp turn west to pass just below me. It was little more than a stone's throw away, or so it seemed. A pilot cutter sped ahead, turned and waited while the giant ship majestically headed for the open ocean. After clearing the last buoy it hove to, swinging broadside to the land allowing the cutter to come alongside to pick up the pilot. If I'd had binoculars I could have seen him jump.

The pilots earn their money. In February 1996 the *Sea Empress* stranded on St Ann's Head, causing a spillage of 72,000 tones of crude oil and catastrophic damage to the Pembrokeshire coast. Thousands of seabirds were killed and 120 miles of beaches contaminated, stretching around the Pembrokeshire coast into Carmarthen Bay to the south. Mercifully the prevailing winds protected the Skomer marine conservation zone to the north. Nevertheless, some beaches were buried under a foot of oil. And although the immediate cleanup took place remarkably quickly, at a cost of £60 million, it was the best part of a decade before the ecology of the shoreline fully recovered.

Since then a much enhanced port control operation means the immediate circumstances that led to the spillage would be unlikely to recur. An inexperienced pilot was allowed to guide the *Sea Empress* in. He took her too close to the north shore, which led to the grounding. That was on a late Friday evening. By the middle of the following day only about 250 tons of oil had been lost. Five Milford Haven tugs had managed to free her from the rocks and there was an option to tow her further out to sea, away from immediate danger. The imminence of a Force 9 gale made this a pressing necessity.

The pilot aboard the *Sea Empress* radioed the Port Authority's Control Room to ask permission from the Harbour Master and received the following, now infamous reply: 'I agree with you but I have a room full of men saying No.' They were men from the salvagers, the oil and insurance companies, the coastguard, and the Department of Transport Pollution Control Unit. Their collective and soon to be mistaken view was that the *Sea Empress* could be emptied of her cargo where she was and then towed to safety. The gale duly arrived, the towlines connecting the tugs broke and the *Sea Empress* was thrown about the rocks for twelve hours, losing most of her cargo of crude in the process.

Lessons have been learnt from the decisions that led up to this disaster. But in some respects they are being forgotten. In the wake of the incident, emergency towing vessels with much greater capacity than those operating in the Haven, were put in place around the coast of the United Kingdom – at Dover, Orkney, Stornoway, and Falmouth. The last provided cover for the Welsh coast.

However, in 2011 the Conservative government scrapped this fleet, as a cost saving measure. Questioned about this, the Maritime and Coastguard Agency said, 'The government believes that responsibility for ensuring the operational safety of ships is properly a matter for the commercial shipping industry.' Meanwhile, other European countries, including Spain, France, Norway, and Germany are maintaining government financed emergency towing vessels. And, of course, since the *Sea Empress* event we have much larger vessels coming into Milford Haven, carrying liquefied natural gas from Quatar, a much more unstable and dangerous cargo (see pages 186-189).

Dismissing these thoughts, I pressed on, leaving St Ann's Head behind, with its lighthouse and outbuildings now converted into holiday cottages. Ahead of me is Mill Bay. Henry Tudor landed here on Sunday 7 August in 1485. This was prior to his march through Wales to defeat Richard III at the Battle of Bosworth a fortnight later. Mill Bay is a tiny creek right at the mouth of the Haven. There couldn't have been much room for his four thousand men, and their horses. Most were French. There were about a thousand Scots and a few hundred Welsh. Many were mercenaries.

Why did he land here? In the first place he could be sure he would be unopposed at such a remote spot. Even so, Richard III had observers at Dale three miles round the headland and news of the landing carried quickly. The king had wind of it in a matter of days.

Henry, or rather Jasper Tudor his uncle, had another good reason to choose Preseli as the launch pad for siezing the throne. Henry was born in Pembroke Castle in 1547 on the other side of the Haven. The Tudors were Lancastrians. Uncle Jasper was nominally Earl of Pembroke. He had fled to France with his

fourteen-year-old nephew in 1461 when Henry IV became the first Yorkist king. Henry died in 1483 and was succeeded by Richard III who was regarded as an usurper by the Lancastrian cause. Henry Tudor, now aged twenty-eight, was their standard bearer since his mother Lady Margaret Beaufort was a member of the Lancastrian branch of the royal family. Henry was half-English, a quarter French, and a quarter Welsh. But that was enough to persuade many of his countrymen to his cause.

For two weeks Henry marched at an average of fourteen miles a day through Wales to England, via Haverfordwest, Cardigan, Aberystwyth, Machynlleth and Welshpool. Along the way he gathered a host of Welsh followers. At Bosworth, near Leicester in the heart of England, much of his army was Welsh speaking. Prominent among them was thirty-six-year-old Rhys ap Thomas who reputedly placed Richard's muddy crown on Henry's head.

Rhys was based at Carew Castle, the highest most navigable point on the Carew river at the eastern end of Milford Haven. He joined Henry at Shrewsbury with about two thousand men from south-west Wales, having marched a different route. They went via Carmarthen, Llandovery, Brecon and Newtown. Rhys led them under his family's banner, blazoned with the historic three ravens of Urien, the sixth century king of Rheged.[6] One contemporary ballad narrated how:

...Rhys ap Thomas draws Wales with him,
A worthy sight it was to see
How the Welsh rose wholly with him
And shogged them to Shrewsbury.[7]

The reason Rhys took a different route was probably to mislead Richard III who thought he had his support. Legend has it Rhys swore to the king that Henry Tudor would only come to Wales 'over my bellie'. But he was already thinking of throwing in his lot with the Lancastrians. He resented the fact that Richard had kept his four-year-old son at court in London, as hostage against his loyalty.

When Henry had successfully taken Dale, it is said Rhys came face-to-face with him a few miles inland on the road to Haverfordwest, at Mullock Bridge. To keep his oath of loyalty to Richard the legend – and it is a legend – is that Rhys lay down under the bridge 'bellie-up', so Henry could ride over him.

At Bosworth Rhys is credited with delivering with his lance axe the final thrust that killed Richard III, by then isolated from his men and unseated from his horse. The poet Guto'r Glyn (1412-1493), referring to Richard's emblem of a boar wrote afterwards that Rhys had 'killed the boar, shaved his head.' Certainly Rhys was well rewarded. Henry knighted him three days after the battle and made him Chamberlain of South Wales. He celebrated these honours with a famous tournament at Carew Castle, an event commemorated regularly for the tourists to this day. In 1505 he was made a Knight of the Garter.

After Mill Bay there are two more to traverse, Watwick and Castlereach Bays, before reaching Dale Point and its magnificent views far into Milford Haven. Here you'll find Dale Fort, built in 1856 as part of a system of twelve fortifications and barracks around the entrance to Milford Haven. They were designed to deter Napoleon III of France from attacking the naval bases in the Haven. But this was not a realistic threat and the Fort's seven large smooth bore muzzle-loaded guns facing out to sea were never fired in anger.

Today the fort is a field centre, founded in 1947 by the Field Studies Council, to introduce Preseli's fauna and flora to streams of visiting school children. Before I passed it my boot kicked into some flora at the edge of the coast path. Lo and behold out sprang a handful of Pembrokeshire early potatoes. A little later I discovered a few mushrooms and collected those as well, though that didn't seem so adventurous.

As the pebbles of Dale's sailing beach came into view, the yachts floating in the harbour reminded me that I'd last walked around the Peninsula exactly twenty years earlier, in 1997. I'd come with my son to escape the events surrounding Princess Diana's funeral. While he went windsurfing I went walking. Later I caught sight of him in the bay and realised his was the only sail on the water. It turned out that the Haven had been closed for the day, as a mark of respect. But no-one had told us.

PICTON'S RENOIR

Picton Castle was built in the late twelfth century. For most of its history it was in the hands of the Philipps family, from about 1485 until 1987. Then the costs of maintenance and taxation prompted them to create the charitable trust that now runs it.

When I walked through the magnificent Great Hall of Picton Castle, about four miles to the east of Haverfordwest, I missed it. The guidebook doesn't mention it and nor at first did my guide – you can't visit Picton Castle unless on a guided tour. It was only when I asked about it towards the end of my visit that I was taken back and had it pointed out.

And there it was, in the Great Hall, quite prominently displayed it has to be said. It's on the wall facing the great Portland stone fireplace. Above that is a large portrait of Sir Robert Walpole, Britain's first Prime Minister. By comparison the painting I was anxious to see, 'Boats on the Seine at Argenteuil', believed to be by Pierre August Renoir, is rather small. It's easy to miss amidst the splendour of the rest of the Great Hall's furniture.

I was keen to see the painting because of the controversy that surrounds it. Two art houses in Paris have had an argument about whether it is, indeed, a genuine Renoir. The Bernheim Jeune Gallery says it is while the Wildenstein Institute refutes this. For what it's worth, which is not very much, I reckon it is. If that could be proved it would be worth a great deal to the Picton Castle Trust, getting on for at least half a million pounds. As it is, the painting is worth very little, which is perhaps why my guide didn't bother pointing it out.

Sir Laurence Philipps, later Lord Milford, bought 'Boats on the Seine at Argenteuil' in 1937. Sir Laurence, who made a considerable fortune as a stockbroker and underwriter, was the great grandfather of Nicky Philipps. Today she is one of Picton Castle charity's trustees and herself a portrait artist, well-known for her paintings of the Royal Family.

She says her late Great Aunt Gwen was convinced that Renoir had given 'Boats on the Seine' to his fellow Impressionist Claude Monet. He kept it at his home in Giverney, famous for its lily ponds. Gwen visited Giverney with Sir Laurence in 1936, twelve years after Monet's death. There they met the artist's stepdaughter Blanche, who told them the painting was by Renoir. He had painted it alongside Monet on the banks of the Seine in 1874. Moreover, she agreed he could buy the work through intermediaries, the Bernheim-Jeune gallery and Arthur Tooth, a London dealer.

In the 1960s, when they needed to renovate Picton Castle's roof, the Philipps family sold most of their collection of Impressionist works, including paintings by Monet, Alfred Sisley and Camille Pissarro. However, 'Boats on the Seine at Argenteuil' was not included. This was because it was unsigned and its provenance could not be guaranteed.

Move on half a century to 2015. Strapped for cash, the Picton Castle Trust decided to try and prove that their painting was a Renoir. They asked programme makers at the BBC television *Fake or Fortune* art series to investigate. In the programme, broadcast in

July 2015, journalist Fiona Bruce and international art dealer Philip Mould set out to establish the authenticity of the Renoir. Mould's first judgement, mirroring my own, was positive. 'Everything about it feels right,' he said. 'This is what the early Impressionists were up to. It's about light, colour, and feeling, about life on the move. The more I spend time with with it the more I feel this has to be a Renoir.'

But that's only an opinion, more informed than my own to be sure, but still just an opinion. In pursuit of facts, Bruce and Mould first established an unbroken paper trail. Researching archives in Paris and London they discovered documentary evidence that the art house Bernheum Jeune bought the painting for 40,000 Francs from Blanche Monet on 10 February 1937. On 23 April the same year they sold it to the London art dealer Arthur Tooth for 85,000 Francs. That was quite a mark-up. Then on 1 June Sir Laurence Philipps bought it from Arthur Tooth for £1,250, another substantial increase. The price was the equivalent of two average houses in those days.

Philip Mould followed up the information that Monet and Renoir had been painting side-by-side on the banks of the Seine in the Paris suburb of Argenteuil when the painting was created. He found an almost identical scene to the one by Renoir, but painted by Monet during the same period. This supported Blanche Monet's story.

He then examined physical evidence from the painting itself. The Musée d'Orsay in Paris has one of the biggest collections of Renoir's paintings in the world. It also has a large store of his memorabilia. Behind the scenes at the museum Mould examined paint boxes, palettes and paints used by the artist. Amongst them was a list Renoir had drawn up in 1877 of the pigments and colours he was using at that time.

Armed with this information he took 'Boats on the Seine at Argenteuil' to Berlin to be examined by the Bruker Corporation, which produces state of the art scientific instruments that analyse materials from drugs to explosives to works of art. One of their instruments scanned the painting to compare the pigments it contains with those on Renoir's 1877 list. There was a close correlation. In particular, they found large traces of vermillion red mercury sulphate, cobalt blue, and chrome yellow. They were all pigments Renoir was using in the 1870s.

Philip Mould then took the painting to the Courthauld Institute in London. Here it was examined by a specialised infra-red camera which revealed a stencilled manufacturer's stamp on the back of the canvas. This showed that the Paris firm Defarge Carpentiers, which Renoir used to obtain his art materials, had supplied the canvas. Not only that, other research on the range of labels used by the firm revealed that this particular one came from the 1871 to 1879 period, precisely the decade in which 'Boats on the Seine at Argenteuil' was painted.

'To my absolute satisfaction we've proved that this picture is by Renoir,' Philip Mould concluded. 'We've established that there is a companion painting to it by his friend Monet, just as Aunt Gwen said. We've established that the pigments in it are the same as those he used in the 1870s, by Renoir's own account. We've found a hidden stamp on the back. That proves that the canvas comes from his supplier in the 1870s. And we have got an unbroken paper trail that goes right back to Blanche Monet. In art world terms that is more than enough evidence. Surely now the Wildenstein Institute must accept this is a Renoir.'

They didn't. After considering the new evidence for a week they still refused to accept its authenticity. They gave three reasons. First, they claimed there was no evidence to support the provenance of the paintings in terms of documentation, such as a letter from Renoir to Monet. Secondly, the painting was not signed. And finally, they declared the painting was poorly executed. Even if it was unfinished it did not fit with Renoir's style.

This was thin gruel. In the first place, it is highly unlikely that the kind of documentation the Wildenstein Institute was demanding would exist. As to the lack of a signature, this is the case with many of the more than four thousand canvases Renoir produced over six decades. This is especially the case with those that were unfinished sketches, as this seems to be. And the last reason is just another opinion.

The programme makers consulted with Professor Anthea Callen, an expert on Impressionism. Her conclusion? 'There are difficulties with the painting,' she conceded. 'The proportions of the objects in the picture are awkward in places. In particular, the larger boat on the right, which is the key focus in the composition, is rather large in relation to the little boats in the background. There's a very sudden jump from foreground to background. And the little figure is rather too large for the size of the sailing boat. And because it is so thinly painted it has a real feel of being unresolved, unfinished, but that may be intentional. I wouldn't necessarily assume that this is anything more than a study, a preparatory study perhaps, but more like an exercise where the artist is learning to paint *en pleine aire*, outside in the landscape which is very difficult to do. It's not a great painting but I would nevertheless think it was a Renoir. He did produce a lot of second rate paintings in addition to being a genius.'

In light of all this, she was asked why the Wildenstein Institute didn't agree with her and the Bernheim Jeune Gallery? 'In one word, rivalry.'

So on the basis of an ancient dispute between two esoteric art houses in Paris, Picton Castle is being deprived of much needed funds to sustain its crumbling structure. But never mind, in 2016 the Heritage Lottery Fund awarded it £645,000 to restore its forty acres of gardens. And who knows? One day a letter may come to light from Monet to Renoir thanking him for the gift of 'Boats on the Seine at Argenteuil'.

DEER PARK

Clambering down the steep cliff in the Deer Park overlooking Skomer Island is tough going, through gorse, bracken, brambles, heather and rock screes. If truth be told, I'd been rather dreading this moment. Though I often pass close by – it's a hauntingly beautiful place – I hadn't been to this exact spot for more than a decade. The last time I came calamity struck.

The Deer Park is the largest promontory hill fort in Wales. Iron age ramparts defended the thin neck on the landward side. Later Lord Kensington built a high stone wall to enclose the Park, though no deer were ever kept. It has splendid views across St Brides Bay to St Davids Head in the north and the Dale Peninsula in the south. As the crow flies Skomer is two miles away, Ramsey and Grassholm islands about ten miles. In season you have a good chance of catching mackerel off its rocks.

It was an early evening in August 2005 and I'd come with my daughter Morwenna, then seven years old. I'd been casting for about an hour, losing expensive tackle rather than catching fish. As I hauled in a cast I took a step backwards and, sensing Morwenna behind me, moved my leg sideways. And stepped into mid-air. I fell about two to three metres, enough to find myself plunging to the ground head first. The heaviest half of you is the top and gravity does the rest. Seeing the ground coming I involuntarily put out my arms. My left elbow took the impact and dislocated. I could see the bulge of the bone. My head had bounced against the rocks and blood streamed from a gash across my forehead.

For a moment poor Morwenna was convinced I was dead. She leapt down beside me.

'Dad!'

'I'm fine,' I said, shakily getting to my feet.

I don't know how we managed to climb the rocks with the fishing tackle, and then over the Deer Park headland to find the car. Morwenna changed the gears as I drove to Talbenny, near Little Haven, using my right arm. Later I was driven to Withybush Hospital in Haverfordwest. By then it was getting dark. We were held up by a number of other vehicles, including a tractor, as we negotiated the narrow lanes. I was glad that we didn't have to travel further, to Carmathen say, to find a hospital.

Early the next morning I was wheeled into the operating theatre. My last memory, as the anaesthetic kicked in, was a circle of curious heads. Later that day I found myself back on the ward in a drowsed, but comfortable state, my arm strapped firmly to my chest. I was being examined by Glan Phillips, the consultant orthopaedic surgeon who had carried out the operation.

'Thanks for sorting me out,' I said.

'No, no,' Glan replied. 'We all want to thank you, for doing so much to save our hospital.'

'Hospital campaigner operated on in Withybush' announced the headline in the *Pembrokeshire Telegraph* a few days later. But that's another story (see pages 85 to 89).

The day I returned to the Deer Park I was surprised to discover that the coastguard hut at the pinnacle of the hill fort was operating again. It was built in 1931 following a ship coming to grief in Jack Sound, the treacherous rock-strewn stretch of water that separates Skomer from the mainland. It closed in 1969, but volunteers re-opened it in 2009. It's now staffed at weekends and bank holidays.

David Hill, who used to work for Westland Helicopters in Yeovil and retired to nearby Marloes, is on duty today. He tells me that they're on the lookout as much for tourists in distress as ships. Their last major call-out was to rescue a man trapped half-way down the cliff at Anvil Point on the headland. A helicopter came from St Athan.

The normal look-out shift is four hours, but David Hill often stays for seven or eight. 'You meet all kinds here', he says. 'In the last week I've met people from Tasmania, Siberia and Switzerland.'

As I leave I glace up at the flag flying from the hut. It has the Welsh colours, red on a green and white background, but I suddenly see that the dragon is, in fact, a red lobster.'

'Is that a joke?' I ask.

'It's Skin Cancer Cymru's flag,' says Hill. 'We support the charity.'

LITTLE HAVEN

On the face of it, little has changed in Little Haven since I was a boy. If you look at old photographs from the 1950s, it still looks much the same. The cliffs are still there, of course, and so too is the Castle pub overlooking the village green and the narrow beach. The two other pubs are still there as well, the St Brides and the Swan though that has gone up-market. In fact, it has been completely rebuilt and is a world away from the spit and sawdust local of the 1950s. But it's still in the same place, opening on to the narrow roadway that leads to the Point, a lookout that gives you sweeping views of St Brides Bay.

Uniquely, Little Haven used to combine fishing with coal mining as its main source of income. The village lies at the westernmost edge of the Pembrokeshire anthracite coalfield and there are the remains of a number of workings that were driven horizontally into the cliffs. The coal was loaded on to coasters from the beach. However, that industry vanished by the mid-nineteenth century. Today Little Haven is full of holiday cottages and makes its living from tourism.

Above the Point is a large house that many years ago was a hotel. Uniformed porters wheeled the luggage of its guests past the Swan and up the fifty yards of the narrow cobbled track. When I was a boy the hotel was in the market for eels. They fetched a shilling each so long as they were skinned, a tricky process.

When we were about ten my cousin Robert and I would fish for them in the stream that flows on to the beach. We used anything for bait, bread, worms, even bacon. Once we got one hooked it would make its escape upstream, dragging the line and us after it. Their strength was prodigious. They'd force us to clamber through the rocky stream bed and undergrowth. More often than not they'd get jammed beneath a rock and refuse all our efforts to pull them out. Either that or they'd wriggle off the hook and get away. On the rare occasion we caught one it would twist dangerously in our hands, exuding slippery mucus. It would arch its back and snap at our arms, its jaws like a pliers and spiky teeth razor sharp.

We would nail its head to a piece of wood, cut behind its ears and spend what seemed like hours pulling away the skin. 'I'm fed up with this old stream,' Robert said one day. 'Let's try that big pool on the beach, I bet there are a load there.'

He was talking about a deep round pool at the side of a large cave that separates Little Haven and Settlands beaches and which can be reached at low tide. We went there with a couple of kitchen buckets and immediately began emptying it. This took quite a time, but eventually we were standing on a layer of large rocks and pebbles. We threw those out as well. Sure enough there were at least a dozen large twisting eels, as well as crabs and dogfish. Whenever I walk across the beach, that moment comes to mind. As does the occasions when my father would strike a tennis ball high in the sky with his racket while my brother and I hovered, straining to be the one to catch it. As I saw the ball descending fast and straight a frisson of fear, a kind of vertigo, coursed through me 'Come on,' my father would cry. 'It's not a cricket ball!' Sometimes he would launch one of those as well, striking it with a cricket bat. My father had a reputation in Little Haven for organising people into teams for a match on the beach. After one of these we had a picnic on Settlands. When we finished my mother sent me to the shore to wash the dishes. I returned to confess that I had lost one in the water. Immediately, my father rounded up everyone to hand, and to my mother's mortification, marched us down to the sea. He made us join hands in a line to search for the errant plate. Sure enough it was found. Once my father dived off the rocks and lost his false teeth. Some days later I was beachcombing along the seaweed and jetsam at the tidal edge and came across them, intact. Dad ran them under the tap and put them straight back in.

Even more eccentric than my father was Gerald Bird, known as Dickie, who ran a boat yard above the beach. He hired out small rowing and sailing craft. For a small boy, the yard was a treasure trove, a crazy chandlery that had taken years to assemble, full of bric-a-brac, metal, bits of wood, oars, discarded engines, sails, tools, grease, old stoves. At the back of the yard were the remains of an army canoe with two large floats attached. Dickie levered them off, lashed them together with a couple of planks, and made me a makeshift raft. I'd paddle it across the Haven at full tide. The floats were full of ping pong balls and unsinkable.

Dickie Bird had the distracted air of someone with an aristocratic lineage. There was talk of links with Bird's Custard, first formulated and cooked in Birmingham by one Alfred Bird in 1837. But Dickie was always short of money. On one occasion the boat yard caught fire because he had connected it illegally to an electricity cable. There were no fuses.

With his sister, who also lived in the village, Dickie launched the Nest, a restaurant of dubious quality. He was the cook, producing platefuls of greasy chips. However, he could not be relied on to finish preparing a meal in timely fashion. Often he was called to his boatyard for some emergency or other. Famously, the hatch that connected the kitchen with the dining area was improvised with an old toilet seat. Dickie once caused a serious incident. He went missing for a few days and there was real concern when his boat was found floating empty in the middle of St Brides Bay. The coast guard and lifeboat were deployed, as well as a naval helicopter. But despite extensive searches nothing was found. Three weeks later Dickie turned up to ask what the fuss had been about. All he had done was board a tanker that had been anchored in the Bay and signed on as a deckhand, just for the hell of it.

I've owned a caravan on a field near the cliff edge at Talbenny to the south of Little Haven for more than forty years. The first one I put there had an open coal fire, gas lamps and no running water. I bought it from a woman in Hengoed in the Rhymney Valley and had it transported to Preseli on the back of a lorry. The trouble was, I inspected it in the dark. The farmer in whose field I had secured a pitch rang me. Did I not realise the van was pink, contravening National Park regulations? The next weekend my father and I went down and painted it white.

I've had more vans since then, all of them second hand. Two were blown over in gales. In 1992, the winter of the great storm, one van was completely flattened. I reckon a great wind came up the side of the cliff, leaving something near a vacuum in its wake. It swept across the field in a line about thirty yards wide destroying everything within it, about a dozen vans. Everything either side was intact. My van was one of those destroyed, turned over like a leaf. All I could rescue was the cooker. As I was extracting it I found a baked bean tin that had been split.

Some years ago, when I was making my will, I agonised about what to do with the caravan. It was more of a problem than the house. How to divide it up amongst the children? Then I thought, 'What's the big deal, it's practically worthless?' But then, on second thoughts, I realised it was worth more than money could buy.

Notes

1. Quoted in Flora Thomas, *The Builders of Milford*, published by the *Pembrokeshire Telegraph*, 1920, page 17. Note: 'culm' is the coal dust that emanated in large quantities from the

mining of anthracite in Pembrokeshire.

2. Mrs John Farrar (Eliza Ware Rotch Farrar), *Recollections of Seventy Years*, Ticknor & Fields, Boston, 1865, p. 39.

3. Ibid. page 39-40.

4. It comes from number 27 of the 42 questions in *Advice and Queries*: 'Live adventurously. When choices arise, do you take the way that offers the fullest opportunity for the use of your gifts in the service of God and the community? Let your life speak. When decisions have to be made, are you ready to join with others in seeking clearness, asking for God's guidance and offering counsel to one another?'

5. Richard Howells (Ed.), *Where the River Bends: An Illustrated History of Hook*, Planed, 2012. *Black Diamond Village*, DVD, Planed, 2012.

6. Rheged was one of the kingdoms of the Old North – Hen Ogledd – the Brythonic-speaking region of what is now northern England and southern Scotland.

7. A.F. Pollard, *The Reign of Henry VII from Contemporary Sources*, 3 vols., London 1913, p. 14.

ISLANDS

RAMSEY

Ramsey Island is six hundred acres of hill and moorlands edging the St Davids peninsula. The name was probably derived from the Vikings, a corruption of the Norse *Hrafn's Ey*, Ravens Island. In Welsh it is called Ynys Dewi, the island of our patron saint, a place for the soul.

However, until recently Ramsey has also been known as Rat Island. That's because for than a century the place was infested with rats. It's not altogether clear how they arrived. Perhaps they came ashore from ships wrecked on the island's fierce rocks. Maybe they jumped from coastal traders that regularly used Ramsey Sound as an anchorage. More likely, they hid themselves in the straw used in the boats that shipped cattle and sheep to and from the mainland.

Whichever way they came, they multiplied by the thousand and wrought havoc on Ramsey's indigenous birdlife. In particular, they saw off the puffins and Manx shearwaters. Until near the end of the nineteenth century both species congregated in their burrows in large numbers on the island. But the rats ate their eggs and drove them out. From then on the island was farmed in desultorily fashion through much of the twentieth century until the RSPB took it over in 1992. This was the critical moment of change. There was to be a confrontation with the rats.

There were a few Manx shearwaters left, just seven-hundred-and-fifty breeding pairs in 1993. But the puffins were all gone. The RSPB brought in Wildlife Management International, a New Zealand firm that had a record of eradicating mice, feral cats, rabbits, but above all rats, from more than twenty islands around the world. In November 1999 they set up 1,200 traps across the island. These were tubes, about three inches across and two feet long. Metal sticks held them above the ground, enough to prevent access by shrews and voles, more benign Ramsey species. For a couple of months, the tubes were filled with harmless bait that rats love, a mixture of beer, wax and chocolate. This was to get them used to entering the traps. Rats are notoriously wary of anything new appearing in their habitat. Then, over Christmas and New Year, the traps were filled with 165 kilos of new bait, as irresistible as chocolate, but poisonous.

The rats were eliminated within a few weeks. And the subsequent revival of the shearwaters has been remarkable. When they were next counted, in 2004, their numbers had doubled, to 1,621 breeding pairs. That went up to 2,387 by 2007, to 3,835 by 2012, and 4,796 by 2015. When they next count, probably in 2020, it's reckoned their number will exceed 6,000.

Counting Manx shearwaters on Ramsey is more problematic than on Skomer (see page 227). Their numbers are relatively few so they don't cover the island to the same extent. Their burrows only line the cliffs a few yards inland. As a result, it's not possible to count the number of birds incubating their eggs in a small area and then extrapolate the total by the acreage of the island. Instead the wardens count the burrows, a tedious process that takes a month.

The Manx shearwaters have had a healthy revival. Not so with the puffins. They fly around the island, but so far none have been enticed ashore to nest. To encourage them plastic decoy puffins have been placed in the cliffs, with accompanying recordings of their cries. Ramsey's wardens reckon that eventually the burrows on Skomer and Skokholm will become impossibly overcrowded. The puffins will have no choice but to nest on Ramsey. But that could take a few years yet.

When I was last on Ramsey, in the 1980s, the pest of the moment was the rabbit. I was with a team working on *Wales This Week*, a television current affairs programme that is still going. In those days there were four reporters, split into pairs. Each produced an investigative half-hour every two weeks. One Monday the programme we had going out that Thursday fell through. As we mulled over the dilemma I idly pulled open the top drawer of my desk. Looking down I saw a press cutting. It was about a young couple and their toddler who had packed in the second-hand book shop they'd been running in Cardiff and moved to live on Ramsey. 'We could do something on them,' I suggested.

In those days there were no mobile phones. So I drove down to St Justinians and persuaded a fisherman to take me across Ramsey Sound. The couple in my press cutting were John and Heather Freeman. They were astonished to see me advancing across their farmyard. They were even more surprised when I told them I wanted to bring a film crew on to the island the next day. Nonetheless, they agreed.

Rabbits were frustrating their efforts to grow hay for their sheep and vegetables in their garden. 'The place is infested with them,' John Freeman told me. 'We've dug fences feet into the ground to prevent them burrowing underneath. And they should be high enough to stop them jumping over. But still they come.'

Rabbits were obviously the main story. But we couldn't get near enough to film them. How did we resolve it? At this distance I can confess. We took the crew to a rabbit farm in Carmarthenshire and filmed some close-ups.

These days, the rabbits on Skomer are regarded as an asset. Together with the sheep they keep the grass in the fields short enough to allow a number of rare birds to survive. One example is Ramsey's star species, the chough. It's a relative of the crow, but with a red beak, red feet and finger-like wings. The island has nine breeding pairs. I saw them twice. There was a lone chough pecking through the short grass in search of insects. I studied him, perhaps it was a her, through some binoculars. The second occurrence was more dramatic. Three pairs wheeled in the air currents above a high cliff edge with the beach far below. The choughs soared, swooped and then raced alongside me, level with where I was standing. Their black, corrugated wings clutched at the sky.

SKOMER

Until this moment I hadn't heard of the short-eared owl. But now, buoyed by the enthusiasm and reverence of the people around me,

I'm staring at one with a kind of reverence myself, through an expensive pair of binoculars. The owl is standing rather irreverently. It has its back to me, on what looks to be a compost tip. But then it turns its head and its yellow eyes gaze directly into mine, owl-like. It stretches a wing and lifts a foot. It seems bored. It's completely unaffected by the suppressed excitement of the people watching it. That's despite their being little more than ten yards away, shrouded with all manner of electronic gear, cameras, enormous lenses, telescopes.

I'm told this is one of four breeding pairs on Skomer Island. There's another pair on Skokholm Island close by, and a pair on Ramsey further to the north, off St Davids Head. And that's it. News of the sighting travels like electricity among the two-hundred-and-fifty or so bird lovers who have landed on Skomer this warm Spring day.

'We're so privileged,' I hear a woman say as she passes me, carefully so as not to take a foot off the path. Although we can't see them, the burrows of thousands of Manx shearwaters, puffins and rabbits are just inches below the ground all around us.

'We're lucky,' says bird expert Dave Astins who is showing me around. 'You can come here for days at a time and never see the short-eared owl.' He takes his binoculars off me carefully – they cost £1,600 – and scans the horizon. 'Look, there's another one! It's

flying! Across that low ridge, over there.' I stare and I do indeed see
what appears to be another short-eared owl, its long wings flapping
slowly as it makes a graceful loop, and disappears.

'We'd be really lucky to see the little owl,' Dave says. 'But that's
even rarer, much more difficult on Skomer.' It seems there are only
two pairs in the whole of Pembrokeshire. But one of them is here.

Dave has been a committed bird watcher for more the thirty years
and in the last month has gone professional. Within a space of a few
weeks he has given up his job with Carmarthenhire's Education and
Children's Service, is in the process of selling his house to downsize,
and will then sell his car, replacing it with a van. All this is to allow
him to devote his life to the thing he loves most, bird watching. 'I'm
changing a lot of things,' he tells me. 'It's liberating.'

He's set up West Coast Birdwatching, to take novices like me on
days (and sometimes nights) to all corners of Pembrokeshire 'to
find the birds you would like to see to improve your identifications
skills.' This might work in the spring and summer, perhaps even
autumn, but what about winter? 'I'll be leading groups abroad,'
Dave says confidently. 'This coming winter I've already got trips to
Oman and the Cape Verde Islands lined up.'

Every time Dave sees a bird, up go his binoculars, and he
identifies it. 'It's a habit,' he says. 'I'm always on the lookout for a
species I haven't seen.' Within the space of half-a-mile he points out
a whitethroat, a warbler that winters in Africa; a dunnock, a
secretive kind of bird that nests round walls and bushes; a linnet, a
small finch; a wheatear, that nests in burrows; a stonechat, 'only one
pair breeding on Skomer this year'; a sedge warbler, that lives
around ponds; and a meadow pipet.

I realise I've been confusing this last bird with the skylark. It
doesn't go quite as high during the song flight, and 'parachutes'
down to the ground. It makes a very different sound, too, short zip,
zip zip cries. Dave has identified 298 different species in
Pembrokeshire. How often does he come across a new one?

'Oh, about two or three times a year.'

Is there one he would particularly like to see today?

'Lots of potential, but a red-rumped swallow wouldn't be out of
the question.'

Skomer is a low-lying island, highest point seventy-nine metres,
covering about three hundred hectares. You can circumnavigate it in
about three hours. In the spring it is a patchwork of bright meadows
of bluebells, pink campion, and sea white campion, all interspersed

with purple clumps of thrift.

We've been walking for about two hours before we encounter a puffin, Skomer's most iconic bird. The island is a global nerve centre for the species. In some places the puffin is under threat from climate change, but not on Skomer. Here their numbers are increasing, from about 20,000 in 2016, to 25,000 in 2017, and 31,000 at the last count, in April 2018.

In Spring half of them are in their burrows incubating their single egg, while their mate takes time off floating on the water or flying about with their energetic beating wings. When their egg hatches in June the parents become frantically busy, delivering sand eels to their ravenous chick. They hold them crossways in their bills, sometimes six at a time. Yet it's a mystery how they catch them. Are they caught in one movement, or singly, and if so, how is each held?

I wonder, too, how the South and West Wales Wildlife Trust that runs Skomer can be so accurate when counting the puffins. How do they do it? For some unknown reason, just before they start laying their eggs, all the puffins come ashore for a night or two during April. Maybe it's to bond and inspect their burrows – they always return to the same one. It's then the Trust takes the opportunity. It brings volunteers on to the island, Dave Astins among them. They're divided, two each to seven areas, where they count the birds.

SKOKHOLM

How to describe wandering across Skokholm island at two in the morning on a dark summer's night? The air is full of unearthly, hoarse staccato noises. Rasping, shrieking calls pivot back and forth. It's like being in a farmyard full of half-crazed cockerels, or being close to an off message foghorn. Overhead there's a flutter of wings, then a soft thump into bracken or turf. A fresh chorus comes from the ground below, more moaning, croaking and wheezing. Momentarily, there's an eerie silence until a little further on the sequence repeats itself, but this time in a different octave.

And so the black night continues, with constant high-pitched cries that seem to instill an anxious sense of urgency among the birds. 'Am I in the right place?' 'Where are you?' 'Are you there?' 'Are you coming? 'Oh, for the Lord's sake, come on!'

This is the sound of thousands of Manx shearwaters flying off the sea under the cover of darkness. They come to lay and incubate their single egg, then to hatch and feed their chicks. Locals call them 'cuckles and cock-lollies'. They also call Skomer and Skokholm isles of the lost souls.

Manx shearwaters are brilliant seabirds, perfectly adapted to spend their lives at sea shearing the waves. But they're hopeless on land. Their legs are set back near the end of their bodies. This is great for paddling, but no good for walking. They land on their tummies and waddle awkwardly along to flop into their burrows. They can be easily picked off, especially by the great black-backed gull, Skokholm's top predator. These gulls can swallow a rabbit, let alone a seabird. That's why Manx shearwaters come in only when it's really dark. They swoop ashore during the early hours, when the moon is on the wane, ideally when there's cloud cover.

Skomer and Skokholm islands are located a few miles off the Marloes peninsula at the southern end of St Brides Bay. They're home to about half the world's population of Manx shearwaters, approaching 400,000 on Skomer and 100,000 on Skokholm. In 2018 it was discovered there are far more of them than had been previously thought. They're counted by playing a recording of their cries into the borrows and waiting for a response. Previously they had only played male recordings. In 2018 they played female calls as well and the male birds responded enthusiastically. On Skokholm it was believed there were about 60,000 breeding pairs. This estimate now shot up to around 100,000.

I'm spending three nights on Skokholm. It's a mile long and half-a-mile wide, 260 acres of bare windswept moorland and high cliffs. The name is Norse for wooded isle, though it's hard to imagine many trees surviving here. It's half the size of Skomer, two miles to the northwest. Three nights is the minimum you can spend, though many stay a week or longer. Sometimes, if there's a heavy south-easterly swell you have to extend your stay. The boat from St Martin's Haven cannot land in these conditions.

No day visitors are allowed which makes Skokholm special. During a year Skomer gets 18,000 visitors, but only 300 land on Skokholm. Usually there are about a dozen people, including the two wardens and their two volunteer assistants, here for three months at a time. When the puffins are hatching, in June and July, there can be up to ten staff and researchers and twenty visitors. But they don't all come for the birds. Many want to experience island life, in search of a kind of secular retreat. About seventy per cent are repeat visitors. Four-hundred-and-forty of them belong to the Friends of Skokholm. Every February they hold a reunion near Cheltenham (presumably equally inconvenient for everybody).

I'm staying in a whitewashed farmhouse whose foundations go back to the eighteenth century. Its main association is with the naturalist Ronald Lockley. The island's people gather here at 9pm each day to share what they've been up to. A plaque by the front door says, 'Remember his incredible love of nature and how he used his brilliant mind to unravel some of her mysteries. Naturalist, author, scientist and farmer, Ronald Mathias Lockley (1903-2000) lived on Skokholm from 1927 to 1940. He started Britain's first Bird Observatory here in 1933. His studies of island wildlife, especially the birds, made Skokholm famous and continue to inspire us all.'

Lined on a shelf in what was his sitting room, are Lockley's sixty complete works. His first book *Dream Island* is a memoir of his early years on Skokholm.[1] He makes everything sound idyllic. The sun shines most of the time. The land is bountiful and the sea full of lobsters. Sailing his seventeen-foot long ketch *Storm Petrel* is a delight. A shipwreck the *Alice Williams* even brings wood to build his house and its cargo of coal is enough to keep his fire going for five years. There are gales, but invariably melodramatic ones. After a year he was joined by Doris who lived next door to him in Cardiff when he was growing up. However, I reckon she had to put up with

a lot. Wildlife came emphatically first for Lockley. He had three marriages and the first two ended in divorce.

His most famous book was a scientific study, *The Private Life of the Rabbit*. Nonetheless it was a major inspiration behind Richard Adams' best-selling *Watership Down*, the anthropomorphic tale of rabbits searching for a new home.[2]

Lockley's current successor is Richard Brown, a no-nonsense Yorkshireman. A small group of us meet him after we land at eight o'clock in the morning, the time dictated by the tide. Over a mug of tea, he gives us an introduction to island life, the communal facilities, the scarcity of water (there are no showers), the mysteries of compostable toilets, where to recharge your mobile, what not to do. The most important instruction is to stick to the network of paths, marked by white-painted poles and pebbles. Step off the paths and in all likelihood you'll invade a puffin's or manx shearwater's burrow.

Richard was an assistant warden on Skomer for two years, and then on Bardsey Island off the Llŷn peninsula for five years. There he met his partner Giselle who had previously worked for the RSPB in Norfolk. They came to Skokholm as wardens in 2013.

Richard leads us to the north coast across fields of turf and bracken, lined by the remains of stone walls. He gives us a rundown of the flora and fauna. Leaving aside the native seabirds, Skokholm is a stopping off point for all kinds of migrating species, including willow warblers, spotted flycatchers, sedge warblers, whitethroats, and chiffchaffs. There are other naturalist delights. The island has the biggest slow worm in the world, all sorts of bugs, moths and butterflies, as well as acres of wildflowers. Richard points to a scarlet pimpernel, a small red flower. 'We've got a blue variety as well,' he says. 'Darwin got excited when he found that if you cross the red with the blue you get a purple version.'

And then there are the famous rabbits, hundreds if not thousands of them. In the 1930s Lockley wanted to farm chinchilla rabbits and tried all means to get rid of the native variety, including introducing myxomatosis, normally fatal for rabbits. But even that didn't work. Myxomatosis is carried by fleas. All rabbits have fleas, except those on Skokholm. No-one knows exactly why. It's assumed the island location has given Skokholm's rabbits a different evolutionary path.[3]

On the west point of the island, where the land juts out into the Atlantic and the next stop is America, stands the lighthouse. Here Richard and Giselle live. It used to belong to Trinity House. In 2005 the South and West Wales Wildlife Trust, which already owned the rest of the island, bought it for £500,000. It seems a lot to me, given that the lighthouse, complete with helicopter landing pad, remains operational. It's automatic, but visited once a year for servicing.

The Trust were keen to buy it because it's surrounded by the most concentrated mass of Manx shearwater burrows on the planet. They're being intensively studied. Scattered around are 213 numbered tiles. Each covers the burrow of a shearwater chick which has been examined, weighed and ringed.

Richard kneels to the ground and lifts tile 147. He reaches carefully inside and draws out a fluffy chick. It doesn't look particularly upset at being disturbed. It pokes its beak out, then withdraws it and shuts an eye. 'I think it's going back to sleep,' Richard says, gently putting it back. Yet within a week or so this small, delicate creature will be travelling to Argentina, entirely alone. It's been assiduously fed by its parents for the past two months and now, at a little over six-hundred grams, is about a third heavier than they are.

Soon the parents will stop feeding it. A week will go by, with the chick flapping its wings at the edge of its burrow to give them strength. When it's getting really hungry, and if it's lucky enough to be near a cliff edge, one dark night it'll push itself off. Otherwise it'll find a ledge or stone and awkwardly launch into the sky. Then it's some six thousand miles non-stop, down the west coast of Africa and across the South Atlantic. Some make the journey in less than a fortnight. They hang around the coast of Brazil and Argentina for a couple of years before making what becomes their annual trip to Skokholm to search out a burrow and find a mate. They're monogamous and in about six or seven years they'll be ready to breed. The oldest recorded Manx shearwater lived for fifty-four years, which means a lot of chicks.

Later in the day I'm sitting in a hide on the north side of the island chatting to volunteer assistant warden Kirsty Franklin. She's from Cornwall and studied Zoology at Cardiff University. In the autumn she starts a PhD on the Mauritius round island petrel, a project funded by the British Ornithological Union.

Kirsty has a powerful telescope with which she constantly scans the horizon. Anything unusual today?

'Spotted a Balearic shearwater, which is pretty rare,' she says. 'Oh, and a comic tern.'

'Comic?'

'Because it was difficult to tell whether it was a common or an arctic tern,' she laughs.[4]

The hide is perched high above Mad Bay, right on the cliff edge. It's called Howard's End, which has nothing to do with E.M. Forster' novel. A carpenter called Howard lost a wheelbarrow and some planks over the cliff while he was building it.

After my second day on Skokholm it begins to feel as if I'm on a long sea voyage. The island is my ship. I spend hours gazing out at the breaking waves, the never-ending swell. Walking the paths is like pacing the deck, up-and-down, keeping to the straight and narrow. Time slips by. I'm sensitive to the slightest change in the weather. Gulls drift on the wind. What is their destination? Like the island they're going nowhere. Except, as with the earth itself, they're turning endlessly in space.

Warden Richard has been on the island for six years, which seems an eternity to me, a kind of space odyssey in itself. What does it feel like?

'I guess you've got to be pretty tough-minded to live on an island,' he replies. 'But I wouldn't choose any other kind of life. People just waste their time on the mainland.'

'Really?'

He smiles. 'Oh yes, doing a million pointless things.'

GRASSHOLM

It's exhilarating to speed in a low-slung powerboat far out on the ocean and see a low-flying flock of gannets coming straight at you. There were about thirty of them, inches separating their narrow black-tipped wings, six feet across. They flapped slowly, seemingly without effort. But it was still enough to drive them forward at a smart pace. I thought they might hit the boat. At the last minute they veered and were gone.

Gannets are graceful birds. They are at their most dramatic when catching fish. They plunge vertically from a hundred feet, a height at which their binocular vision can spot their prey in the sea far below. They hit the water at sixty miles per hour, sending up a shower of spray. A split second before impact their wings dislocate close against their bodies to streamline entry. A secondary eyelid protects their eyes. Internal nostrils close to stop water ingress. Reinforced skull, strong neck muscles, and air sacs cushion the impact. The momentum takes them as far as eighty feet below the surface. They can hold their breath for forty-five seconds. They catch anything from cod, sardines and mackerel to sand eels. They swallow them under water, rising to float on the surface to ease their digestion.

I'm with Ffion Rees and we're racing towards Grassholm. It's ten miles offshore beyond Skomer, the fourth largest gannet colony in the world. Despite its small size, a mere twenty-two acres, it's home to about a hundred thousand gannets.

Ffion is a feisty woman. Brought up in Pembrokeshire, she studied at Aberdeen University, and then taught English in Vienna. But she always came home in the summer to mess about with boats. She spent a number of years training people on powerboat courses in places as far afield as Bangladesh, Indonesia, and Oman. In 2015 she crewed on a yacht on her first Atlantic crossing. A year later she set up her wildlife boat-tripping company, Falcon Boats. Which is how I come to be a passenger on her large, rigid inflatable powerboat that planes across the water.

Ffion's a sea creature. She has been working on the ocean for twenty years: 'I remember saying once: I can't spend the rest of my life driving a boat around Ramsey and Grassholm. Well, it would appear I can.' The reason has something to do with the ever-changing quality of the sea. 'It has more moods than I have myself. No two trips are alike. Between the tides, the weather, and the seasons, nothing's ever the same.'

A distant spot on the horizon, Grassholm comes steadily into view. Half of the island is shiny white, made by the gannets themselves, the guano that solidifies their nests. It's more than noticeable downwind. The nests, a beak's distance from each other, are uniformly spaced across the island. Gannets are aggressive birds. Hundreds of them soar and swoop above us, making a cacophony of sound.

Gannets have been on Grassholm for a century. Before that it was home to puffins. In 1890 their number was estimated to be about half-a-million. But by 1946 these had fallen to two-hundred and soon disappeared altogether.

Grasses, especially red fescue, had grown on the island's bare rock, flourishing in the salt air. They grew each summer and died back each winter to form a soil-less haystack about two feet thick above the rock. This became a maze of tunnels for the burrowing puffins. Eventually, however, the weather and the weight of the birds caused the flimsy grass roofs to fall in. The tenements became too exposed for nesting purposes.

The puffins retreated to Skomer and Skokholm and were replaced by the gannets. They build their nests differently. They make raised pods out of anything they can find, seaweed in particular. By the 1930s there were about 20,000 nesting pairs. Since then the number has grown steadily to reach today's prodigious proportions. Perhaps Grassholm is full up.

The island has long caught the imagination of storytellers. In earlier times it was known as *Ynys Gwales* (the Welsh Island). It features in one of the most famous episodes of the *Mabinogi*, mythical stories compiled in the twelfth and thirteenth centuries from earlier oral traditions. In one of them the giant Bendigeidfran, King of Britain, leads an army to Ireland to rescue his sister Branwen who has been mistreated by her husband, an Irish king. A furious battle ensues in which Bendigeidfran is mortally wounded. Only seven of his men survive. He orders them to cut off his head and return it to Britain.

They take it to Harlech where for seven years they are entertained by the head that continues to speak. Later they move to Ynys Gwales where they live for a further eighty years in a kind of idyll, unaware of the passage of time. However, they are enjoined never to open a door facing southwards towards Cornwall. Eventually, of course, one of them does. As a result, they are suddenly made aware of the misfortune and grief that has befallen

them. The story ends with their taking Bendigeidfran's head, now
fallen silent, to London. There they bury it facing France to ward
off invasion.

It is a story that has fascinated writers and artists down the
centuries. One of the latest is the artist Iwan Bala who has produced
many images of an island on a distant horizon. The outline he draws
is based on a map of Wales turned on its side, with the peninsulas
of St Davids and the Llŷn pointing upwards, like mountains. The
shape is also reminiscent of the contours of Grassholm, the *Ynys
Gwales* of his imagination. As Iwan Bala has explained:

> The iconic island is a barren piece of land that needs revitalising, a
> large percentage of its mass is submerged, either hidden or
> drowned. It's an image of duality, a place on to which we can project
> our hopes and our disappointments. But it is also separated from
> the viewer by a stretch of water, and suggests an unattainable and
> 'fantasy island' like 'Gwales' in the Welsh myth cycle the *Mabinogi*,
> a free Wales, free of care, but also a diverting reverie, a mirage. It
> marks a stage in the complex and confusing process of
> decolonisation.[5]

In the face of such exalted interpretations it comes as an anti-climax
to have to report that these days Grassholm is akin to a rubbish
dump. This has happened because of the gannets. But it's not their
fault. Normally, they would collect floating seaweed to build their
nests. But over recent decades they have tended to collect plastic,
which they mistake for seaweed. So much so that more than eighty
per cent of the island's nests now contain plastic, getting on for
nineteen tons.

Most of it is fishing gear. Synthetic rope is the biggest culprit,
followed by mono-filament netting and line, some of it doubtless
from far beyond Welsh shores. But there's also domestic stuff,
including packaging tapes, crisp packets, plastic bags, party
poppers, and balloons.

As the gannet chicks grow and begin to move around, some
become entangled. Strands of fibre slowly wind around their legs
and tighten like a tourniquet. Some chicks, even a few adults,
become trapped. Every October an RSPB team lands on
Grassholm and frees up to a hundred birds.

It's a graphic instance of environmental degradation, but little
can be done about it. Removing the plastic would destroy the

gannet habitat in the process. And in any event it's reckoned that if it was removed, the gannets would bring the plastic back within five to ten years.

On my trip out to the island, one pristine, hot June day, the ocean was glassy calm. We picked up three helium balloons, floating bright blue, green, and red on the water. One of them had birthday greetings on the side.

'Every time I come out I pick up something like this,' Ffion said. 'Goodness knows what's hiding beneath the surface.'

Notes

1. R.M. Lockley, *Dream Island, A Record of a Simple Life*, Witherby 1930.
2. R.M. Lockley's *The Private Life of the Rabbit* was published by Andre Deutsch in 1964, and Richard Adams' *Watership Down* by Rex Collings in 1972.
3. This has happened with the vole on neighbouring Skomer island. Though closely related

to the Bank Vole, found on the mainland, the Skomer Vole's larger size, lighter colour and differences in skull and teeth, are sufficient for it to be considered an island race or sub-species. The Skomer Vole's different evolutionary path is attributed to the absence of ground predators.

4. The artic tern is slightly smaller than the common tern. An authoritative guide (Lars Svensson, *Collins Bird Guide*, 2009) says its flight is 'more elastic and gracefully bouncing' than the common tern's, although 'the flight of the latter is just as elegant'.

5. Iwan Bala, 'Horizon Wales: Visual Art and the Postcolonial', in Jane Aaron and Chris Williams (Eds.), *Postcolonial Wales*, University of Wales Press, 2005, page 248.

WORKS CONSULTED

Allen, Richard, 'Nantucket Quakers and the Milford Haven Whaling Industry', in *Quaker Studies* 15/1, 2010.

Bailey, Anthony, *Stories in Stone*, Preseli Heritage Publications, 2000.

Barber, Chris, *Megaliths of Wales*, Amberley Publishing, 2017.

Bradford, Phil, and Denyer, Andrew, *The Dale Peninsula coast path*, www.Walking-Guides.co.uk, 2012

Breverton, Terry, *The Book of Welsh Saints*, Glyndwr Publishing, 2000.

Breverton, Terry, *Wales: A Historical Companion*, Amberley Publishing, 2009.

Charles, B.G., *George Owen of Henllys: A Welsh Elizabethan*, National Library of Wales Press, 1973.

Condry, William M., *The Natural History of Wales*, Bloomsbury, 1990.

Curtis, Tony, *Real South Pembrokeshire*, Seren 2011.

Davies, Damian Walford and Eastham, Anne, *Saints and Stones*, Gomer, 2002.

Davies, Janet, 'The Fight for Preseli', in *Planet No 58*, August-September, 1986.

Davies, John, 'The inheritance of Waldo and D.J.' in Osmond, John (Ed.) *The Preseli Papers*, Plaid Cymru, 2007.

Davies. John, Jenkins, Nigel, Baines, Menna and Lynch, Peredur, *The Welsh Academy Encyclopaedia of Wales*, University of Wales Press, 2008.

Davies, John and Delyth, Marian, *Wales – the 100 Places to See Before You Die*, Y Lolfa, 2010.

Davies, R.R. (Ed.), *The British Isles 1100 – 1150: Comparisons, Contrasts and Connections*, John Donald, Edinburgh, 1988.

Davies, Sioned (trans.) *The Mabinogion*, Oxford University Press, 2007.

Sybil Edwards, *The Story of the Milford Haven Waterway*, Logaston Press, 2009.

Elis-Gruffydd, Dyfed, *Wales: 100 Remarkable Vistas*, Y Lolfa, 2017.

Evans, Gwynfor, *For the Sake of Wales*, Welsh Academic Press, 1996.

Evans, Russell, *A Brief History of Rhydwilym Baptist Church 1668-2018*, Capel Rhydwilym, 2018.

Fern, Susan, *The Man Who Killed Richard III*, Amberley Press, 2014.

Fowler, Bill, Cramp, Elizabeth, and Walker, Audrey, *The Last Invasion Tapestry: The Story Behind a Community Project*, Pembrokeshire County Council, 2007.

Goddard, Christopher and Evans, Katherine, *The Wales Coast Path: A Practical Guide for Walkers*, St Davids Press, 2016.

Green, Francis, 'The Pictons of Poyston', in *West Wales Historical Records*, Vol X, 1924.

Griffith, Stephen, *A History of Quakers in Pembrokeshire*, Gomer, 1995.

Heath, Julian, *Sacred Circles: Prehistoric Stone Circles in Wales*, Llygad Gwalch, 2010.

Hilling, John B., *Cilgerran Castle, St Dogmael's Abbey, Pentre Ifan Burial Chamber, Carreg Coetan Arthur Burial Chamber*, Cadw, 2000.

Howell, David W., *Nicholas of Glais, The People's Champion*, Clydach Historical Society, 1991.

Howells, Richard (Ed.), *Where the River Bends: An Illustrated History of Hook*, Planed, 2012.

Jenkins, Dafydd, *Writers of Wales – D.J. Williams*, University of Wales Press, 1973.

John, Brian, *Pembrokeshire*, Greencroft Books, 1984.

John, Brian, *Pembrokeshire Coast Path*, Aurum Press, 1990.

John, Brian, *Martha Morgan's Little World – The Essential Companion to the Angel Mountain Saga*, Greencroft Books, 2006.

John, Brian, *The Bluestone Enigma – Stonehenge, Preseli and the Ice Age*, Greencroft Books, 2008.

John, Terry, *The Civil War in Pembrokeshire*, Logaston Press, 2008.

Jones, Bobi, 'Stories of the Land, *Planet* 67, February/March 1988.

Jones, Francis, *Historic Pembrokeshire Homes and Their Familes*, Brawdy Books, 2001.

Kinross John S., *Fishguard Fiasco – An Account of the Last Invasion of Britain*, Logaston Press, 2007.

Lockley, R.M., *Dream Island: A Record of a Simple Life*, H.F.&G. Witherby, 1930.

Lockley, R.M., *I Know an Island*, George Harrap, 1938.

Lockley, R.M., *Pembrokeshire*, Robert Hale, 1957.

Lockley, R.M., *Wales*, Batsford, 1966.

Llwyd, Alan, *The Story of Waldo Williams – Poet of Peace*, Barddas Publications, 2010.

Mac Giolla Chriost, Diarmait, *Welsh Writing, Political Action and Incarceration: Branwen's Starling*, Palgrave Macmillan, 2013.

McKay, K.D., *A Vision of Greatness – The History of Milford 1790-1990*, Brace Harvatt Associates, 1989.

Miles, Dilwyn, *The Pembrokeshire Coast National Park*, David and Charles, 1987.

Molloy, Pat, *And They Blessed Rebecca: An Account of the Welsh Toll-gate Riots 1839-1844*, Gomer Press, 1983.

Molloy, Pat, *Operation Seal Bay*, Gomer Press, 1986.

Morgan, Kenneth O., *Modern Wales: Politics, Places and People*, University of Wales Press, 1977.

Muller, Mark, *People Who Shaped Haverfordwest*, Haverfordwest Civic Society, 2009.

Nash, George, *The Architecture of Death: Neolithic Chambered Tombs in Wales*, Logaston Press, 2006.

Nicholas, James, *Waldo Williams*, University of Wales Press, 1975.

Osmond, John Ed., *The Preseli Papers*, Plaid Cymru, 2007.

Owen, Hywel, and Morgan, Richard, *The Dictionary of Place Names of Wales*, Gomer, 2007.

Rees, Derek, *Rings and Rosettes: The History of the Pembrokeshire Agricultural Society 1784-1977*, Gomer Press, 1977.

Rees, Derek, *The Pembrokeshire County Shows 1959-2009: 50 Years at Withybush*, Pembrokeshire Agricultural Society, 2009.

Rees, Ffion, *Ramsey Island and Beyond*, Graffeg, 2017.

Seymour, John, *The Fat of the Land*, Faber and Faber, 1961 (re-published by Carningli Books, 2011).

Seymour, John, *About Pembrokeshire: Gwlad yr Hud – Land of Enchantment*, T.J. Whalley & Associates, 1971.

Seymour, John, *I'm a Stranger Here Myself – The Story of a Welsh Farm*, Faber and Faber, 1978 (re-published by Carningli Books, 2011, www.pantryfields.com).

Svensson, Lars, *Collins Bird Guide*, 2009.

Thomas, Ifor, *Body Beautiful*, Parthian, 2005.

Thomas, Ned, *The Welsh Extremist*, Victor Gollanz, 1971.

Wiliam, Eurwyn, 'Concealed Horse Skulls: Testimony and Message', in Trefor M. Owen (Ed.) *From Corrib to Cultra: Folklife Essays in Honour of Alan Gailey*, Institute of Irish Studies Queens University Belfast, 2000.

Williams, Glanmor, *Wales c1415-1642: Recovery, Reorientation and Reformation*, Clarendon Press and University of Wales Press, 1987.

Williams, Herbert, *The Pembrokeshire Coast National Park*, Webb and Bower/Michael Joseph, 1987.

Williams, Waldo, *The Peacemakers: Selected Poems* (translated with an Introduction by Tony Conran), Gomer, 1997

Wimbush, Paul, *The Birth of an Ecovillage – Adventures in an Alternative World*, FeedARead Publishing, 2012.

Wint, Sarah, *Sunshine Over Clover: Gardens of Wellbeing*, Orphans Press, 2016.

Wrench, Tony, *Building a Low Impact Roundhouse*, Permanent Publications, 2014.

Wyn, Hefin, *Battle of the Preselau*, Clychau Clogog, 2008.

Wyn, Hefin (Ed.) *O'r Witwg I'r Wern / Ancient Wisdom and Sacred Cows*, Cymdeithas Cwm Cerwyn, 2011.

THE PHOTOGRAPHS

ACKNOWLEDGEMENTS

My first thanks are to Peter Finch, Editor of the *Real* series, and Mick Felton, Editor at Seren, for commissioning *Real Preseli*. As ever my partner Ceri Black offered much encouragement, read the manuscript in draft, and made many helpful suggestions.

Hefin Wyn was a constant source of advice, especially in my exploration of Mynydd Preselau. Brian John, a veteran chronicler of Pembrokeshire, pointed me in a number of directions. Others who guided me on particular themes and in specific places include: Dave Astins, Vernon Beynon, Richard Brown, Ray Burgess, Vicki Cummings, Llinos and Cynog Dafis, Bonni Davies, David Doorbar, David Ellis, Bishop Wyn Evans, Rev Chris Gillam, Rev Jenny Gough, Jane Griffiths, Elizabeth Haines, Simon Hancock, Richard Howells, Clive James, Terry John, Meirion Jones, Andrew Kerrison, Bob Marshall-Andrews, Vicki Moller, Clive Morgan, Fran Morgan, Jamie Owen, Myles Pepper, Glen Peters, Glen Phillips, Derek Rees, Ffion Rees, Robert Rhys, Richard Russill, Anne Seymour, Rhys Sinnett, Ifor Thomas, Boyd Williams, Tao and Hoppi Wimbush, Sarah Wint, Hatty Woakes, and Tony Wrench.

This book is dedicated to my grandchildren – Ewen, Seren, Ioan and Osian – in the confident expectation that they will find Preseli as a rewarding experience in the course of their lives as I have found it in mine.

THE AUTHOR

John Osmond is a writer and journalist, having worked for newspapers and broadcasters in Wales over the past five decades. He was a political correspondent with the *Western Mail* during the 1970s, Editor of *Arcade Wales Fortnightly* in the early 1980s, and Deputy Editor of *Wales on Sunday* during its launch period between 1988-90. In the 1980s he also went into television, becoming a producer with HTV Wales. Later he ran his own television production company, producing documentaries for the BBC, S4C, Channel 4 and STV. In 1996 he was made inaugural Director of the Institute of Welsh Affairs, a position he held for seventeen years.

He is a Fellow of Cardiff Metropolitan University and has been awarded an Honorary MA by the University of Wales.

Born and brought up in Abergavenny, John spent a great deal of time during his youth in Preseli where a number of relatives lived. He has owned several caravans near the cliff edge at Talbenny, near Little Haven, since the early 1970s. He was a candidate for Plaid Cymru in the Preseli Pembrokeshire constituency in the 2007 National Assembly election, the 2015 Westminster general election, and again at the National Assembly election in 2016.

John graduated from the University of Bristol and began his career in journalism with *Yorkshire Post Newspapers* in the 1960s. Since then he has published widely on Welsh politics and culture. His first novel, *Ten Million Stars Are Burning*, was published by Gomer in 2018.

INDEX

Other Titles in the series: